DOS 4 Made Easy

DOS 4 Made Easy

Herbert Schildt

Osborne **McGraw-Hill**

Berkeley, California

Osborne **McGraw-Hill**
2600 Tenth Street
Berkeley, California 94710
U.S.A.

For information on translations and book distributors outside of the
U.S.A., please write to Osborne **McGraw-Hill** at the above address.

A complete list of trademarks appears on page 329.

DOS 4 Made Easy

1234567890 DODO 898

ISBN 0-07-881448-0

Acquisitions Editor: Jeff Pepper
Copy Editor: Kay Luthin
Word Processor: Bonnie Bozorg
Proofreader: Juliette Anjos
Production Supervisor: Kevin Shafer

CONTENTS

PREFACE

This book is for anyone who wants to learn how to use DOS version 4, which is a complex program with many commands and options. No prior experience with computers is necessary for learning DOS in this book. The text presented here distills DOS into its most useful components and concentrates on getting you familiar with DOS as quickly and easily as possible. By the time you finish this book, you will be using DOS like a pro!

There are really two sides to DOS version 4: the Shell and the command prompt. This book looks carefully at both of these. It begins with the Shell because it is easiest to understand. Once you have learned about the Shell, you can move to the command prompt for more complex DOS usage. As you progress, you'll learn the more advanced DOS commands that give you real power over the system. The later chapters explain how to configure your system and how to manage your floppy- and fixed-disk drives—including backing up the fixed disk.

This book is a tutorial with many hands-on examples and experiments. It is highly recommended that you have a computer available so that you can work along with the text.

—HS

1

COMPUTER BASICS

Before you begin your exploration of DOS, it is important that you understand a few things about your computer, including the computer's individual pieces and how these pieces work together to form the complete system. Although you do not have to understand how a computer works to use it, it does help to have some familiarity with its basic operation.

This chapter uses IBM-style computers for illustration, but the information is applicable to virtually all IBM-compatible computers.

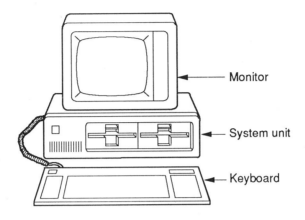

FIGURE 1-1   The basic elements of a computer

THE PARTS OF YOUR SYSTEM

All microcomputers consist of at least the following three items:

- The system unit
- The keyboard
- The monitor (video display screen)

These items, shown in Figure 1-1, represent the minimal amount of equipment needed to create a functional computer. In addition to these, most computer systems include a printer. Many computer systems also have a modem, which allows two computers to communicate over a telephone line. Your computer could contain other devices, such as a mouse.

THE SYSTEM UNIT

The *system unit* is the heart of the computer. It is composed of the following items:

- The central processing unit (CPU)

- Memory

- Disk drives

- Various adapters and options

All other pieces of the computer plug into the system unit through connectors on the back. (If your computer is not set up and ready to run, refer to the installation guide provided with your system.)

The CPU

The *central processing unit,* or *CPU,* is the brain of the computer. It performs all of the analytical, computational, and logical functions that occur inside the system. It operates by executing a *program,* which is a list of instructions. (You will learn more about programs shortly.)

Memory

The computer's memory stores information that will be processed by the CPU. The memory of your computer is made up of bytes. Although the origin of the term *byte* is lost in the past, it essentially means one character. Therefore, if someone says to you that your computer has about 640,000 bytes of memory, it means that it can store approximately 640,000 characters.

You will often hear two terms associated with the memory of the computer: *RAM* and *ROM.* RAM stands for "random access memory." This is the kind of memory your computer has the most of, and it may be used to store and retrieve any type of information. Always remember that anything stored in RAM is lost when the computer is turned off.

The other type of memory contained in your computer, ROM, stands for "read-only memory." The contents of this sort of memory cannot be changed; they can only be read. ROM stores the information that the computer needs when it is first turned on. In a way, ROM in a computer is similar to instinct in an animal. Unlike RAM, the contents of ROM are not lost when the computer is turned off.

You will often see the letter "K" after a number when the amount of RAM in a computer is referred to. For example, most computers today come with 640K of RAM. "K" usually stands for 1000; therefore, 640K is short for 640,000. Similarly, in the computer world "K" indicates the number of bytes. When used with computers, "K" more precisely stands for 1024 bytes.

Disk Drives

A *disk drive* is used to read and write information to or from a disk. The disk actually holds the information, and the drive is the mechanism that reads or writes data to or from it. (You will learn more about disks in the next section.) Data that is stored on a disk is not lost when the computer is turned off. Since anything that is in the RAM of the computer is lost when the power is turned off, information that is important and that you wish to keep must be stored on a disk.

All disk drives have two elements in common. First, they use a *read/write head* to read and write information to and from the disk. This head is similar to the play/record head on a cassette tape recorder. Second, all disk drives have a means of spinning the disk. Because information is spread over the

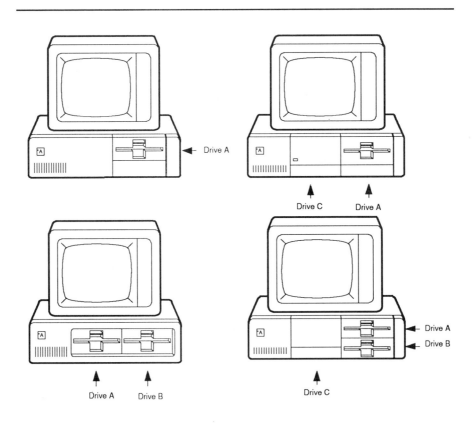

FIGURE 1-2   Disk-drive configurations

surface of the disk, the disk must turn so that all of the information on it can be accessed.

There are two basic types of disk drives: *floppy* and *fixed*. They are housed in the system unit. Most system units are configured in one of these four ways:

- One floppy-disk drive

- Two floppy-disk drives

- One floppy-disk and one fixed-disk drive

- Two floppy-disk drives and one fixed-disk drive

These configurations are illustrated in Figure 1-2.

Before the advent of the IBM Personal System/2 Models 60 and 80, the system unit of most personal computers sat on the desk beneath the monitor. With the Model 60 and Model 80, however, the system unit is usually placed on the floor, away from the monitor and keyboard. The disk drives are mounted sideways in the system unit. These models may also come with an external 5 1/4-inch drive to allow the easy exchange of information with older IBM PC and AT computers.

The drives in a system are labeled by letters, as you can also see in Figure 1-2. The fixed-disk drive is usually drive C. Floppy-disk drives use floppy disks (also called "diskettes") as their storage media. A floppy disk is a thin, flat, removable magnetic disk that stores information.

There are two types of floppy disks. The older type, which is at present the most common, is the 5 1/4-inch minifloppy, used by the IBM PC, XT, AT, and compatibles. A new type of floppy disk, the 3 1/2-inch microfloppy, is used by IBM's newer Personal System/2 line of computers. Floppy-disk elements are shown in Figure 1-3.

Minifloppy Disks

The 5 1/4-inch minifloppy disk, as shown in Figure 1-3, consists of the magnetic media that actually store the information, and a stiff jacket that protects the magnetic media from harm. The computer accesses the magnetic media through the read/write opening. The index hole is used by the computer to properly align the disk.

Perhaps the single most important feature of the floppy disk is the *write-protect notch*. When the write-protect notch is left uncovered (as shown in the figure), information can be both written to and read from the disk. However, when this notch is covered by means of a write-protect tab (supplied along with the disk), the computer can only read the information on the

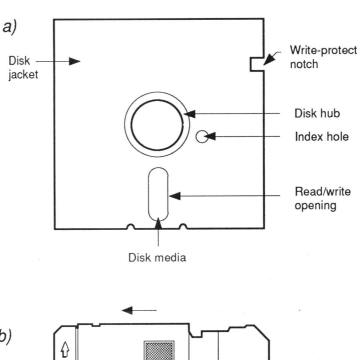

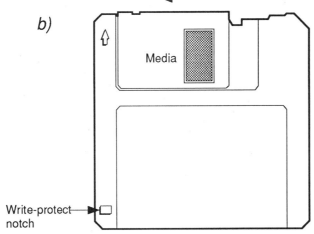

FIGURE 1-3   Elements of (*a*) 5 1/4-inch minifloppy and (*b*) 3 1/2-inch
microfloppy disks

disk, not write to the disk. Covering the write-protect notch is a good way to prevent important information from being destroyed accidentally.

You insert a minifloppy disk into a disk drive with the write-protect notch to the left and the read/write opening facing forward. Before the computer can use the disk, the drive door must be closed or latched. There are two basic types of 5 1/4- inch minidrives in general use; the method of closing the drive door for both is shown in Figure 1-4.

The floppy disk must be turning in order for the disk drive to read or write information from or to it. When you close the drive door, you are doing three things. First, you are telling the computer that there is a disk in the drive; second, you are securing the disk to the turntable that actually spins it; and

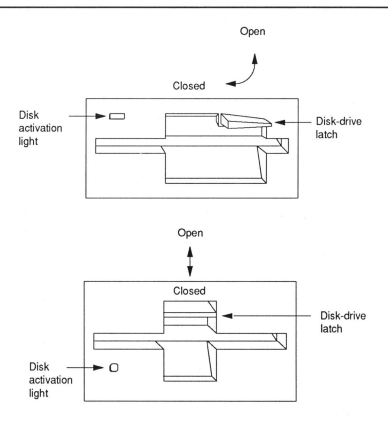

FIGURE 1-4   Closing the drive door

finally, you are enabling the read/write head of the drive to access the floppy disk.

Microfloppy Disks

The IBM PS/2 line of computers uses 3 1/2-inch microfloppy disks. In principle, these work the same way as minifloppy disks, except that they are smaller and provide more protection for the magnetic media. As Figure 1-3 shows, a microfloppy disk has a shutter that covers the read/write opening. This shutter is opened by the computer only when access to the disk is required. This protects the magnetic media from harm while the floppy disk is outside of the computer and from dust while it is inside the computer.

The write-protect notch in a microfloppy disk has a built-in slider that is used to cover the notch. In a microfloppy disk the write-protect notch works opposite to the way it works in a minifloppy disk. When the notch is open, the disk is write protected; otherwise, it is not.

The microfloppy-disk drive does not use a latch; instead, the disk drops into place. To eject the disk from the drive, you press the disk eject button on the front of the drive.

Handling Floppy Disks

No matter what type of floppy disk you have, you must take care to protect it from harm. The basic rules are simple: No dust, no magnets, and no folding (see Figure 1-5). Motors in devices such as vacuum cleaners and floor waxers set up strong magnetic fields that, given the right circumstances and proximity, can erase a disk. Never store your disks in the bottom drawer of your desk, where they stand the greatest chance of being affected by these appliances.

Fixed Disks

Many computers contain a special type of disk called a fixed disk. (You will also see this referred to as a "hard disk.") A fixed disk is a high-speed, large-capacity disk. It cannot be removed from the fixed-disk drive; hence, the term "fixed."

A fixed disk can hold substantially more information than a minifloppy or microfloppy disk can. For example, a minifloppy or microfloppy disk typi-

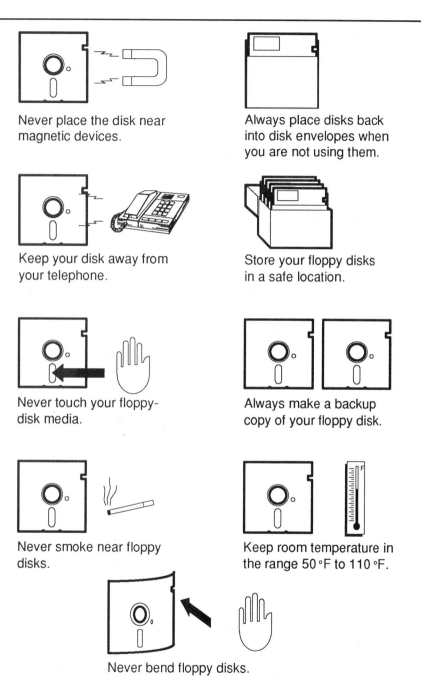

FIGURE 1-5 Protecting your disks

cally holds between 360,000 and 1,440,000 bytes of information, whereas a fixed disk holds between 10,000,000 and 70,000,000 bytes.

One million is often referred to by the prefix "mega." You will often hear the amount of storage available on a fixed disk referred to in terms of megabytes (or MB for short). For example, a disk drive that can hold 20,000,000 bytes of information will be called a 20-megabyte or 20MB drive.

Fixed disks cannot tolerate jolting vibrations or sharp shocks. A hard blow to the computer while it is accessing a fixed disk can damage the magnetic media because the read/write head of a fixed disk is positioned extremely close to the surface of the media. If you jar the computer sharply, the head could actually come into contact with the media and make a scratch, which could cause a loss of information. You don't have to walk around on tiptoes when you are using a fixed disk, but you should respect a fixed disk for what it is: a highly sophisticated piece of equipment.

THE MONITOR

The *monitor* is the television-like screen that usually sits on top of the system unit (except in the IBM Models 60 and 80, where the system unit is usually on the floor instead of on the desk). The computer uses the monitor to display information; in other words, it is your window into the computer.

The monitor plugs into the back of the system unit. There are two basic types of monitors: black-and-white (monochrome) monitors and color monitors. For the most part, it doesn't matter which type you have.

THE KEYBOARD

The *keyboard* allows you to communicate with the computer. There are two basic styles of keyboard commonly associated with microcomputers: PC XT-style keyboards, and AT-style keyboards. The XT-style keyboard was the first one developed by IBM. Later, the IBM AT computer was developed with a slightly different keyboard. PS/2 keyboards are similar to the AT keyboard. Both types are shown in Figure 1-6.

For the most part, these keyboards are like a typewriter's keyboard. However, there are a few special features that you should be aware of. The 10 keys on the far left of the XT-style keyboard, labeled F1 through F10, or the 12 keys on the top row of the PS/2-style keyboard, labeled F1 through F12, are called *function keys*. These, as well as other special keys, are gray instead of white like the rest of the keys.

(a)

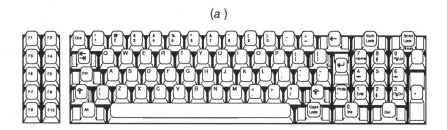

IBM PC

(b)

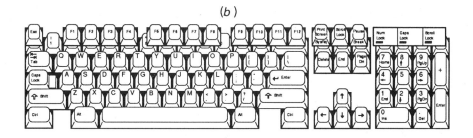

IBM PS/2

FIGURE 1-6   The two most common keyboard styles: (a) the PC XT style and
(b) the PS/2 style

The other gray keys have special meanings that depend upon what the
computer is doing. The ESC (escape) key can be used to cancel certain operations. The CTRL (control) and ALT (alternate) keys are used to generate special characters not readily available at the keyboard. The CAPS LOCK key
operates the same way as it does on a typewriter, making all letters uppercase.

The numeric keypad has two separate purposes: it allows you to enter
numbers rapidly, and it allows you to control the movements of the cursor
on the screen. The NUM LOCK key determines whether the arrow keys or the
digit keys are active. By pressing the NUM LOCK key, you can toggle between

the two uses of the number pad. The PRTSCR key causes what is currently on the computer screen to be printed by the printer. The SCROLL LOCK-BREAK key cancels certain computer operations. You will learn more about these special keys later as you learn more about DOS.

THE MOUSE

A *mouse* is an alternative input device. Unlike the keyboard, which lets you type in information, the mouse lets you select various options. A mouse consists of a small hand-held unit with one, two, or three buttons and a small ball on the bottom. As you move the mouse across your desk, a small locator symbol, called the *mouse pointer,* moves across the screen. A typical mouse is shown in Figure 1-7.

Early versions of DOS did not support the mouse; however, DOS version 4 is designed to take full advantage of it. Although you do not need a mouse to fully utilize DOS, it does make several tasks much easier.

THE PRINTER

Most computer installations include a printer. As you might expect, a printer is used to create permanent output from the computer. It is possible that your computer will have more than one printer connected to it, because different printers are used for different purposes.

The most common type of printer is called a *dot-matrix* printer. This sort of printer creates printouts quickly, but its print quality is not as good as that

FIGURE 1-7   A typical mouse

of a typewriter. Another type of printer is called either a *daisywheel* or *letter-quality* printer. It creates high-quality output and is generally used in word-processing applications. Finally, you might have a laser printer attached to your computer. It is capable of producing typeset-quality output and is used when only the very best quality will do.

No matter what type of printer you have, if it is connected to the computer in the standard way, everything you learn in this book will be applicable to your printer.

THE MODEM

In order for a computer to communicate with another computer over telephone lines, a piece of hardware called a *modem* is needed. There are two types of modems: *internal* and *external*. An internal modem is a special circuit card that plugs into the inside of the computer; all you will see is a telephone cord plugged into the back of the system unit. An external modem sits outside the system.

DOS cannot directly communicate with a modem. If a modem is part of your computer, you will need a special communications program to run it.

SOFTWARE

So far, this chapter has only discussed the different pieces of hardware that make up a computer system. However, there is a wise saying in the computer business: "A computer without software is, at best, an expensive doorstop." *Software* consists of programs, and programs run your computer. Without programs, the computer hardware can do nothing, because it doesn't know what to do. The computer hardware can do nothing that it isn't told to do; it is the software's job to make the computer do useful things. You will probably use several programs, including word processors, accounting packages, and spreadsheets.

You do not need to know how to program in order to fully utilize DOS, but it is useful to understand what a program is and how a computer executes programs. A program consists of a sequence of instructions that the computer follows. When a program is run, all of its instructions are loaded into the memory of the computer. To begin execution, the CPU fetches the first instruction and does what the instruction tells it to do. Next, it gets the second instruction, and performs that task; then it gets the third instruction, and so on. The program ends when the last instruction is executed.

Computer programs are represented in *machine code* that the computer can directly read and execute. Except for very experienced and knowledgeable programmers, most people cannot read and understand machine code. For this reason, most programs are written in what is called a *high-level language,* which is quite like English. This high-level version of the program is translated into machine code by a special program called a *compiler.*

WHAT IS DOS
AND WHAT DOES IT DO?

First and foremost, DOS is a program; it is part of the software that your computer needs to function. But it is a very special program, because it is the program that is in charge of the computer's hardware. With very few exceptions, any other program that runs on your computer does so with the help of DOS. Stated a different way, DOS is the program that controls the basic hardware components of the computer. Programs of this type are called *operating systems.* In fact, the name "DOS" is an acronym for "Disk Operating System."

Although DOS controls other programs that run in the computer, DOS is under your control and exists primarily to give you a way to communicate your instructions to the computer. You give instructions to DOS by means of commands that it will recognize. For the most part, these commands consist of regular, English-like words. For example, ERASE, COPY, and PRINT are a few actual DOS commands.

There are two ways in which you can give a command to DOS. First, you can select a command from DOS's menu-driven interface, which is usually called the *DOS Shell,* or the Shell for short. The Shell presents you with lists of things that DOS can do and you simply select the desired operation. For beginners, this is the easiest way to communicate with DOS.

The second way you can give a command to DOS is to request a *command prompt.* You give DOS commands from the command prompt by typing the name of the command at the prompt. Previous versions of DOS did not have the Shell, and the command prompt was the only way in which to communicate with DOS.

Once you have become very familiar with DOS you may find the command-prompt method preferable to the Shell because it is faster than selecting items from a menu. Because it is easier to learn, the first few chapters of this book focus on the DOS Shell. Later in the book the command-prompt interface is discussed.

DOS Versions

Like most things, DOS has changed over time. Since its creation, it has been improved and enhanced. Each time DOS was revised, a new version number was assigned to it. The first version of DOS was 1.00. The latest DOS version is 4.00, which introduces the menu-driven interface. This book is about DOS version 4.00, but much of what you will learn is applicable to other versions.

In versions of software, the number preceding the decimal point is called the *major revision number*. This number is changed only when major alterations take place. The numbers to the right of the decimal point are called the *minor revision numbers,* and they indicate versions that differ only slightly from the previous one. When you see the term "DOS 4" in this book, it stands for DOS 4.00 and the minor-revision versions that will soon follow it.

SUMMARY

You should now be familiar with:

- The various pieces of a computer system
- The concepts of programs and software
- The function DOS serves in the computer
- The way DOS version numbers are organized

In the next chapter you will learn to start the computer and learn about the DOS menu-driven interface.

2

AN INTRODUCTION TO THE DOS SHELL

This chapter introduces the DOS Shell, which is a menu-driven interface that lets you control DOS. It is called a "shell" because it encloses DOS like a shell. The Shell makes it easier for beginners to run DOS because it effectively masks the low- level functioning of DOS from you. Keep in mind that many things introduced in this chapter will be more thoroughly explored later in this book, after you know more about DOS.

Before you can examine the DOS Shell, you will need to get DOS started on your computer. If you don't know how, the following section will show you. For this and the remaining chapters in this book, it will be best if you are seated at your computer so that you can try the examples.

LOADING DOS

Exactly how you get DOS running on your computer depends on what kind of disk drives your computer has. Before beginning, find the proper category in the sections presented here, and follow the appropriate instructions. If you will be loading DOS from a floppy-disk drive, DOS will be on one, two, or four floppies.

The following instructions assume that your computer is turned on.

Loading DOS from a Fixed Disk

If your computer has a fixed disk and DOS has been properly installed on it, then DOS will load automatically. You do not have to put any disk into drive A of your computer. If for some reason DOS has not been loaded onto your fixed disk, refer to the appropriate instructions for loading DOS from a floppy disk.

Loading DOS from a 1.44 MB Floppy

If DOS has been installed on a 1.44-megabyte PS/2-compatible microfloppy, then all of DOS is contained on that one disk. It should be labeled "Startup." Insert this disk into drive A, and press the CTRL, ALT, and DEL keys at the same time. Leave the Startup disk in drive A.

Loading DOS from Two 720K Floppies

If DOS has been installed on two 720-kilobyte PS/2-compatible microfloppies, then DOS is split between the one labeled "Startup" and the one labeled "Shell." To start the Shell, put the Shell disk in drive A, and press the CTRL, ALT, and DEL keys at the same time. Leave the Shell disk in drive A.

Loading DOS from Four 360K Floppies

If DOS has been installed on four 360-kilobyte minifloppies, then DOS is split between the Startup, Shell, Working 1, and Working 2 disks. To start the Shell, put the Startup disk in drive A, and press the CTRL, ALT, and DEL keys at the same time. Next, remove the Startup disk and put the one labeled "Shell" into drive A. You will see a prompt on the screen that looks like this:

A>

Type **DOSSHELL**. You will see the DOSSHELL command on the screen next to the prompt. If you make a typing error, use the BACKSPACE key to correct it. Once you have correctly entered the command, press ENTER. This causes the shell to be loaded. Leave the Shell disk in drive A.

WHAT IF THINGS LOOK DIFFERENT?

Precisely what happens when DOS begins execution is determined, in part, by whether DOS is loaded from a fixed disk or from a DOS floppy disk. This is because DOS can be customized to better fit the needs of a specific working environment. (You will learn how to customize DOS later in this book.)

If the computer you are using has been in use for a while and is used by other people, it has probably been customized to some extent. Most customizations will not affect the way you control DOS or use it to help you run programs, but it can cause some things to appear differently on the monitor— or not to appear at all.

This book assumes that DOS has been installed with IBM's standard installation instructions. As you read this chapter, if you find that your screen looks nothing like what is being shown here, you have two choices. First, you can reinstall DOS so that the standard default installation is used. Your screen will then show the examples as they appear in this book. Second, you can just ignore the differences and relate what is presented here to what you see on your screen. Often, the differences are so small that the second solution is the better choice. There is, however, one exception.

It is possible to configure DOS version 4 in such a way that the DOS Shell is not activated. This will not usually be the case. However, if this has been done, talk to the person who installed DOS on your machine, and explain to him or her that you are new to DOS and would like to use the Shell to make learning easier; the installer should be able to reactivate it easily.

If you are on your own and the DOS Shell does not appear when DOS is loaded, refer to IBM's DOS installation instructions and reinstall DOS using the IBM-recommended procedure. Please remember one thing: the DOS Shell is available only with DOS version 4 or later. If you have an earlier version, there will be no Shell.

TEXT VERSUS GRAPHICS

The DOS Shell can be configured to run in two different modes: *text mode* and *graphics mode*. If your computer only has a monochrome video adapter, then the Shell will be configured for text mode. Otherwise, it will be configured for graphics mode operation. The differences between these two modes are slight, but the graphics mode version does present a more visually appealing display.

THE DOS SHELL: AN OVERVIEW

The DOS Shell consists of three main parts:

- The Start Programs screen

- The File System

- The on-line, context-sensitive help system

When the Shell begins execution, you will see a screen that looks like the one shown in Figure 2-1. This is called the Start Programs screen. As its name implies, the Start Programs screen is the one you use to start the execution of a program. You will also use this screen to activate the File System.

Three items are displayed at the top of this screen. From left to right, they are the current system date, the title of the screen, and the current system time. If the date and time are not set correctly, don't worry; later in this chapter you will learn how to set them.

The next line down contains two items. On the left is the *action bar*, which on this screen consists of three options: Program, Group, and Exit. Notice that the "P" of Program, the "G" of Group, and the "x" of Exit are highlighted. These are the *hot keys* associated with each option, which can be used to

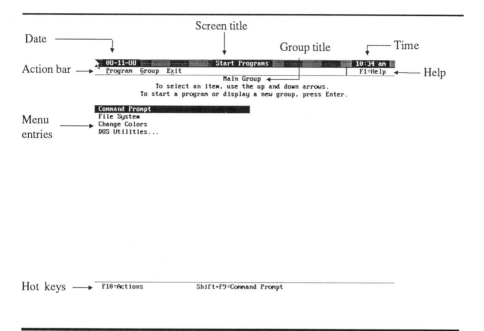

Figure 2-1   The Start Programs screen

select an option. On the right side of the second line is a reminder that you can activate the on-line help system by pressing the F1 key.

The third line contains the group title, which in this case is "Main Group." The instructions under the group title tell you how to select an item by means of the cursor keys.

The next few lines contain the items that are in the Main Group by default. These items are Command Prompt, File System, Change Colors, and DOS Utilities. It is possible to add items to the Main Group, so your display may show some additional options.

Selecting Command Prompt activates the DOS command prompt. The File System entry activates the File System, which is a menu-driven alternative to the command prompt that allows you to maintain your files. The Change Colors entry allows you to change the colors used by the Shell. This entry will only be present if you have a color display adapter. Finally, selecting DOS Utilities activates a menu of DOS commands from which you can choose.

The bottom line of the Start Programs screen contains two hot-key reminders: that pressing F10 activates the action bar and that pressing the SHIFT key at the same time you press F9 activates the DOS command prompt.

MOVING THE HIGHLIGHT
AND MAKING A SELECTION

As stated in Chapter 1, the DOS Shell supports both the keyboard and the mouse as input devices. You can run the Shell by using only the keyboard, but the mouse makes a handy addition. This section explores how to move the highlight about the screen and make a menu selection—first, by using the keyboard, and second, by using the mouse.

Using the Keyboard

When the Start Programs screen is first displayed, the highlight is on the Command Prompt selection in the Main Group. To move the highlight to another selection, use the up or down arrow key. Move the highlight down one line now. (If it doesn't move, press the NUM LOCK key.)

The highlight should now be resting on the File System entry. Try pressing the down arrow key a number of times. As you can see, the highlight continually cycles between the entries in the Main Group list. At this time, move the highlight to the **DOS Utilities** entry.

To make a selection from a menu, position the highlight on the item you want and press ENTER. To try this, make sure that the highlight is on the **DOS Utilities** entry and then press ENTER. After a few seconds, the group title will change to "DOS Utilities..." and a new list of options will be displayed. You will learn about these options later; for now, just press the ESC key to return to the Main Group.

To activate the action bar, press the F10 key. Try this now. As you can see, the Program option is highlighted. You can move the highlight around by using the left and right arrow keys. To select an option, press ENTER when the highlight is over the desired object. To deactivate the action bar, press

F10 a second time. The F10 key acts as a toggle, changing the part of the screen that is active each time it is pressed.

Using the Mouse

Using the mouse to select a menu item or an action-bar item is somewhat easier than using the keyboard. To move the highlight, move the mouse pointer to the item you want and click the left button one time. (The right button of the mouse is not used by the DOS Shell; however, it is possible that you will have application programs that do use it.) The mouse pointer will either be a small arrow or a solid box, depending upon what sort of video adapter your system has. To try this, move the mouse pointer to the **DOS Utilities** entry and press the left button one time.

To select an item, move the mouse pointer to the desired item and *double-click* the left button. A double click is two presses in quick sucession. You must be careful not to move the mouse between the two clicks. (If the mouse is moved between the first and second click, no command will be activated.) To try this, make sure that the mouse is positioned over the **DOS Utilities** entry and double-click. As you can see, this activates the **DOS Utilities** group. If it doesn't work the first time, try it again. It can take a couple of tries to get the hang of double-clicking.

Keep in mind that only items in the Start Programs menu (or one of its group menus) require a double click. Other types of menus, which you will see in the next section, allow selections with just a single click.

To cancel the DOS Utilities group, move the mouse pointer to the **Esc=Cancel** entry on the bottom line and click once (in other words, single-click). Do this now.

Unlike the keyboard, with a mouse you do not have to press F10 to activate the action bar. Instead, simply move the mouse pointer to the option you want and click once. Try this with the Program option. You will see a drop-down menu that contains further options. (The action bar and its menus will be discussed in the next chapter.) Now move the pointer to somewhere on the screen that is blank, and click once. As you can see, the drop-down menu is removed from the screen. In general, until you have actually made a selection from a menu, you can change what you are doing simply by moving the mouse to some other part of the screen and clicking once.

Keep in mind that you can intermix keyboard and mouse commands. The DOS Shell doesn't care which you use at any point in time.

THE ON-LINE HELP SYSTEM

The Shell's on-line Help System is context sensitive. This means that it will tell you information about whatever it is that you are doing at the time. More specifically, it gives you information about whatever you have highlighted. Once the Help System is activated, you may also request information about other topics if you wish.

Keep in mind that, in general, the information displayed by the Help System is intended to act as a reminder. It cannot be substituted for a good working knowledge of DOS.

To activate the Help System, either press F1 or move the mouse pointer to the **F1=Help** item on the second line and click. For example, move the highlight to the **DOS Utilities** option and then activate the Help System. A small window that tells you about the DOS Utilities option appears. The window will look like the one shown in Figure 2-2. At the top of the window is the name of the item for which you are receiving help. To the far right of the window is the *scroll bar,* which is used by the mouse to scroll the text in the window up or down. (If the Shell has been configured for text mode operation, then an up and down arrow symbol will be substituted for the scroll bar.) You will look more closely at the operation of the scroll bar shortly.

A list of the hot keys that relate to the Help System is shown at the bottom of the window. You can activate an operation by pressing the hot key or by using the mouse to single-click on its entry in the list. Pressing F1 while a help window is displayed causes information about the Help System to be shown. Pressing F9 displays a list of all of the Shell's hot keys. Pressing F11 displays an index of help topics from which you can select.

After you select a topic, information about it will be shown. The only way to deactivate the Help System is by pressing the ESC key or by clicking on the Esc=Cancel entry.

Press ESC to deactivate the help window at this time.

WINDOWS

In the preceding section, you saw the help window. As you use more of the Shell, you will see several examples of windows, so it is important to know more about them.

A *window* is a portion of the screen that is dedicated to one specific task. If you think of the screen as a desk, then you can think of a window as a piece of paper on that desk. For example, if you activate the help window again, you can see that it overlays a portion of the screen. This is like laying one piece of paper over another. When you deactivate the help window, the previous contents of the screen are restored. This process of overlaying and restoring is common to all windows used by the Shell.

There can be many windows on the screen at the same time, but only one will be active at any time. For example, the File System uses several windows.

If the information contained in a window exceeds its height, then the window will include a scroll bar, or if your system is configured for text operation, then pictures of an up and down arrow will be displayed.

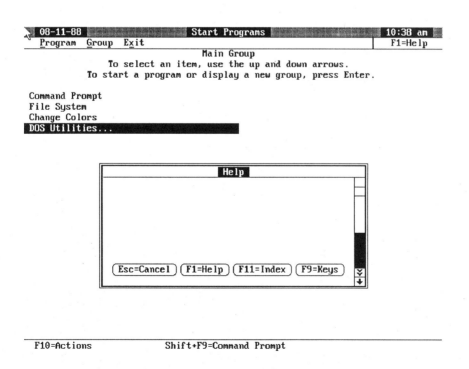

Figure 2-2   The general form of the help window

All scroll bars work the same no matter what the window is used for. The components of the scroll bar are shown in Figure 2-3.

Scroll bars only work with the mouse. To move up one line, position the mouse pointer over the up arrow on the bar and click once. To move up one full window, click on the double up arrows. A similar process is used to move down a line or a window. Activate the help window (if it is not already activated), and try using the scroll bar if you have a mouse. Notice that the slider box moves up or down in the direction of the scroll. The slider box's position in the scroll bar is directly related to the position in the total text of the text currently in view. For example, when the slider box is in the middle of its range, the text on the screen is in the middle of the total text.

You can use the mouse to *drag* the slider box to a new position. To do this, position the mouse on the slider box, and press and hold down the left button. Next, move the mouse, and an outline of the box will follow. When you release the left button, the box will be moved to the new location and the text on the screen will be moved by the same amount. You should try this now.

In a text-only system, the scroll bar is replaced by up and down arrow symbols. To scroll the text by means of the mouse, just click on the direction in which you want to scroll the text. Each time you click, the text will move one line.

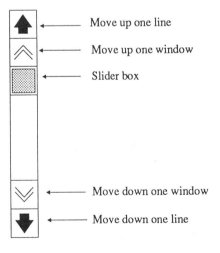

Figure 2-3   The components of the scroll bar

If you do not have a mouse, you can use the up and down arrow keys to scroll the text one line or use the PGUP and PGDN keys to scroll the text one full window.

Deactivate the help window at this time.

ENTERING INFORMATION

As important as menus are to the DOS Shell, there will still be many times when you will need to enter information that cannot be selected from a menu. For example, to set the time or date, you need to enter information—it is not possible or practical to use a menu for this. Because the entering of information is so important, it is necessary to understand the process.

There are many times when DOS will request information. To satisfy the request, type your response at the keyboard. DOS, however, will not have any idea of what you are typing until you enter it by pressing the ENTER key. In other words, until you press ENTER, DOS does not know what you have typed. There is a very important advantage to this approach: it allows you to correct mistakes. DOS requires that the information and commands you give it be in a precise format; it does not accept misspellings, for instance.

If you see that you have made a typing error—or if you change your mind about the information you want to enter—you can correct it if you have not yet pressed ENTER by using the BACKSPACE key, which is the gray key with the arrow pointing to the left (labeled BK on some keyboards). Each time you press BACKSPACE, the cursor backs up one space, erasing whatever was in that space. Once you have erased your error, you simply begin typing again.

As far as DOS is concerned, uppercase and lowercase letters are the same; that is, anytime you communicate with DOS, you can enter the information without worrying about the case of the letters. However, keep in mind that many programs that run under DOS are case sensitive and require entries to be in either uppercase or lowercase characters.

SETTING THE TIME AND DATE

If your system does not have a built-in clock, then the time and date displayed on the Start Programs screen will most likely be wrong. In this section you will learn how to set the time and date. Even if the time and date are correct on your system, you should follow along with this section; it is a good example of how you give commands to DOS using the Shell.

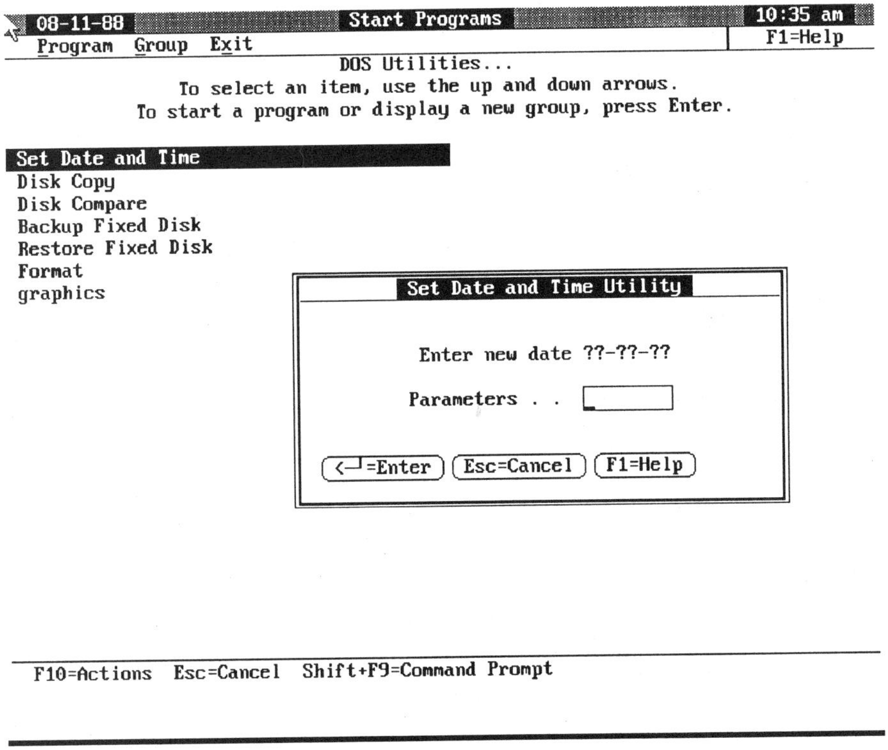

```
▓08-11-88▓▓▓▓▓▓▓▓▓▓▓▓▓▓▓Start Programs▓▓▓▓▓▓▓▓▓▓▓10:35 am▓
 Program  Group  Exit                                  F1=Help
                         DOS Utilities...
              To select an item, use the up and down arrows.
          To start a program or display a new group, press Enter.

 ▓Set Date and Time▓▓▓▓▓▓▓▓▓▓▓▓▓▓▓
  Disk Copy
  Disk Compare
  Backup Fixed Disk
  Restore Fixed Disk
  Format
  graphics            ┌──────Set Date and Time Utility──────┐
                      │                                     │
                      │                                     │
                      │      Enter new date ??-??-??        │
                      │                                     │
                      │      Parameters . . ┌──────┐        │
                      │                     └──────┘        │
                      │                                     │
                      │  ┌─────────┐ ┌──────────┐ ┌───────┐ │
                      │  │<─┘=Enter│ │Esc=Cancel│ │F1=Help│ │
                      │  └─────────┘ └──────────┘ └───────┘ │
                      └─────────────────────────────────────┘



 F10=Actions  Esc=Cancel  Shift+F9=Command Prompt
```

Figure 2-4   The Set Time and Date window

To set the time and date, first select **DOS Utilities** from the Main Group. You will see a menu that looks like this:

```
Set Date and Time
Disk Copy
Disk Compare
Backup Fixed Disk
Restore Fixed Disk
Format
```

You will only see the backup and restore options if your system has a fixed disk.

Select the **Set Date and Time** item. You will see a window like the one in Figure 2-4. You will also see the cursor blinking after the beginning square bracket on the line that says "Parameters." The DOS Shell uses this word in this context to mean the date. Enter the correct date at this time, using numbers. If you live in an English-speaking country, then enter the date using the format *month- day-year*. If you live in a non-English-speaking country, enter the date using the form common to your country. Separate the parts of the date with a dash. Whatever you type will appear between the two square brackets. (Remember, if you make a mistake, use the BACKSPACE key to make a correction.) When you are done, press the ENTER key.

After you enter the date, you will be prompted for the correct time. DOS displays the time in the normal 12-hour clock format with A.M. and P.M. symbols. However, DOS requires that you *enter* the date in a 24-hour clock format. This means, for example, that 9 A.M. will be entered as **9**, but 1 P.M. must be entered as **13**, 2 P.M. as **14**, and so on.

DOS allows you to enter only the hour and minute; you cannot set the seconds. Enter the correct time now, separating the hours from the minutes with a colon. When you have done this correctly, press ENTER. If you enter the time or the date information incorrectly—that is, in a format that DOS cannot understand—you will be reprompted for a correct entry.

Once the time and the date have been set, the screen will clear. You will see the message

Press any key to continue . . .

Do as it says. The screen will clear again, and the Start Programs screen will reappear. Press ESC to return to the Main Group.

MAKING BACKUP COPIES OF YOUR MASTER DOS DISKS

If your system is new and you are in charge of it, the most important first step you can take is to back up the DOS disks. Floppy disks can be destroyed or lost easily; for this reason, it is imperative to have more than one copy of the DOS disks. If the backup has already been made by someone else, you should still read this section just so you will know how to do it should the need arise. In general, you should never work with the original DOS master disks, but always with the backups, which are your **work disks**. It is best to keep the DOS masters in a safe place so they will not be destroyed accidentally.

To begin the backup procedure, select the **DOS Utilities** option from the Main Group. Next, select the **Disk Copy** option from the **DOS Utilities** menu. You will see the window shown in Figure 2-5.

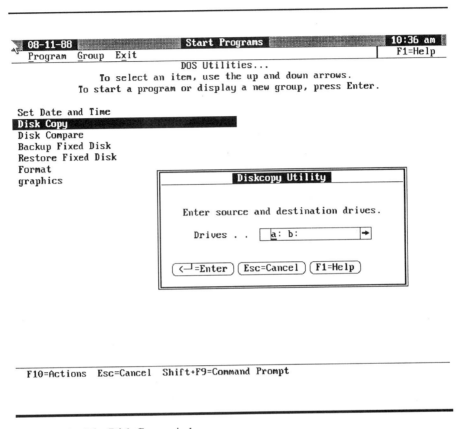

Figure 2-5   The Disk Copy window

The exact backup procedure is different for systems with two floppy-disk drives and those with one floppy-disk drive. Read the section that applies to the configuration of your computer. If your copy of DOS is on more than one disk, be sure to copy all of the DOS disks by repeating the following procedures.

Backup with Two Floppy-Disk Drives

If your system has two floppy-disk drives, put a DOS master disk in drive A and a blank disk in drive B. Since the **Disk Copy** option uses these two disk drives by default, simply press ENTER to begin the copying process. The screen will clear, and you will see the following messages:

> Insert SOURCE diskette in drive A:
> Insert TARGET diskette in drive B:
> Press any key to continue . . .

Make sure that the disks are in the proper drives, and then press any key to start the process.

The disk-copy process will display some information about what it is doing, but don't worry about it now. Later, you will be able to understand what this information means. The copy process takes a few minutes on most computers, so be prepared for this. When the copy is complete, you will see the message

> Copy another diskette (Y/N)?

If you wish to make another copy of the DOS disk, type **Y**, and the copy process will be repeated; otherwise, type **N**. As you will see, there are many DOS commands that require yes or no ("Y/N?") responses.

Backup with One Floppy-Disk Drive

If your system has only one floppy-disk drive you should change the drive information in the Disk Copy window to **A: A:** and press ENTER. You will see this message:

> Insert SOURCE diskette in drive A:
> Press any key to continue . . .

You will use drive A for both the source and destination disks by swapping them in and out as prompted by the disk-copy process. Put a DOS disk into drive A, and close the drive door. After that, strike any key.

DOS will first read the contents of the DOS disk into the memory of the computer. Once this has been done, you will see the message

> Insert TARGET diskette in drive A:
> Press any key to continue . . .

At this time, remove the DOS disk from the computer, put the blank floppy disk into drive A, and press a key. DOS will copy the information it read from the DOS disk onto the blank disk.

The disk-copy process will display some information about what it is doing, but don't worry about it now. Later, you will be able to understand what it means. The one-drive copy process can take a few minutes, so be patient.

When the copy is complete, you will see the message

Copy another diskette (Y/N)?

If you wish to make another copy of the DOS disk, type **Y**, and the copy process will be repeated; otherwise, type **N**.

What to Do If Something Goes Wrong

Once in a while an error will occur when you are copying a floppy disk, and you will see an error message. This is usually caused by a faulty target disk. The first thing you should do is try the entire process again. Things will sometimes straighten themselves out. If this doesn't work, try a new target disk. If this *still* doesn't work, you should seek advice from a coworker or the supplier of your computer.

Labeling Copies of the DOS Disks

Any floppy disk that contains information should have a stick-on label attached it. The label should include the following items:

- A brief description of what is on the disk
- The copy number
- Your name
- The date

The reason for the description is obvious: you must have some way to remember what is on the disk. A good title for the DOS backup copy is "DOS backup disk." Since you might want to have several backup copies, using a copy number is a good idea. You can indicate this by calling the first copy Copy 1, for example. Include the date the disk was first put in service. In this way you will be able to keep disks with similar descriptions separate. Finally, in large offices, disks have a way of getting lost, so your name helps to ensure that your disk will find its way back to you.

A good layout for the DOS backup label is shown here:

DOS backup diskette
Copy: 1
Return to: Herb Schildt
Date: 2/28/88

Be sure to prepare the label before you put it on the floppy disk. Once the label is on, you should use only a felt-tipped pen to make changes or corrections to it. Using a ballpoint pen or a pencil may result in lost data because of damage to the magnetic surface.

RESTARTING DOS

It is not necessary to actually turn your computer off and then on again in order to load DOS. Pressing the CTRL, ALT, and DEL keys at the same time causes the computer to reload DOS and begin running it. Try doing this now. If you are loading DOS from a floppy disk, be sure to put the appropriate disk into drive A. When DOS restarts, you may have to reenter the correct date and time because, as far as DOS is concerned, the computer was just turned on—DOS has no way of knowing that it was just running a few seconds ago.

You are probably wondering why you would want to restart DOS. First, causing DOS to be reloaded also causes the computer to stop whatever it is doing. Therefore, if the computer begins to do something you think it shouldn't, you can always stop this by reloading DOS. In a sense, pressing the CTRL, ALT, and DEL keys is an emergency stop signal. For now, since you don't know much about DOS yet, if you think that you have accidentally done something that you shouldn't have, just reload DOS.

You also may need to reload DOS if a program you are running fails. Fortunately, because of the high quality of software available today, program failures are rare. However, they can still occur. A mistake in a computer program is called a *bug*. Some bugs are just annoyances, but others are so bad that they can actually cause the computer to stop running. When the computer stops, DOS cannot run, which means you must restart the computer by reloading DOS. You probably won't have to do this very often.

Finally, in extremely rare situations, a program error can stop the computer so completely that the only way to restart it is to turn the computer itself off and then on again.

TURNING OFF THE COMPUTER

When you are ready to turn your computer off, remember to do one thing first: remove all floppy disks from the drives. When the power is shut off, there is a fraction of a second in which the electricity stored in the power supply of the computer "bleeds" out. During this time of decreasing power, the computer's electronics are in an unstable state; the disk drive could write random information onto your disk and destroy valued data. Most computers today have safeguards built in to prevent this, but no safeguard is completely effective.

SUMMARY

At this point you should know how to

- Start the computer and load DOS
- Move the highlight and make a menu selection
- Use the Shell to set the time and date
- Make a backup of the DOS disks
- Reload DOS
- Safely turn off the computer

In the next chapter you will learn more about DOS files and directories.

3

FILE SYSTEM
BASICS

Before you can go much further in your study of DOS, you need to understand how the Shell's File System operates. However, in order to understand the File System, you will need to know something about the way DOS organizes information on a disk.

This chapter introduces several important concepts and terms. It lays the groundwork for much of the rest of the book, so a careful reading is suggested.

WHAT IS A FILE?

In the previous chapter, the term "file" was used without any definition. Now it is time to define it formally. A *file* is a collection of related information stored on either a floppy or a fixed disk. (For the rest of this discussion, the word "disk" will refer to both a floppy disk and a fixed disk.) The magnetic media of a disk is essentially the same as the recording tape used in an audio tape recorder. The process of placing information onto the disk is very similar to making a tape recording; reading the information from a disk is similar to playing a tape recording.

A disk can hold several files. For example, the same disk might contain a letter, a mailing list, and a general ledger, each in its own file. Because these items are in separate files, there is no chance that they will become mixed up. Figuer 3-1 illustrates a simplified view of the way files are stored on a disk. (As you will see later, file storage is really a little more complicated than this.)

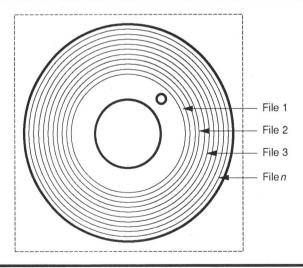

Figure 3-1   A simplified view of files stored on a disk

Information is stored on a disk in much the same way that it is stored in memory: byte by byte. For example, a file might contain the sentence "This is a test." The individual characters (bytes) that make up that sentence are stored on the disk. Disk files are concrete, physical entities. They are as real as paper files. Anything you can do with a paper file can be done with a disk file. This includes copying it, changing it, adding to it, changing its name, and—unfortunately—losing it. If you keep this in mind, you will have no trouble running DOS.

FILE NAMES

Each file on a disk must have a unique name to identify it. A file name can consist of two parts. The first part, traditionally called the *filename,* is what you will think of as the name of the file. It may be from one to eight characters long. The second part of a file name is called the *extension,* and it is optional. The extension helps you create groups of similar files or distinguish two files with the same filename from one another. The extension may be up to three characters long. The filename is like a person's first name, and the extension is like a person's last name.

To fully specify a file you must use both the filename and the extension. The filename is separated from the extension by a period. An example of a file name is TEST.TST.

Most file names are made up of letters and the digits 0 through 9. However, you can use any character you like, except for these:

. " / \ [ ] : | < > + = ;

Control characters are also not allowed. (A control character is generated by holding down the CTRL key and pressing another key. You will learn more about these characters later.)

THE CURRENT DRIVE

Most computers have more than one disk drive, but only one disk can have the focus of DOS at any one time. You can explicitly tell DOS what disk to use, as you did when you made backup copies of the DOS disks. For example, if you had two floppy-disk drives, you in effect told DOS to switch its focus between drives A and B when it copied the disks. If you do not explicitly tell

DOS which disk to use, it will use the disk in the currently active drive, which is usually referred to as the *logged-in disk.*

If you are running DOS from a floppy disk, then by default, drive A is the logged-in disk. If you have a fixed disk, then by default drive C is logged in. You will learn soon how to change the current drive.

DOS'S TREE-STRUCTURED DIRECTORY

The directory of a disk is a little like a book's table of contents: it tells you what the disk contains. The directory lists the names of the files, as well as each file's length and the time and date of creation.

Although all disks have at least one directory, a disk can contain several directories, with each directory containing a group of related files. The one directory that will always be on a disk is called the *root* directory. This directory is created by the formatting process.

You can also define *subdirectories* of the root directory. A subdirectory is a directory within a directory. You can think of the root directory as enclosing the subdirectory. A subdirectory holds a group of related files. For example, a subdirectory could hold all of a certain employee's files—no matter how divergent in purpose and use those files are. Another subdirectory might hold wage information for all the employees of a company. The exact nature of the relationship of files within a subdirectory is purely subjective. DOS doesn't know or care how the files are related; it simply treats a subdirectory as a group.

It is common for a subdirectory to have its own subdirectories. In fact, assuming there is sufficient disk space, any directory can contain a subdirectory.

If you think of the root directory as a filing cabinet, subdirectories are its drawers, with each drawer labeled and used for a specific purpose. Within each drawer, files can be further organized by topic, which is analogous to a subdirectory within a subdirectory.

Since subdirectories are simply directories contained within other directories, the term "subdirectory" is relative and describes a relationship between two directories. Throughout this chapter and the rest of the book unless specific clarification is required, the term "directory" will refer to any type of directory—root or subdirectory. The directory that encloses a subdirectory is called the *parent* directory. The only directory that does not have a parent is the root.

The disk directory structure used by DOS is called *tree structured* because, when drawn in a diagram on paper, the root and subdirectories resemble the root system of a tree. For example, if you diagrammed the directory struc-

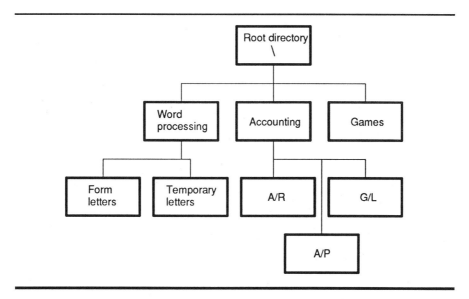

Figure 3-2   A diagram of a tree-structured directory

ture of a disk used by a small hypothetical insurance office, it might look like the one shown in Figure 3-2. Here, the root directory contains three subdirectories: WORDPROC (for word processing), ACCOUNTS, and GAMES. WORDPROC, in turn, contains two subdirectories of its own: FORMLET and TEMP, for form letters and temporary letters. The ACCOUNTS subdirectory contains three subdirectories: AR (accounts receivable), AP (accounts payable), and GL (general ledger). The GAMES subdirectory has no further subdirectories.

Tree-structured directories allow related groups of files to be treated as units of increasing specialization. For example, the directory for word processing branches from the root because word processing is a logically separate task from accounting and games. Word processing itself contains two distinct types of documents: reusable form letters and disposable, single-use correspondence. As you move down the tree from the root, each directory becomes more specialized in what it contains.

PATHS AND PATH NAMES

Each directory has a unique *path* from the root to itself. For example, in Figure 3-2, the path to the GL directory, beginning at the root, is first to AC-

COUNTS and then to GL. In the language of DOS, you specify a path by using a *path name*. The path name for the GL directory is \ACCOUNTS\GL. The first backslash is DOS's name for the root. Subsequent backslashes act as separators between the path name and the file name.

The full path name for a file takes this form:

drive_specifier: \ *path* \ *filename*

For example, if the directories in Figure 3-2 are on drive A, then the full path name for the GL directory is

A:\ACCOUNTS\GL

When no drive specifier is present, the logged-in drive is used.

ACTIVATING THE FILE SYSTEM

Now that you have learned something about DOS files, directories, and paths, it is time to learn about the File System. To activate the File System, select the File System option from the Main Group menu on the Start Programs screen. If you are running DOS from a floppy disk, you will see a screen that looks similar to Figure 3-3. If you are running DOS from a fixed disk, then entries in the Directory Tree window and the file names in the File List window will be different.

NAVIGATING IN
THE FILE SYSTEM

As you can see, the File System contains several windows. By default, the Directory Tree window is active. Only the active window is the focus of keyboard input. To activate a different window by using the keyboard, press the TAB key. Each time this key is pressed, a different window is activated in round-robin fashion, and the highlight is moved to the active window. If you have a mouse, you can activate any window at any time by single-clicking the mouse in the window you want to activate.

```
████ 08-11-88 ████████████████ File System ████████████ 4:09 pm ████
  File  Options  Arrange  Exit                          │ F1=Help
  Ctrl+letter selects a drive.
  ▣A  ▣B  ▢C  ▢D

  A:\
┌─────────────────────────┬──────────────────────────────────────┐
│     Directory Tree      │              *.*                     │
│                         │                                      │
│ ✓A:\                    │ ▨012345  .678         109   06-17-88 │
│                         │ ▨0E191012          17,138   08-09-88 │
│                         │ ▨0E291255           2,269   08-11-88 │
│                         │ ▨10061E4D           2,221   08-10-88 │
│                         │ ▨4201    .CPI       6,404   06-17-88 │
│                         │ ▨4208    .CPI         641   06-17-88 │
│                         │ ▨5202    .CPI         402   06-17-88 │
│                         │ ▨ANSI    .SYS       9,148   06-17-88 │
│                         │ ▤APPEND  .EXE      11,170   06-17-88 │
│                         │ ▤ASSIGN  .COM       5,785   06-17-88 │
│                         │ ▤ATTRIB  .EXE      10,247   06-17-88 │
│                         │ ▤AUTOEXEC.BAT          99   08-04-88 │
│                         │ ▤BASICA  .COM      36,205   06-17-88 │
│                         │ ▤CHKDSK  .COM      17,771   06-17-88 │
│                         │ ▤COMMAND .COM      37,637   06-17-88 │
│                         │ ▤COMP    .COM       9,491   06-17-88 │
│                         │ ▨CONFIG  .SYS         114   08-04-88 │
│                         │ ▨COUNTRY .SYS      12,838   06-17-88 │
│                         │ ▤DEBUG   .COM      21,606   06-17-88 │
│                         │ ▤DISKCOMP.COM       9,889   06-17-88 │
│                         │ ▤DISKCOPY.COM      10,428   06-17-88 │
└─────────────────────────┴──────────────────────────────────────┘
  F10=Actions  Shift+F9=Command Prompt
```

Figure 3-3   The File System screen

As in the Start Programs screen, you can activate the on-line Help System at any time by pressing F1. The action bar can be activated by pressing F10. Although its selections are different from the action bar in the Start Programs screen, its operation is the same.

When active, the Drive Identifier window highlights the currently logged-in drive. You can select a different drive by using the left and right arrow keys and pressing ENTER when the highlight is on the drive you want. If you have a mouse, you can simply click once on the drive you want to log in. When you switch drives, the information in the other windows is updated automatically to reflect this change; for example, you will see the new disk's directory.

The Path window shows the current path name but does not allow you to change it. The path changes automatically when you select a new directory.

Scroll bars allow the mouse to be used to scroll the contents of the Directory Tree and File List windows. You may also use the up and down arrow keys or the PGUP and PGDN keys to scroll these windows.

To select a directory by means of the keyboard, position the highlight on the one you want and press ENTER. To select a directory by means of the mouse, simply position the mouse pointer on the one you want and click once.

When a new directory is chosen, the contents of that directory are displayed in the File List window. If your computer has a fixed disk and has been in use for a while, it will almost certainly contain a fairly complete directory structure. However, if you are running DOS from a floppy disk, it may not have any subdirectories, so don't be surprised if you don't see any. In a later chapter you will learn how to create your own subdirectories.

To select a file by means of the keyboard, position the highlight on the file you want and press the space bar. To select a file with the mouse, position the mouse pointer on the file you want and click once.

To exit the File System and return to the Start Programs window, either select the Exit option on the action bar or press F3.

A Note to Fixed-Disks Users

If DOS was installed on your computer with the defaults suggested by IBM, you should see a directory called DOS in the Directory Tree window. You should move the highlight to that directory and press ENTER. What you see in the directory listing area should then be similar to these examples.

THE DIRECTORY LISTING

Assuming that DOS has been installed on your computer in the usual way, the directory listing displayed in the File List window contains files that come with DOS. The entry for each file contains three elements: first, the filename followed by the file's extension; next, the length of the file in bytes; and finally, the creation date of the file. For example, for DOS version 4, the first file in the list is 012345.678, which is 109 bytes in length and was created on 6-17-88.

You have probably noticed the *.* symbol at the top of the directory listing. Don't worry about this now; you will learn its meaning later.

If the Shell is running in graphics mode, then a fourth element is included in the directory listing for each file: a small rectangular icon at the start of each filename, which tells you if a file is a program file. If the icon shows a computer screen, then the file contains a program. If it shows a piece of paper with a corner turned over, the file does not contain a program. In text mode, no icons are shown.

When a file is selected, its icon is highlighted in graphics mode. In text mode, a small triangle is put in front of the filename.

All files listed in the same directory have unique names; two files cannot have the same filename and extension. However, two files in different directories *can* have the same names; of course, their path names will differ.

When DOS displays file names, it puts spaces between the file's name and its extension. However, whenever you need to tell DOS about a file, you must not have any spaces in the name. For example, to tell DOS about a file with a filename of EXAMPLE and an extension of .TST, you would use

EXAMPLE.TST

FILE TYPES

Three types of files can be stored on a disk:

- Text files
- Data files
- Program files

To run DOS correctly, you should become familiar with these types and their differences.

Text Files

A *text file* contains information that you can read. It consists solely of characters that can be displayed on the screen. Text files are often created by word processors; in most cases, you will make and maintain text files yourself.

Text files may have any previously unused filename and any extension. However, no text file should use the extension .EXE or .COM, because these extensions are reserved for program files.

Data Files

A *data file* contains information that a program, not a person, can read. Most of the information in a data file cannot be displayed on the monitor because it is in a form only the computer can understand. The special internal representation used by the computer for data is sometimes referred to as binary representation of data.

Data files are created and maintained by programs. For example, an inventory management program will create and maintain a data file that holds inventory information. As with text files, data files may be assigned any previously unused filename and any extension except .EXE, .COM, or .BAT. Many data files use the extension .DAT.

Program Files

Program files contain programs that the computer can execute. Unlike the two other file types, in DOS all program files use the extension .COM, .EXE, or .BAT. Although there are some differences between program files that use the .COM, .BAT and .EXE extensions, you only need to know that they are program files and are functionally the same. Most program files are created by programmers, although you will learn to create some very simple ones yourself.

Many of the programs you will use fall into the category of *application programs*. As the name implies, an application program is a program that applies itself to a specific task. For example, a general ledger program is an application program in the area of accounting. In short, an application program solves a specific problem or performs a specific task.

Reserved Extensions

DOS reserves a few file-name extensions for special purposes, just as .EXE and .COM are reserved for program files. For example, the .SYS extension indicates files that only DOS uses. The file extension .BAT indicates a *batch file,* which contains a sequence of commands for DOS to perform. (You will learn how to create batch files in Chapter 8.) The extensions .CPI and .PIF are reserved by DOS for hardware-specific information. Finally, the extension .BAS indicates BASIC program files. It is best not to use any reserved extensions in the file names that you create.

INTERNAL AND EXTERNAL COMMANDS

DOS commands are divided into two major groups: *internal* commands and *external* commands. An internal command is a command that is contained in the part of DOS that stays loaded in the memory of your computer. When you enter an internal command, DOS responds almost instantly. DOS internal commands are those commands that you are most likely to need frequently as you use the computer.

An external command is not loaded into memory with the rest of DOS; rather, it remains on a DOS disk or on the fixed disk if DOS has been installed on it. DOS includes many little-used commands; instead of having these consume memory that your application programs could use, DOS leaves them on the disk until they are needed. This conserves the computer's memory.

If you are running DOS from floppy disks, you might need to switch disks to get access to an external command. Also, because external commands are loaded by DOS as needed, there is a slight delay before DOS responds when you use the command. After an external command has executed, it is no longer kept in memory; it must be reloaded each time that it is used.

If your computer has a fixed disk, switch to drive C and select the DOS directory. If you are using floppy disks, make sure the DOS Shell disk is in drive A and that drive A is currently logged in. The directory shown in the Directory Tree window is used by DOS. This is where the external commands are stored. Not all files are external commands—just those that end in .COM, .EXE, or .BAT. The other files are data files used by DOS. Keep in mind that an external command is a program supplied by DOS.

The name of the DOS external commands are the same as the filename part of a file's name. For example, CHKDSK.COM corresponds to the DOS command CHKDSK, which is used for checking the status of a disk.

Although the most common DOS functions have been made into menu entries, you will probably at some time need to specify a command that is not in an entry. You will look closely at adding commands to the Shell later; generally, this involves specifying the command's name and any options the command may require.

The internal and external command names are shown in Table 3-1.

A CLOSER LOOK
AT HOW DOS STORES FILES

In the first part of this chapter you learned that DOS stores files on a disk in much the same way as songs are recorded on a record. Although understanding the exact method DOS uses to store a file is not necessary for using DOS, understanding the concepts behind file storage will help you interpret certain DOS error messages that refer to them. Also, many books, user

Internal commands	External commands
CHCP	APPEND
CHDIR (CD)	ASSIGN
CLS	ATTRIB
COPY	BACKUP
CTTY	CHKDSK
DATE	COMMAND
DEL (ERASE)	COMP
DIR	DOSSHELL
ERASE (DEL)	DISKCOMP
INSTALL	DISKCOPY
MKDIR	FASTOPEN
PATH	FDISK
PROMPT	FIND
RENAME (REN)	FORMAT
RMDIR (RD)	GRAFTABL
SET	GRAPHICS
TIME	JOIN
TYPE	INSTALL
VERIFY	KEYB
VOL	LABEL
	MEM
	MODE
	MORE
	NLSFUNC
	PRINT
	RECOVER
	REPLACE
	RESTORE
	SELECT
	SHARE
	SHELL
	SORT
	SUBST
	SYS
	TREE
	XCOPY

TABLE 3-1   DOS's Internal and External Commands

manuals, and magazine articles assume that you have a basic understanding of the way DOS files are stored.

Information is recorded on a disk in concentric circles called *tracks*. (When the disk drive loads a program, you can sometimes hear the read/write head moving between tracks.) Each track, in turn, is composed of a number of *sectors*. (The exact number varies and is not important.) DOS uses sector sizes of 512 and 1024 depending on the type of disk. Figure 3-4 shows how sectors and tracks are laid out on a disk.

When DOS records a file on a disk, it does not necessarily use sectors and tracks that are adjacent to each other. DOS may scatter a file throughout the disk's surface. This is why even a small amount of physical damage to a disk can destroy several files.

The smallest accessible unit of disk storage, the sector, is 512 or 1024, but this does not mean that the smallest file size you can have is 512 bytes. On the contrary, you can have files of any length, including 0 bytes. No matter how short a file is, the full sector is allocated to it, and the rest of the space is not used. For this reason, several small files can sometimes fill up a disk faster than a few large ones. When a file longer than one sector is stored on a disk, there must be some way for DOS to know which sector goes with which file. DOS accomplishes this by storing the location of each sector in a *file allocation table,* sometimes called the *FAT*. DOS refers to this table when it accesses a file.

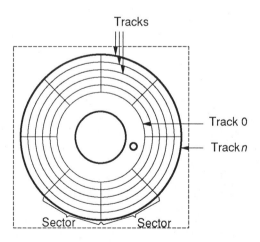

FIGURE 3-4   Sectors and tracks on a disk

The exact physical position of the tracks and sectors on a disk is determined when the disk is *formatted*. When you made a backup of the DOS master disk, the copy procedure automatically formatted the disk before it placed information on it. All disks must be formatted before being used. When a disk is not formatted, DOS and the computer have no way of knowing where to put information. The DOS command to format a disk will be discussed later.

A DOS ERROR MESSAGE

If it is not active, activate the File System at this time. Next, open the drive door on drive A, and then select the drive A in the Drive Identifier window.

Because the drive door is open, DOS will not be able to read the disk directory, and it will generate the error window shown in Figure 3-5. Insert a disk, close the drive door, and select option 1 in the window at this time. As you can see, the directory can now be read and displayed.

In general, DOS error messages can occur for a variety of reasons. Some errors, like the one you just generated on purpose, can be fixed by changing something; you will usually want to change whatever is wrong and then try the operation again. However, there are some types of errors that cannot be rectified at the time (for example, if you are trying to log onto a broken disk drive). For these types of errors, select the second option and do not retry the operation.

DOS can generate other types of error messages. The most important of these will be discussed when the need arises.

FORMATTING DISKS

To follow along with the examples in the next chapter you will need a blank formatted disk. Let's make one now.

Before you can use a disk to store information, the disk must be formatted. The formatting process prepares the disk by setting up the tracks and sectors that DOS uses to store information. If you try to use an unformatted disk, DOS will issue an error message.

To format a disk, deactivate the File System by pressing F3. Next, select the DOS Utilities option from the Main Group. Then, select Format. You will see the Format window displayed. It will look like the one shown in Figure 3-6. By default, the Format option formats the disk in drive A. (You can change it to drive B if you like.) The formatting option uses an external command called FORMAT, so this command must be on the disk that you are using.

Warning: The FORMAT command must be used with care because the formatting process destroys any data that may already exist on a disk. If you

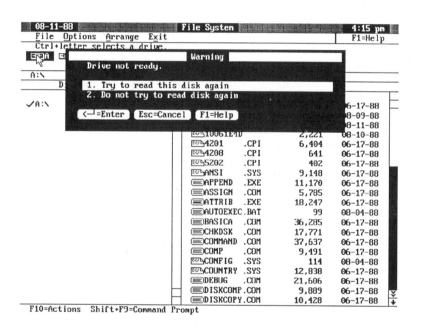

FIGURE 3-5   A DOS error window

are preparing a new disk for use, then there is no data to destroy. However, if you accidentally format a disk that contains data, that data will be lost forever. **Caution:** Unless you really know what you are doing, never format your fixed disk. Generally, the fixed disk will already be formatted and will not need to be formatted again. Doing so will irreversibly destroy all files on the disk.

For now, remove any disk that might be in drive A and put in the blank disk you are going to format. Press ENTER. The screen will clear and you will be told to insert the blank disk into drive A and press ENTER. This is a double check and is a safety feature that helps prevent you from accidentally formatting the wrong disk. As the formatting procedure executes it continually displays the amount of the disk that has been formatted. Since it takes about a minute to format a disk, it lets you know that the computer is still working.

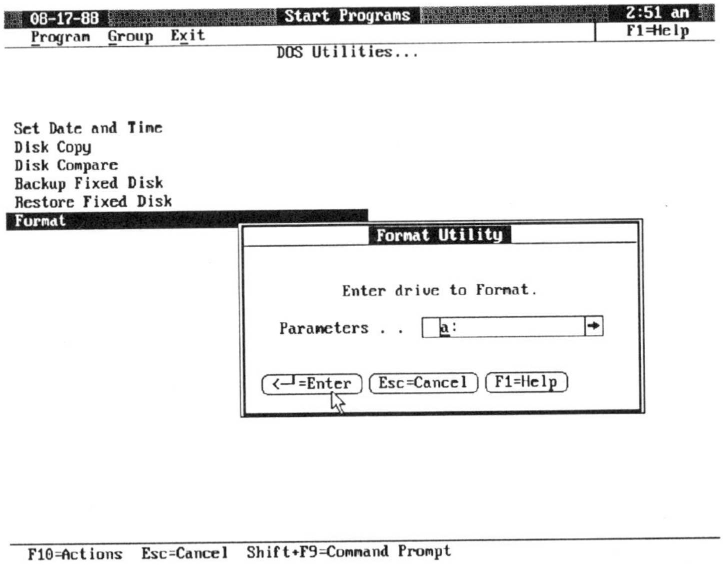

Figure 3-6. FORMAT utility screen

When the formatting process is finished, this message will be displayed:

```
Format complete
Volume label (11 characters, ENTER for none)?
```

The *volume label* is more or less the disk's name. Although not required, volume labels can be useful in certain situations. Use the name MYDISK for this disk's volume label and press ENTER. (More on volume labels later in this book.) Next, you will see something similar to this:

```
362496 bytes of total disk space
362496 bytes available on disk

    1024 bytes in each allocation unit
     354 allocation units available on disk

Volume Serial Number is 0A41-16D6
Format another (Y/N)?
```

The messages actually displayed may differ from that shown in several ways. First, there are several different types of floppy drives in use in IBM PC and compatible computers. These drives have different storage capacities. So if the number of bytes of total or available disk space differs, do not worry about it. The message also may differ if part of the floppy disk was bad and could not be formatted. Although this is not a common occurrence, you are sure to encounter it at some point. If you do, the number of bytes of total disk storage will differ from the amount available, and you will see another line that tells you the exact number of unusable bytes. It is usually best to discard a disk with bad sectors and use a new one because such a disk often will deteriorate over time. The number of bytes per allocation unit and the number of allocation units per disk depend upon the type of the disk drive. (An allocation unit is the same thing as a sector.) Finally, the volume serial number will almost certainly be different.

Since you need only one disk, respond by typing **N**. The format command will be discussed later in this book because it allows several options.

SUMMARY

You should now understand

- What a file is
- How file names are constructed
- The purpose of the directory
- The differences between text, data, and program files
- How to activate the File System
- How to change the current drive
- The difference between internal and external commands
- What tracks and sectors are
- How to interpret various DOS error messages

Now that you have seen how DOS stores files and maintains directories, and you understand the differences between files, you will use the File System in the next chapter to manipulate those files. You will also learn to run external DOS commands and application programs.

4

USING THE FILE SYSTEM

In Chapter 3 you learned many important concepts. In this chapter you will learn to apply those concepts by actually using the File System. This chapter introduces several of the most common and fundamental DOS File System operations. You will learn how to start a program and how to view and print files. You will also learn how to copy and erase a file and how to change the way in which the directory is displayed. By the time you finish this chapter, you will be able to run your application programs.

To follow along with the examples in this and subsequent chapters, you will need a blank, formatted floppy disk. If you have not yet made one, refer to the end of Chapter 3 for instructions.

STARTING A PROGRAM

Activate the File System at this time. If you are running DOS from a floppy disk, make sure that a DOS disk is in drive A, and log on to drive A. If you are using a fixed disk, log on to drive C and select the DOS directory.

It is very easy to start a program with the File System. You first highlight the program you want to start in the File List window, and then you press ENTER. If you are using a mouse, you can instead simply double-click on the program you want to execute.

For an example of this, let's execute a DOS external command. As you learned in the last chapter, DOS external commands are actually programs that are supplied by DOS. Thus, the basic method used to execute an external command will also apply to any application program you have.

If DOS has been installed according to the instructions supplied by IBM, you will see the CHKDSK.COM file about two-thirds of the way down in the File List window. This is the DOS program that reports on the status of your disk. To execute the CHKDSK command contained in this file, position the highlight on the file name and press ENTER. If you have a mouse, you can double-click on CHKDSK.COM to execute it. You will see a screen that looks something like the one shown in Figure 4-1. This window tells you that it has opened the CHKDSK.COM file.

Opening a file is different from selecting a file. When you select a file by pressing the space bar or by single-clicking the mouse on the desired file, you are telling the Shell that you are interested in this file and that you may want to do something with it in the future; but the file itself is not directly affected. However, when a file is opened, it means that DOS is doing something with the file. The distinction may seem blurred at this point, but as you learn more about how the File System operates, it will become clearer.

Inside the File Open window, the cursor is positioned at the Options line. Some programs require that certain additional information be passed to them. For example, a word-processing file may need to know the name of the file you want to edit. You will use the Options line to enter any such information.

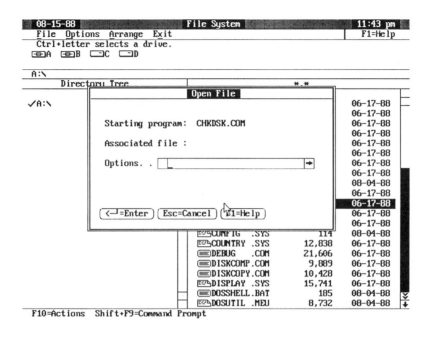

FIGURE 4-1   Executing an external DOS command from the File System

It is not necessary to enter any options for the CHKDSK command, so press ENTER at this time. The screen will clear, and the disk drive will be accessed. (For some systems, this command may take a few seconds to finish execution.) The CHKDSK command will display a lot of information about the state of your disk drive, as well as the amount of memory in the computer. For the moment, ignore this information. You will look closely at CHKDSK a little later.

When CHKDSK has finished, you will be told to press ENTER to return to the File System. In general, when a program you started by using the File System finishes, you will be prompted to press ENTER. The File System does not restart automatically; it allows you time to read any information that may be reported by the program before the screen is overwritten. Press ENTER at this time to return to the File System.

For the example just given and the other examples in this chapter, you are using the DOS directory or disk. However, when you want to run an application program, you will probably need to switch to a different directory or disk (or both) because DOS will not contain the application.

A CLOSER LOOK AT THE FILE SYSTEM ACTION BAR

As you can see, the File System action bar has four options: **File**, **Options**, **Arrange**, and **Exit**. Each of these options displays a drop-down menu when selected. The following sections present an overview of what each option does.

The File Option

Most of the **File** options relate to a file that you have selected in the File List window. In order to follow along, activate the File List window and move the highlight to the first file, which is called 012345.678. Then press the space bar. You will see a short text file that was created when DOS was installed on your system. (If you don't see this file, then select the DOSSHELL.BAT file.)

Tab to the File System Action Bar, highlight **File**, and press ENTER or single-click on the **File** option while using the mouse. Select the **File** option now. Your screen will look like Figure 4-2. The first option, **Open**, starts a program running. Selecting this option accomplishes the same thing as starting a program by means of the File List window. The **Open** option is only useful for program files; you cannot run a nonprogram file with it.

You can use the next option, **Print**, to print the contents of a text file if you have a printer. The **Associate** option is used to link one file to another. You will examine this option later in the book. The **Move** option lets you move a file from one place to another. You can move a file between disks or between directories. When you move a file, it is erased from its original position after being copied to its new place.

The **Copy** option is like **Move** except that the original file is not erased. The **Delete** option lets you remove (erase) a file from a disk. It also lets you remove a subdirectory. **Change Attribute** is used to change one or more of a file's attributes. Every file has associated with it a set of parameters that tell DOS certain things about the file. Some of these can be set by you.

The **Rename** option enables you to change the name of a file.

The **View** option lets you see the contents of a file. This is most useful with text files. Program files with the extension .EXE or .COM contain codes

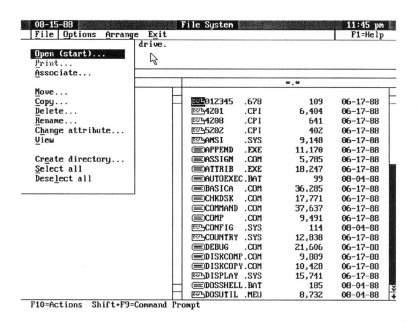

FIGURE 4-2   The File options

that the computer can read, so viewing one of these is of little value except to programmers. Also, some types of data files cannot be read because the information in them is in a special form.

The **Create Directory** option allows you to create a new subdirectory. **Select All** selects all of the files in the current directory, and **Deselect All** deselects all of the files in the current directory.

Press ESC now to remove the File menu from the screen.

The Options Entry

Select the **Options** entry at this time. The first option is **Display Options**. It is used to change the way the files are displayed in the File List window.

File Options lets you change the way certain file operations take place. The Show Information option displays information about the current disk and directory.

Press ESC now to cancel the Options option.

The Arrange Option

Select the Arrange option. The first entry in the menu is Single File List. This option will not be active at this time because, by default, a single file list is displayed.

Selecting the Multiple File List option splits the screen horizontally and lets you display two separate directories. When you select the System File List option, the directory structure of the disk is ignored and all files on the logged-in disk are displayed.

Press ESC now to cancel the Arrange option.

The Exit Option

The Exit option's menu has two items. The first causes the File System to be terminated and the Start Programs screen to be redisplayed. The second option resumes the File System and has the same effect as pressing the ESC key.

MAKING A SELECTION FROM A PULL-DOWN MENU

To make a selection from a pull-down menu, first highlight the item you want and then press ENTER. You can also select an option by positioning the mouse pointer on it and clicking once. Finally, you can press the letter key for the highlighted letter of the item you want.

When a menu item cannot be activated, it will be shown in low-intensity gray if the Shell is running in graphics mode. In text mode, an inactive selection has an asterisk where its hot key would normally appear. A menu item will be deactivated by the Shell when the item is not an appropriate choice in your current activities.

As you look at the pull-down menus associated with the File System, you will notice that some entries have three periods after their names and others do not. Whenever you will be prompted for additional information after you select an item, the item is followed by three periods. Items that do not have the periods after their names are activated the moment you choose them.

VIEWING AND PRINTING A FILE

Now that you have seen the various elements of the File System, it's time to put them to work. Select the 012345.678 file if it is not already selected. Remember, to select a file, activate the File List window, move the highlight to the file, and then press the space bar, or if you are using a mouse, move the mouse pointer to the desired file name and click once. When a file is selected, its icon is highlighted in graphics mode or a small triangle is put in front of its name in text mode.

To view the file, activate the action bar and select **File**. From the menu select **View**. You will see the screen shown in Figure 4-3. The 012345.678

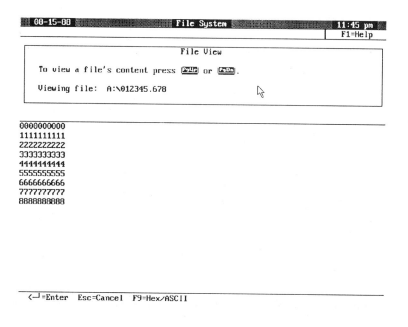

FIGURE 4-3　The View utility

file is short; if this were a long file, you could use the PGUP and PGDN keys to view all of its contents in the display area. Pressing ENTER also has the same effect as pressing PGDN.

If you press F9 while using the **View** utility, the display will show the contents of a file in a format that is used by programmers. Each letter in the file will be shown in its internal machine representation, in *hexadecimal* format. (Hexadecimal is a number system used by programmers that is based on 16 instead of 10.) Unless you are a programmer, you will never use this version of the **View** utility. However, feel free to try it at this time. The F9 key is a *toggle,* which means it switches between the two displays each time it is pressed.

Press ESC to cancel the **View** utility. Notice that the **File** option is no longer active. Note also that the 012345.678 file is no longer selected. In general, once the Shell has completed a file command, it deselects all files.

To print a file on the printer, use the **Print** option in the **File** pull-down menu. To try this, select 012345.678 again, activate the **File** menu again, and select **Print**. As you can see, the file will be printed. Remember, your computer must have a printer for this command to work.

DRIVE SPECIFIERS
AND PATH NAMES

Drive specifiers and path names were introduced in the previous chapter; you will now take a closer look at them. Until now, you have been selecting files by using the File List window and selecting drives by using the Drive Identifier window. However, many DOS commands require you to enter one or more file names, and it is possible for the file to be on a drive other than the currently logged-in drive.

To tell DOS which drive a file is on, use a *drive specifier,* which consists of the drive letter, a colon, and the file's name. For example, if the TEST.TST file is on drive B, you can give DOS this information by using the drive specifier

    B:TEST.TST

When no drive specifier is present, DOS automatically uses the logged-in drive.

When you select a directory from the Directory Tree window, you are in effect telling DOS to use this directory for all operations unless told otherwise. If you want to access a file in a *different* directory, you must use the full directory path name of the file. This tells DOS to ignore the logged-in directory and to use the one specified with the file name.

Remember, all path names begin with a leading backslash, and each directory in the path is separated from the next by a backslash. Also, the file name is separated from the path name by a backslash. For example, if the path to the TEST.TST file is \GAMES\ARCADE, then this is how you would fully specify the file:

\GAMES\ARCADE\TEST.TST

Of course, if TEST.TST is not on the logged-in drive, you must add a drive specifier to the name. For example, if TEST.TST is on drive D, this is its full path name:

D:\GAMES\ARCADE\TEST.TST

Remember, both the drive specifier and the path are optional. When either or both are absent, DOS will use the current drive and/or the current path.

COPYING A FILE

As you continue to use your computer, you will find that one of the most common tasks you perform is the copying of files. It is very easy to copy a file by using the File System. You can make multiple copies of a file (with different names, of course) on the same disk and copy a file to another disk. The general procedure is to first select a file in the File List window. Next, activate the **File** option and select **Copy**. You will then be prompted for the destination.

Try an example of this procedure now. Select the file that is called CHKDSK.COM. Next, activate the action bar and select **File**. From the drop-down menu, select **Copy**. You will then see a screen similar to the one shown in Figure 4-4.

Notice that the name of the file you selected is on the "From" line and the cursor is blinking on the "To" line. If you are using a fixed disk, the "To" line will contain D:\DOS. (Remember, your DOS directory may have another name.) If you are running DOS from a floppy disk, the "To" line will display A:\. These are the default path names. However, you can specify any path name you like.

Advance the cursor to the end of whatever is on the "To" line. You can do this by pressing the right arrow key several times or by pressing the END key

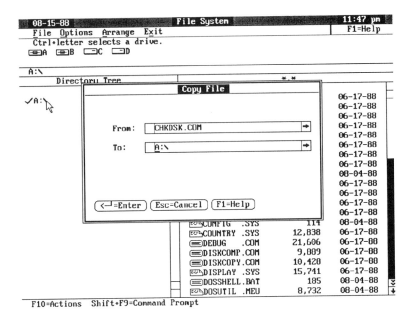

FIGURE 4-4   The Copy File window

once. If you are running DOS with a fixed disk, enter a backslash at the end of the line. Next, enter the file name **CD.TST**. At this point, the "To" line should look like one of the two shown here:

```
C:\DOS\CD.TST
A:\CD.TST
```

After you have entered the file name correctly, press ENTER to begin the copying process. When this process has completed, you will see a directory entry for CD.TST directly above the one for CHKDSK.COM. Notice that the only difference between the two entries is their names. Everything else is the same. The copying operation makes an exact copy of the original file.

Unlike an audio tape, in which each copy gets progressively worse, a copy of a disk file is exactly the same as the original. The information in the file does not degrade with each copy.

The file-copying operation is most often used to copy a file to another disk for backup purposes. In general, you will always want at least two copies of important files in case one should be destroyed; three or four copies are even safer. Assuming that you have at least two drives in your computer, copying a file to another disk is an easy process.

The Copy option allows you to specify the disk drives of both the source and destination files by using their drive specifiers. For example, if you have a fixed disk and a floppy-disk drive, insert the blank formatted disk in drive A. To copy CHKDSK.COM from the fixed disk to the floppy disk, select CHKDSK.COM on the fixed disk and use the following for the "To" line:

A:CHKDSK.COM

If you are running DOS from a floppy-disk drive, you can copy from drive A (the current drive) to drive B. First select CHKDSK.COM, and then use the following on the "To" line:

B:CHKDSK.COM

If you have two floppy-disk drives, put the blank formatted disk in drive B. If you only have one disk drive, you can use the form of the "To" line just given, but you will have to swap disks in and out as prompted.

The method of copying CHKDSK.COM just shown is seldom used in practice because a shorter form exists. When the destination file is going to have the same name as the source file, only the destination drive specifier needs to be used—there is no need to specify the file name again. For example, this will work fine for the "To" line:

B:

The only time that you need to specify a name for the destination file is when it will not be the same as the source file's name.

As you will see later, this copying operation has other functions besides the ones discussed here. However, let's leave it for a while and look at how to erase files.

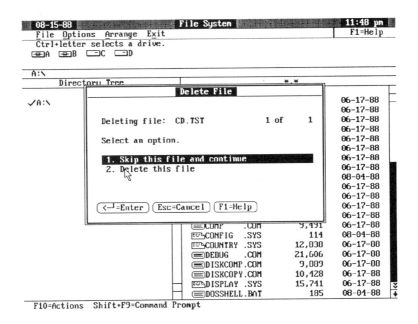

FIGURE 4-5   The Delete File safety check window

ERASING FILES

You often need a file only for a short period of time, or you may want to put
a disk to a different use and need to remove the files that no longer matter.
Either way, it is easy to remove a file from a disk by using the File System.

To try an example, erase the CD.TST file that you created in the previous
section. First, select the file from the File List window. Next, activate the action bar and select **File**. From the drop-down menu, select the Delete option.
You will then be shown the file you are going to delete. If it is the correct file
(as it should be if you selected the right file), then press ENTER. (If it is not
the right file, press ESC and try again.)

At this point you will see a window like the one in Figure 4-5. Erasing a
file is a one-way operation; you can not bring it back once it is gone. DOS
gives you a second chance to change your mind before it erases the file. The
safety check window has two options. The first lets you abort the deletion

operation and is the same as pressing ESC. The second option tells DOS to go ahead and erase the file. Since you do, in fact, want to erase the file, select the second option.

You can delete more than one file at a time by first selecting all of the files you want to erase and then activating the **Delete** option.

When you erase a file, you should consider it permanently and irreversibly gone. You may read in various magazine advertisements that it is possible to recover an accidentally erased file. In practice, however, this is seldom true. If you are an experienced DOS user and know exactly what you are doing and you try to recover the file *immediately* after erasing it, you can sometimes be successful, but this requires the use of special programs not supplied with DOS. The rule, therefore, is to be very careful about what you erase, because once a file is gone, it's gone.

RENAMING A FILE

If you have been following along with the examples, then you will have copied CHKDSK.COM to a previously blank disk. Make sure that this disk is in drive A at this time.

To rename a file, you first select the file you want to change the name of in the File List window and then select the **Rename** option in the **File** menu. You will then be prompted for the new name of the file. To try this, let's give the copy of CHKDSK.COM you put on the disk the new name TEST.COM.

Select drive A in the Drive Specifier window. Next, select the file CHKDSK.COM in the File List window. Activate the action bar, and choose **File**; then select **Rename**. You will be prompted at this point for the new name for CHKDSK.COM. Enter **TEST.COM** and press ENTER. You will see that the name change takes place. To change the name back to CHKDSK.COM, repeat the procedure.

If you are running DOS from the fixed disk, select drive C at this time and activate the DOS directory. If you are using floppy disks, put your DOS disk back in drive A now.

CHANGING THE WAY
FILES ARE DISPLAYED

You can change which files are displayed in the File List window and the order in which they are displayed by using the **Options** entry. Select **Options** at this time. The first entry in the pull-down menu is **Display Options**. Select

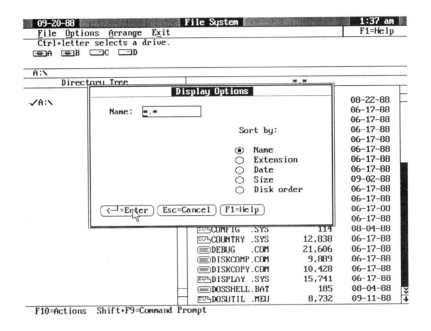

FIGURE 4-6   The Display Options window

it at this time. You will see the Display Options window, which looks like the one shown in Figure 4-6.

The Display Options window contains two items. The first is the Name field, which is used to specify the name of the file or files you want to see displayed in the File List window. By default, the name is *.*, which tells DOS to display all files.

The second item in the window is the Sort By menu. When files are shown in the File List window they are by default sorted in alphabetical order, based on their names. You can change the way in which the files are sorted by selecting an option from the list.

To switch between the Name and Sort By options, press the TAB key or click once with the mouse on the desired item.

Looking for Specific Files

Until now, the Shell has displayed the entire contents of the current directory in the File List window. However, you can use the Name option to find a specific file by entering its name, which is sometimes called the *file specifier*. This method allows you to quickly determine whether a file is in the directory or not. For example, enter the file name **SORT.EXE** at the name prompt and press ENTER. The File List window will clear, and then only the SORT.EXE file will be displayed. (SORT.EXE is DOS's sort command.) To have the entire directory displayed again, activate the Display Options option and enter ***.*** in the Name field.

When you specify a file name, DOS attempts to find a file in the current directory that matches that name. If you specify a file that is not in the directory, you will see this message:

No files match file specifier

If you think that the file you requested really is in the directory, you may have made a typing error. If, after a second try, DOS still claims the file is nonexistent, try listing the entire directory; you may have forgotten the file's name.

Wild-card File Names

Up to this point, you have learned how to list either the entire directory or a specific file. However, DOS allows you to list groups of related files. You can also list a file without knowing its full name. To accomplish these tasks requires special *wild-card* characters that can be used in place of an actual file name. Let's start with an example.

Assume that you want to list the names of all of the files on a disk that share the .EXE extension. To do this, enter the following at the Name field of the Display Options window:

*.EXE

This causes DOS to display all files with an .EXE extension. The output will be as shown in Figure 4-7.

```
 09-20-88                        File System                    1:38 am
  File  Options  Arrange  Exit                                │ F1=Help
 Ctrl+letter  elects a drive.
  ▭A   ▭B   ▭C   ▭D

 A:\
        Directory Tree          │              *.EXE
 ✓A:\                           │  ≡APPEND   .EXE    11,170    06-17-88
                                │  ≡ATTRIB   .EXE    18,247    06-17-88
                                │  ≡FILESYS  .EXE    11,125    06-17-88
                                │  ≡FIND     .EXE     5,983    06-17-88
                                │  ≡IFSFUNC  .EXE    21,637    06-17-88
                                │  ≡JOIN     .EXE    17,457    06-17-88
                                │  ≡MEM      .EXE    20,133    06-17-88
                                │  ≡NLSFUNC  .EXE     6,910    06-17-88
                                │  ≡REPLACE  .EXE    17,199    06-17-88
                                │  ≡SHARE    .EXE    10,285    06-17-88
                                │  ≡SHELLC   .EXE   153,975    06-17-88
                                │  ≡SORT     .EXE     5,914    06-17-88
                                │  ≡SUBST    .EXE    18,143    06-17-88
                                │  ≡XCOPY    .EXE    17,087    06-17-88



 F10=Actions  Shift+F9=Command Prompt
```

FIGURE 4-7   Directory display with the *.EXE file specifier

When used in a file name that is part of a DOS command, the asterisk is a special character that tells DOS to match any sequence of characters. It means that any character can occupy the position of the asterisk and all character positions after it. Note that the filename and extension are separate, so the asterisk applies only to the part of the name in which it is used. This is the reason that the Shell uses *.* by default in the Name field.

You can use the asterisk to find files whose names have one or more initial characters in common by specifying those characters followed by an asterisk. For example, enter this file specifier:

S*.EXE

DOS will display all files that begin with the letter "S" and have the .EXE extension—in this case, SHARE.EXE, SHELLC.EXE, SORT.EXE, and SUBST.EXE. Note that any sequence of characters may follow the "S".

You cannot use the asterisk to find files whose filenames begin with different characters but end with the same characters. For example,

*ST.EXE

will *not* find all files with filenames that end in ST. Instead, it will display all files that have the extension .EXE. This is because the asterisk matches any and all characters from its position in the name to the end.

You can use the asterisk wild card in the extension field of a file name. For example, the command

S*.*

reports all files that begin with "S" and that have any extension. Now try some examples on your own.

The second wild-card character is the question mark (?), which will match any one character in its position. Unlike the asterisk, it matches *only* one character—not a sequence of characters. For example, the following file specifier will find all files that end with the characters "DISK":

?DISK.*

To this, DOS responds with FDISK.COM and VDISK.SYS.

For another example, assume that these files are on your disk (they aren't, actually):

TEST1A.DAT
TEST2A.DAT
TEST3A.DAT
TEST1B.DAT
TEST2B.DAT

The file specifier

TEST?A.DAT

will find the TEST1A.DAT, TEST2A.DAT, and TEST3A.DAT files.

Now try some examples of your own with the ? wild-card character.

As you will see later in this book, wild-card characters are very useful in several DOS commands because they allow you to handle related groups of files easily.

```
╔══════════╗              ╔══════════╗              ╔══════════╗
║ 08-15-88 ║              ║File System║             ║ 11:55 pm ║
╚══════════╝              ╚══════════╝              ╚══════════╝
 File  Options  Arrange  Exit                       │ F1=Help
 Ctrl+letter selects a drive.
 ▭A  ▭B  ▭C  ▭D

 A:\
─────────────────────────────────────────────────────────────────
        Directory Tree                            *.*
─────────────────────────────────────────────────────────────────
  ✓▓▓▓                         ▤012345   .678        109    06-17-88
                               ▤SHELL    .ASC          0    08-04-88
                               ▤AUTOEXEC.BAT          99    08-04-88
                               ▤DOSSHELL.BAT         185    08-04-88
                               ▤SHELL    .CLR       4,438    08-11-88
                               ▤IBMBIO   .COM      32,810    06-17-88
                               ▤IBMDOS   .COM      35,984    06-17-88
                               ▤COMMAND  .COM      37,637    06-17-88
                               ▤DISKCOPY.COM       10,428    06-17-88
                               ▤FFORMAT .COM       22,923    06-17-88
                               ▤KEYB     .COM      14,759    06-17-88
                               ▤MODE     .COM      23,040    06-17-88
                               ▤SYS      .COM      11,472    06-17-88
                               ▤ASSIGN   .COM       5,785    06-17-88
                               ▤BASICA   .COM      36,285    06-17-88
                               ▤COMP     .COM       9,491    06-17-88
                               ▤DEBUG    .COM      21,606    06-17-88
                               ▤DISKCOMP.COM        9,889    06-17-88
                               ▤EDLIN    .COM      14,249    06-17-88
                               ▤GRAFTABL.COM       10,271    06-17-88
                               ▤GRAPHICS.COM       16,733    06-17-88
─────────────────────────────────────────────────────────────────
  F10=Actions   Shift+F9=Command Prompt
```

FIGURE 4-8   The DOS directory sorted by extension

Changing the Sorting Order

Select the **Display Options** entry in the **Options** menu. First, reset the file
specifier in the Name field to *.* and press TAB (not ENTER). Pressing the
TAB key activates the Sort By window.

   By default, the directory is sorted by the file names. However, you can
also have the directory sorted by extension, date, or size. You can also request that the contents of the directory not be sorted, which is accomplished
by choosing the **Disk Order** entry. To see the effects of changing the sorting method, choose to sort by extension and press ENTER. The directory will
then look like that shown in Figure 4-8.

```
 08-15-88                        File System                   11:56 pm
 File  Options  Arrange  Exit                                  F1=Help
 Ctr ┌──Show Information──────────────┐
 ⊐A  │                                │
     │                                │
 A:\ │                                │
     │          ◻                     │
     │                                │
                                        * . *
 ✓A:\                          ⊞012345  .678      109   06-17-88
                               ⊞SHELL   .ASC        0   08-04-88
                               ⊜AUTOEXEC.BAT       99   08-04-88
                               ⊜DOSSHELL.BAT      185   08-04-88
                               ⊞SHELL   .CLR    4,438   08-11-88
                               ⊜IBMBIO  .COM   32,810   06-17-88
                               ⊜IBMDOS  .COM   35,984   06-17-88
                               ⊜COMMAND .COM   37,637   06-17-88
                               ⊜DISKCOPY.COM   10,428   06-17-88
                               ⊜FFORMAT .COM   22,923   06-17-88
                               ⊜KEYB    .COM   14,759   06-17-88
                               ⊜MODE    .COM   23,040   06-17-88
     │                         ⊜SYS     .COM   11,472   06-17-88
     │ ┌Esc=Cancel┐ ┌F1=Help┐  ⊜ASSIGN  .COM    5,785   06-17-88
     │ └──────────┘ └───────┘  ⊜BASICA  .COM   36,285   06-17-88
     └────────────────────────┐⊜COMP    .COM    9,491   06-17-88
                               ⊜DEBUG   .COM   21,606   06-17-88
                               ⊜DISKCOMP.COM    9,889   06-17-88
                               ⊜EDLIN   .COM   14,249   06-17-88
                               ⊜GRAFTABL.COM   10,271   06-17-88
                               ⊜GRAPHICS.COM   16,733   06-17-88
 F10=Actions   Shift+F9=Command Prompt
```

FIGURE 4-9   The Show Information window

DISPLAYING FILE INFORMATION

Select the 012345.678 file in the File List window at this time. Activate the
action bar and choose **Options**. From the **Options** menu select **Show Information**. You will see the window shown in Figure 4-9.

The Show Information window displays information about the selected
file, the current directory, and the logged-in disk. You will learn more about
this window later in the book, but keep in mind that the number of selected
files will be shown under the "Selected" heading. This can be useful when
you are not sure how many files have been selected—especially before a
deletion operation.

Press ESC to exit the Show Information window at this time.

```
                         File System
 File  Options  Arrange  Exit                    | F1=Help
 Ctrl+letter selects a drive.
 ▭A  ▭B  ▭C  ▭D
                              ▨
 A:\
          Directory Tree            |        *.*
 ✓A:\                               |
                                    | ▨012345  .678    109  06-17-88
                                    | ▨SHELL    .ASC     0  08-04-88
                                    | ▤AUTOEXEC.BAT     99  08-04-88
                                    | ▤DOSSHELL.BAT    185  08-04-88
                                    | ▨SHELL    .CLR  4,438  08-11-88


 ▭A  ▭B  ▭C  ▭D


          Directory Tree            |        *.*
 ✓A:\                               |
                                    | ▨012345  .678      109  06-17-88
                                    | ▨SHELL    .ASC       0  08-04-88
                                    | ▤AUTOEXEC.BAT       99  08-04-88
                                    | ▤DOSSHELL.BAT      185  08-04-88
                                    | ▨SHELL    .CLR    4,438  08-11-88
                                    | ▤IBMBIO  .COM   32,810  06-17-88
                                    | ▤IBMDOS  .COM   35,984  06-17-88
                                    | ▤COMMAND .COM   37,637  06-17-88
                                    | ▤DISKCOPY.COM   10,428  06-17-88

 F10=Actions  Shift+F9=Command Prompt
```

FIGURE 4-10   Screen appearance when Multiple File List has been selected

ARRANGING THE SCREEN

You can have the Shell display the directory in one of three ways by using the **Arrange** action-bar option. Select **Arrange** at this time. You will see the three options listed in its menu. The first option, **Single File List**, causes a single directory to be displayed. This option will be deactivated, because the directory is already displayed in this format.

The **Multiple File List** option splits the screen and allows you to display the contents of two different directories or disks at the same time. Choose this option now; your screen will look like the one shown in Figure 4-10.

Once the screen has been split, you can change which directory or disk (or both) either directory window is displaying. You might want to try this now. Remember, use the TAB key to activate the various windows. You might

```
08-15-88                        File System                     11:58 pm
File  Options  Arrange  Exit                                   F1=Help
Ctrl+letter selects a drive.
 ⌐═╕A   ⌐═╕B   ⌐═╕C   ⌐═╕D

A:\                        ↳
                                           *.*
File
  Name  : 012345.678      ▓▓012345   .678        109   06-17-88   12:00pm
  Attr  : ...a            ▓▓SHELL     .ASC          0   08-04-88    2:00pm
Selected          A       ≣AUTOEXEC .BAT          99   08-04-88    2:40pm
  Number:         1       ≣DOSSHELL .BAT         185   08-04-88    2:42pm
  Size  :       109       ▓▓SHELL     .CLR      4,438   08-11-88    2:24pm
Directory                 ≣IBMBIO   .COM      32,810   06-17-88   12:00pm
  Name  : ROOT            ≣IBMDOS   .COM      35,984   06-17-88   12:00pm
  Size  :   963,706       ≣COMMAND  .COM      37,637   06-17-88   12:00pm
  Files :        62       ≣DISKCOPY .COM      10,428   06-17-88   12:00pm
Disk                      ≣FFORMAT  .COM      22,923   06-17-88   12:00pm
  Name  : DOS400          ≣KEYB     .COM      14,759   06-17-88   12:00pm
  Size  : 1,457,664       ≣MODE     .COM      23,040   06-17-88   12:00pm
  Avail :   478,720       ≣SYS      .COM      11,472   06-17-88   12:00pm
  Files :        62       ≣ASSIGN   .COM       5,785   06-17-88   12:00pm
  Dirs  :         1       ≣BASICA   .COM      36,285   06-17-88   12:00pm
                          ≣COMP     .COM       9,491   06-17-88   12:00pm
                          ≣DEBUG    .COM      21,606   06-17-88   12:00pm
                          ≣DISKCOMP .COM       9,889   06-17-88   12:00pm
                          ≣EDLIN    .COM      14,249   06-17-88   12:00pm
                          ≣GRAFTABL .COM      10,271   06-17-88   12:00pm ⌄
                          ≣GRAPHICS .COM      16,733   06-17-88   12:00pm ↓
F10=Actions   Shift+F9=Command Prompt
```

FIGURE 4-11   Screen appearance when System File List has been selected

find the **Multiple File List** option useful when you are copying files between directories.

The **System File List** option causes the entire contents of the disk to be displayed, bypassing the directory structure of the disk. Try this option now. Your screen will look similar to that shown in Figure 4-11. Notice that information about the file currently highlighted is shown. As you move the highlight around, the information changes to reflect the new file. Note also the directory that contains the file is displayed.

A system file list is particularly useful when you forget in which directory a file is. To find the file, activate the **System File List** option. Next, using the **Display Options** selection in the **Options** menu, change the file-name specifier to that of the file you want to find. If the file is on the disk, its name will appear in the File List window. To try this, activate Display Options and enter **CHKDSK.COM** for the file specifier. As you can see, it will be found.

SUMMARY

In this chapter you learned about some of the File System's most important and frequently used operations. You learned

- How to start a program
- The various action bar options
- How to view or print a text file
- The purpose of drive specifiers
- How to copy files
- How to erase and rename files
- How to change the directory display
- How to use wild-card file specifiers
- How to arrange the screen

The next chapter will explore some of the File System's more advanced features. You will learn to create and manage directories, change file attributes, and copy files across directories.

5

ADVANCED FILE SYSTEM FEATURES

Now that you know your way around the File System and can perform many of the most common operations, it is time to unlock some of the system's more advanced features. Even though many of these features are quite powerful, they are not difficult to master.

For the examples in this chapter you will need a blank formatted disk. You can use the one you created for Chapter 4 if you like; simply erase any files you may have copied to it. (To erase a file, just follow the procedure described in Chapter 4.)

Activate the File System, and then put the blank disk in drive A. Log in to drive A at this time. (This instruction applies to fixed disk users as well.)

WORKING WITH DIRECTORIES

In Chapter 3 you learned that subdirectories can help your organization and efficiency. Now it is time you learned how to use them. To create a subdirectory with the File System, you must use the Create Directory option in the File menu.

In this section, we will create on the disk in drive A the directory structure shown in Figure 5-1. (This is the same directory structure that was used to introduce directories in Chapter 3.) Be sure that you are logged in to drive A before you begin these examples.

Creating the WP and
WP\FORMLET Subdirectories

Activate the action bar and select **File**. From the **File** menu, select **Create Directory**. You will see the Create Directory window shown in Figure 5-2.

The prompt will be at the line that says "New directory name." At this time enter **WP** and press ENTER. "WP" is short for word processing, which is too long to be a directory name. In the Directory Tree window you will see that the WP directory has been added off the root.

To create the FORMLET directory under the WP directory, first select the WP directory in the Directory Tree window. Next, activate the action bar and select **File**. From the **File** drop-down menu select **Create Directory**. When prompted for the directory name, enter **FORMLET** and press ENTER. (FORMLET is short for form letters.) After the operation completes, you will see this directory tree displayed

```
A:\
 └── WP
      └── FORMLET
```

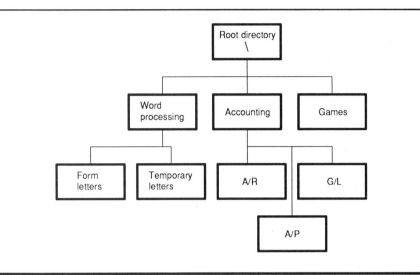

FIGURE 5-1   Example directory structure

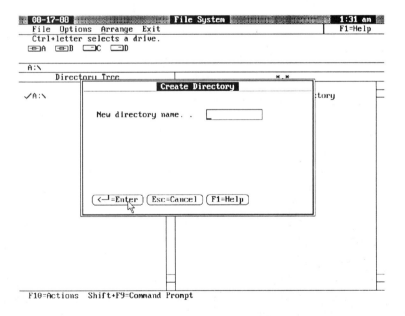

FIGURE 5-2   The Create Directory window

General Rules
For Creating Subdirectories

When you use the Shell to create a subdirectory, you must first select the directory under which you want the subdirectory to be. When you created the FORMLET directory under WP, for example, you first had to select the WP directory. The directory you specify in the Create Directory window will always be created under the directory currently selected in the Directory Tree window.

The DOS Shell does not let you enter a drive specifier or a path name when you enter the name of the directory you want to create. For example, select the root directory at this time, and activate the Create Directory option. When prompted for the directory, try entering **WP\TEMP** and pressing ENTER. As you can see, the message "Access denied" is displayed. Press ESC at this time.

Creating the Rest
Of the Subdirectories

Let's create the rest of the subdirectories that you will need. First, select the WP directory, and activate the **Create Directory** option. Enter **TEMP** for the name and press ENTER.

Next, select the root directory and then create the ACCOUNTS directory. With the root still selected, create the GAMES directory. The tree in the Directory Tree window should now look like this:

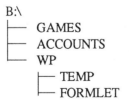

```
B:\
  ├── GAMES
  ├── ACCOUNTS
  └── WP
        ├── TEMP
        └── FORMLET
```

Now fill in the ACCOUNTS subdirectories. Select the ACCOUNTS directory in the Directory Tree window, and then create the AR (accounts receivable), AP (accounts payable), and GL (general ledger) subdirectories at this time. When you have finished, your screen should look similar to that shown in Figure 5-3.

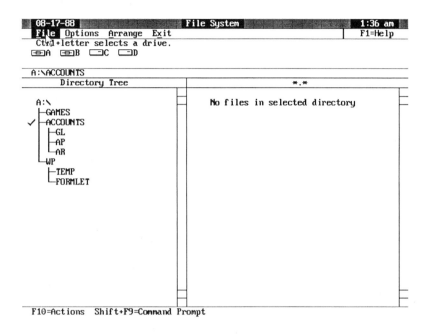

FIGURE 5-3   The example directory structure as shown on the screen

Removing a Directory

To remove a directory, first select the directory you want to remove and then use the **Delete** option in the **File** menu. There is one restriction on removing directories: the directory must be empty. It can contain no files or other sub-directories.

Select the GL directory in the tree at this time. Since it is empty, remove it now. You will see a safety check window, which gives you a second chance to consider keeping the directory. Go ahead and delete the directory at this time. You will see that the GL directory no longer appears in the Directory Tree window. Before continuing, recreate the GL directory in the accounts directory.

If you try to remove a directory that contains files or has its own subdirectories, you will be told that access is denied, and you must abort the operation by pressing ESC. If you do, indeed, want to remove that directory, you must erase all of its files and remove all of its subdirectories first.

COPYING FILES BETWEEN DIRECTORIES

When you copy a file from one directory to another, you must be sure to fully specify the destination path name. For example, let's copy the 0123456.678 file into the FORMLET subdirectory of WP. If you have a fixed disk, switch to drive C and select the DOS directory. If you are running DOS with two floppy disks, put the DOS disk in drive A and the disk whose directory structure you just created into drive B. If you have only one floppy disk, put the DOS disk in drive A and follow the instructions for a dual floppy system. In this case, DOS will prompt you to swap disks.

If you are a fixed-disk user, you should select the 012345.678 file and then activate the **Copy** option in the **File** directory. When prompted for the destination, enter this at the "To" line:

A:\WP\FORMLET

If you are a floppy-disk user, you should select the 012345.678 file and then activate the Copy option in the File directory. When prompted for the destination, enter this at the "To" line:

B:\WP\FORMLET

Then, remove the DOS disk and put the newly created disk into drive A.

Select drive A, and then select the FORMLET directory. You will see that the 012345.678 file is, indeed, in the directory.

To copy a file from a subdirectory to the root directory, use the backslash as the destination path. For example, to copy the 012345.678 file from FORMLET to the root, first activate the FORMLET directory and select 012345.678. Next, activate the Copy option in the File menu, and use this as the destination:

A:\

Remember, the leading backslash is DOS's name for the root directory. If you check the root at this time, you will see that the file has been copied there.

As you have learned, no two files on the same disk, sharing the same path name, can have the same name. Within any directory, therefore, no two file names can be the same. However, files in other directories can have similar names. DOS keeps similar names straight because it always associates a path name with a file name.

Let's do one last exercise, copying the 012345.678 file from the FORMLET subdirectory of WP to the WP directory itself, this time giving the destination file a different name. Select the FORMLET directory, and select 012345.678. Next, activate the Copy option in the File menu and use this for the "To" line:

A:\WP\TEST.TST

When you check the WP directory, you will see that the TEST.TST file is there and that its contents are the same as the 012345.678 file in the FORMLET directory.

Replacing a File

Put the disk containing your directories in drive A, and copy 012345.678 from FORMLET into WP, calling the destination file TEST.TST again. This time, before the copying begins, you will see the safety check window shown in Figure 5-4.

Whenever you attempt to copy a file to a destination that already has a file by that name, you will see this window. It is very easy to accidentally replace a file that you did not mean to replace, so this window gives you a chance to reconsider.

THE CURRENT DIRECTORY

If you have a fixed disk, try this: log in to drive C and select the DOS directory. Next, log in to drive A and select the GAMES directory. Now log back in to the C drive. Notice that the DOS directory is selected. Log in to A. Notice that the GAMES directory is selected. If you have two floppy-disk drives, put the DOS disk in A and the directories disk in B, and try the same process.

This exercise illustrates that DOS remembers which directory is active for each disk drive in the system. In the absence of a path name, DOS uses the

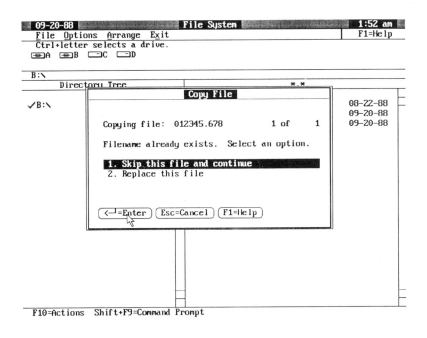

FIGURE 5-4   The safety check window displayed for replacing a file

active directory. Certain DOS commands and options, like Copy, make use
of this fact, as you will see a little later in this chapter.

DIRECTORY CAPACITIES

The root directory of a disk can hold a fixed number of entries based on the
capacity of the disk. (An *entry* is either a file or subdirectory name.) Table
5-1 shows the number of entries for the most common floppy disk formats.
The root directory of the fixed disk can hold 512 entries.

Unlike the root directory, a subdirectory can hold as many entries as available disk space allows. This is because DOS continues to allocate space on
the disk to hold the entries. In general, however, you should not have extremely large directories because they are difficult to manage. Once you

Disk capacity (in bytes)	Maximum entries
160/180K	64
320/360K	112
720K	112
1200K	224
1440K	224

TABLE 5-1   Directory Capacity of Disks

have about a hundred entries, it is time to create a new subdirectory and move some files to it.

MANAGING YOUR DIRECTORIES

Although you will look more closely at the topic of directory management later in this book, a few pointers will help you now. First and foremost, subdirectories should be used to hold logically related groups of files. Files can be related to each other in several different ways. For example, if a computer is shared by a number of people, then creating a subdirectory for each individual is probably a good idea.

Even though all of the files in a user's subdirectory may be quite different in purpose from one another, they are all related because they belong to that user. However, if a computer is being used by one person for several separate tasks, as in the example presented earlier in this chapter, then the subdirectories are best organized by functional areas. The way the computer is used should dictate the directory design.

It is important to remember that each subdirectory uses disk space, and that creating an unnecessarily large number of subdirectories wastes this space. Also, subdirectories that are deeply nested and require long path names slow DOS's access time for any files they contain. You must balance these factors against the advantages that subdirectories have to offer.

MOVING A FILE

If the directories disk you created from the previous section is not in drive A, put it there now. Make sure that you are logged in to drive A at this time.

You have learned how to copy a file; now you will learn how to move a file. Moving a file is exactly like copying it, except that once the copy has taken place, the original file is deleted.

To move a file, first select the file you want to move and then use the **Move** option in the **File** menu. For example, switch to the FORMLET directory and select 012345.678 at this time. Next, activate the **File** menu and select the **Move** option. Use this for the destination:

    A:\GAMES

Press ENTER. This moves the file to the GAMES directory and removes it from the FORMLET directory.

The Move operation is really just a convenience. You can accomplish the same thing by first copying the file and then deleting it.

CHANGING A FILE'S ATTRIBUTES

All files have associated with them a number of *attributes*. Some of these attributes are meaningful only to DOS and may not be changed by you. However, three of them can be set. Before you learn how to change a file's attributes, however, you need to know what they mean.

The three file attributes that you can set are

- Hidden
- Read-only
- Archive

Each attribute is either on or off. If the hidden attribute is on, then the file will still be displayed in the Shell's File List window, but it will not appear in a directory listing at the command prompt. This attribute is off by default.

When the read-only attribute is set (on), the file can be read but cannot be modified or erased. This attribute is off by default. If you wish to safeguard a file from accidental erasure or intentional tampering, setting the read-only attribute is a very good idea.

When the archive attribute is set, the file will automatically be copied by a backup operation. The process of backing up a disk will be discussed later in this book.

To change a file's attributes first select the file or files you want to change and use the **Change attribute** option of the **File** menu. You will next be prompted whether you want to change all selected files at the same time or individually. Generally, it is best to change each file individually so that you know exactly what you are doing. Finally, you will see the **Change Attribute** window, which allows you to change the attributes associated with the selected file.

If you want to try changing a file's attributes, you can experiment using the 012345.678 file on your directories disk. Remember, you can view a file's attributes using the **Show information** option in the **Options** menu.

ASSOCIATING FILES

You can associate a program file with a group of other files which share a common extension. For example, a word-processing program can be associated with all files that have the .WP extension. After this association has been made, each time you open a .WP file, the word-processing program is automatically executed and you can begin editing the file. (Remember, to open a file you either position the mouse pointer on it and double-click or move the highlight to it and press ENTER.)

To see an example of associated files, return to the DOS directory on drive C if you have a fixed disk, or put the DOS disk in drive A if you are running DOS from a floppy disk. Next, find the EDLIN.COM file in the File List window, and select it. EDLIN is the DOS text editor. You will learn how to use it later in the book, but for now it will help demonstrate associated files.

Next, activate the **File** menu and select **Associate**. You will see an Associate File window like the one shown in Figure 5-5. You will be prompted for the extensions of the files you want to associate with the editor. At this time, enter **678** (with no period before the 6) and press ENTER. You will now see a window that asks you if you want to be prompted for options when you open an associated file. For this example, no options are needed, so choose option 2. EDLIN is now associated with any file that ends in 678.

To see how the association works, open the 012345.678 file. The screen will clear and you will see the following:

```
End of input file
*
```

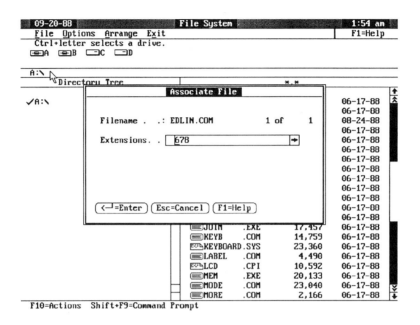

FIGURE 5-5   The Associate File window

The asterisk is EDLIN's prompt. You can list the file by typing **L** and pressing ENTER. To leave EDLIN, enter **E** (for exit) and press ENTER. Do this at this time. You will be told to press ENTER once again to return to the File System. Do this now.

To disassociate a set of files from a program, select the program file and then activate the Associate option. When prompted for the extensions, you will see the current associations. Simply remove the one you no longer want. Try this now by removing 678 from EDLIN's association list.

How you will use the **Associate** option—or whether you will use it at all—depends on why you are using the computer. For example, another area that lends itself to associated files is a spreadsheet program; you could associate the spreadsheet with its files. However, associated files may not make much sense if you use the computer primarily for an accounts payable program, for example.

SELECTING AND DESELECTING ALL FILES

If you want to perform a file operation on all of the files in a directory, you can select them all by using the **Select All** option in the **File** menu. Try it now. As you can see, all of the files are selected. Activate the File menu.

When all of the files are selected, you can perform the following operations:

- Print
- Associate
- Move or Copy
- Delete
- Rename
- Change Attributes

Do not try any of these options at this time, because none of them make any sense for all of the files in your DOS directory or disk. However, when you begin to manage your own directories, the Select All option may be very useful. For example, you could copy all of the files in a directory to another disk in one step.

To deselect all files use the **Deselect All** option in the **File** menu. Deselect all files at this time.

The **Deselect All** option is useful when you are working with a directory that contains many files and you are not sure which files have been selected. By using **Deselect All**, you can ensure that no files are selected.

ELIMINATING THE SAFETY CHECK WINDOWS

As you have seen in these examples, whenever you delete a file or replace a file in a copy operation, a safety check window is displayed. It gives you a chance to change your mind. However, once you become experienced with DOS and the Shell, this extra step can become tedious. For this reason, the Shell lets you disable the safety check windows by using the **File Options** selection in the **Options** menu.

Select this option now. As you can see, three options are in the window:

- Confirm on Delete
- Confirm on Replace
- Select Across Directories

By default, both the **Confirm on Delete** and the **Confirm on Replace** options are on. If you deselect the **Confirm on Delete** option, no safety window will be displayed when you delete a file or a directory. Deselecting **Confirm on Replace** means that there will be no safety check window when you copy a file to a destination that already contains a file by the same name.

As long as you know what you are doing, there is no harm in deactivating these safety check windows. However, you might want to leave them active for the first few weeks you run DOS, just to avoid making a disastrous error.

SELECTING FILES
ACROSS DIRECTORIES

By default, when you change directories, any files selected in the previous directory are automatically deselected. However, you can change this by selecting the **Select Across Directories** option in the **File Options** menu. When this option is activated, the files that you have selected stay selected until you explicitly turn them off.

The principal advantage of keeping files selected is that it allows you to perform operations on files in different directories at the same time. For example, if you have three different word-processing directories, you might want to print files from each directory.

A SECOND LOOK AT
COPYING FILES

You learned how to copy a file in the previous chapter. However, there two more things that you should know about this operation.

Copying Groups of Files

The **Copy** option in the **File** menu allows you to copy groups of files as well as individual files. First, select all of the files you want to copy. Next, activate the **Copy** option in the **File** menu, and specify the destination. All of the specified files will be copied. For example, assuming that you have a fixed disk, put the directories disk created in the first part of this chapter into drive A, and log in to the DOS directory of drive C. Next, select a few small files, and activate the **Copy** option. For the destination, simply enter **A:** and press ENTER. This copies the selected files into the root directory of the disk in drive A.

You can also move multiple files in the same way. Simply select those you want to move, and activate the **Move** option.

Copying Without a Path Name

If in a copy or move operation you use as the destination specifier only a drive specifier with no path name, then the file will be copied into whatever directory was last selected on the target disk. As you know, DOS remembers which directory you were last logged in to for all the drives in your system. It uses that directory for all operations concerning that disk if no other path name is present. The example given here is for a fixed-disk system; if you are running DOS from floppy disks, make the appropriate changes.

Put the directories disk created earlier into drive A. Log in to the GL directory. Switch to drive C, and select the DOS directory. Now copy the 012345.678 file, using **A:** as the destination. Do not put a backslash after the colon.

After the copy has completed, switch to drive A. You will see that the file was copied into the GL directory. For comparison, repeat the procedure, but this time use **A:** as the destination. Since the first backslash in a path name stands for the root, the file is copied into the root.

A CLOSER LOOK AT THE
SHOW INFORMATION WINDOW

If you have fixed disk, select the DOS directory. If you are using floppies, put your DOS disk in drive A. Next, activate the Show Information option in the Options menu. You first saw the Show Information window in the previous chapter; let's explore it a little more thoroughly now.

The Show Information window is divided into four main sections: File, Selected, Directory, and Disk. The File section displays the name of the currently selected file (if any) and shows that file's attributes. When the hidden attribute is on, the letter "h" is displayed. When the read-only attribute is set, an "r" is shown. When the archive attribute is on, an "a" is displayed.

The Selected section tells you which disk is active and how many files (if any) are currently selected. It also tells you the size of those files.

The Directory section shows you the name of the directory, the amount of space the files in that directory take up, and the number of files.

The Disk section reports the name of the disk, the capacity of the disk, and the number of bytes not currently in use. It also displays the number of files and directories on the disk.

RUNNING OUT OF DISK SPACE

All disks have a finite amount of storage capacity. Because of this, it is possible to fill one up. If a disk is full or nearly full and you try to copy a file to it that is bigger than the amount of free space on the disk, you will see this error message in the Copy File window:

Disk is full.

If this occurs, your only option is to cancel the copying operation. Next, you must decide whether to use a new disk or to remove unneeded files from the disk. Then you must repeat the copy process.

You can determine the amount of free space on a disk by selecting the **Show Information** option in the Options menu.

SUMMARY

In this chapter you learned about several advanced File System features, including

- Creating subdirectories
- Removing a directory
- Copying files between directories
- File attributes
- Associating files
- Eliminating safety check windows
- Copying groups of files and copying without a path name

The next chapter wraps up our discussion of the Shell. It includes information on how to configure the Shell and how to print the screen, and it also discusses special editing keys.

6

USING THE SHELL

This is the last chapter of this book that deals exclusively with the Shell. In it, you will learn how to add programs and groups to the Start Programs window, to customize the Program Startup Prompt window, to print the screen, and to use some special editing keys.

GROUPS AND SUBGROUPS

The Shell uses the Main Group and subgroups to organize the Start Programs window. The Main Group can contain both programs and subgroups. For example, by default, the Main Group contains one subgroup, DOS Utilities, and three programs: the Command Prompt program, the File System, and the Change Colors program. In contrast, a subgroup can only contain programs.

The Main Group and subgroup format allows you to put related programs into their own group. For example, you might create a word-processing group and put a word processor, a spelling checker, and a thesaurus program in that group. The Shell lets you manage and structure your programs by allowing you to keep related programs in separate groups.

Note: Do not confuse subgroups with subdirectories. The subgroup in which a program appears in the Start Programs window has nothing whatsoever to do with what directory the program is in on the disk.

ADDING A PROGRAM
TO THE MAIN GROUP

If you have not yet done so, activate the Shell and make sure the Start Programs screen is displaying the Main Group.

DOS allows you to add a program to a group so that you can execute it from the Start Programs window instead of having to use the File System. Not only can this be very convenient, saving you time and keystrokes, but it can also help ensure that the program is started correctly.

Since all of DOS's external commands are programs, as an example let's add CHKDSK to the Main Group. Activate the action bar and select the **Program** option. You will see a menu with the following entries:

Start
Add
Change
Delete
Copy

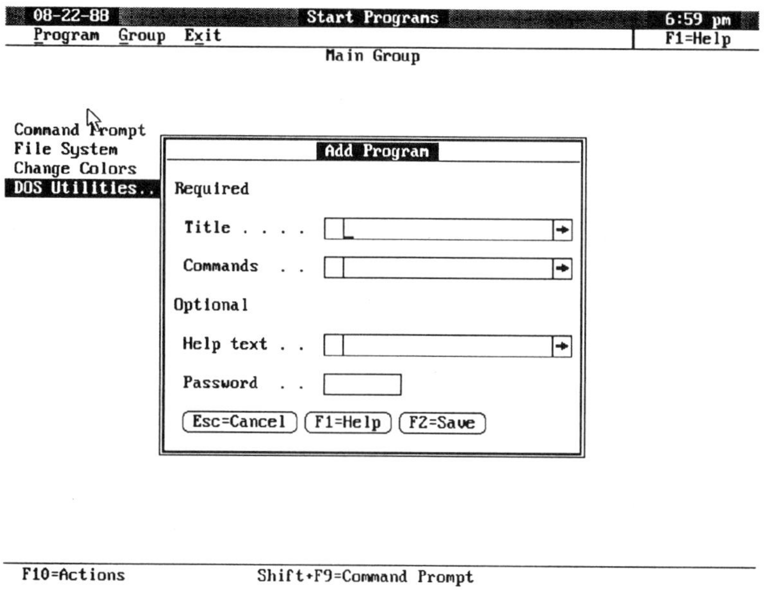

```
 08-22-88                    Start Programs                6:59 pm
   Program  Group  Exit                                    F1=Help
                            Main Group


Command Prompt
File System            ┌──────── Add Program ────────┐
Change Colors          │                             │
DOS Utilities..        │  Required                   │
                       │                             │
                       │    Title . . . .  ┌──────────┤→│
                       │                             │
                       │    Commands  . .  ┌──────────┤→│
                       │                             │
                       │  Optional                   │
                       │                             │
                       │    Help text . .  ┌──────────┤→│
                       │                             │
                       │    Password  . .  ┌──────┐   │
                       │                             │
                       │  (Esc=Cancel) (F1=Help) (F2=Save) │
                       └─────────────────────────────┘


 F10=Actions              Shift+F9=Command Prompt
```

Figure 6-1   The Add Program window

Select the **Add** option. Your screen will look like the one shown in Figure 6-1. Each program has four fields of information associated with it. The first two fields must contain information; the second two are optional.

The first piece of information you must enter is the title of the program that will be displayed in the window. For CHKDSK, enter **"Check the disk"** as the title and press ENTER. The second item you must enter is the command you want to execute. In its simplest form (and in this example), the Commands line contains only the name of the program. Enter **CHKDSK** now.

You can also enter some helpful information about the program at the Help text field. This information can be up to 478 characters long. As you enter text past the end of the window, the text will automatically be scrolled to the left for you. If you want, you can use this text for the help information:

> The CHKDSK program checks the disk drive for errors. It also reports
> the size of the disk, the size of memory, and amount of each that is free.

When this text is displayed, the Help System will automatically format this message for you.

You can give a program password protection if you like. If you do, each time you try to run the program, you will first be prompted for the password. For now, just leave the Password field blank; we will come back to passwords a little later on.

If you have entered anything incorrectly, you can go back to a field by pressing the TAB key an appropriate number of times.

Once you have entered all of the information correctly, press the F2 key to install the program in the Main Group. A moment later you will see the "Check the disk" title appear at the bottom of the list. Try to run the program at this time. The screen will clear and the CHKDSK program will run, displaying its result on the screen. Then, without hesitation, the Shell will be reactivated; you will not need to press any key. However, this means that you will not have time to read all of the information on the screen. Also, notice that when the program begins you are not prompted for program parameters as you are when you run a program from the File System. In fact, the CHKDSK program *can* take additional parameters; you will see how to add them (and other features) in the next section.

If you entered help text, try this: highlight the "Check the disk" title and then press F1. Your help text will appear.

You usually will not want to add many programs to the Main Group, but rather to subgroups, so that you can keep your programs organized. However, you will probably want to add a few programs to the Main Group. For example, if your most common task is using a spreadsheet, then you will want to be able to start that spreadsheet from the Main Group in order to save yourself the extra step of first selecting a subgroup before selecting the program.

A FIRST LOOK AT PROGRAM STARTUP COMMANDS

As you saw in the previous section, when the CHKDSK program began execution, it did not prompt you for any parameters; when it terminated, the Shell was immediately redisplayed and you did not have enough time to read the output of the CHKDSK program. While this behavior may not be a problem for some types of programs, it certainly will be for most.

To rectify these problems, the Shell supports a large number of *program startup commands*, called *PSCs* for short. Although the understanding of many of these commands requires a greater knowledge of DOS than you currently have, you can understand and use a few of the most important ones now.

All program startup commands must be separated from each other by a special command separator. This separator is a pair of vertical bars. They are generated by pressing the F4 key.

Adding a Prompt for Program Parameters

To make the Program Parameters prompt window appear, you must put a beginning and ending set of square brackets after the program's name on the Commands line of the Add Program window. The Commands line for CHKDSK should look like this:

```
CHKDSK [ ]
```

This causes the default Program Parameters prompt window to appear. Anything you enter in this window is passed automatically to the program.

To try this, you will need to change the Commands line for CHKDSK. First, position the highlight over CHKDSK's title. Next, activate the action bar and select **Program**. Select the **Change** option. This displays CHKDSK's information on the screen in the Change Program window.

The TAB key is used to switch fields. Press it one time to activate the Commands line. Once the cursor is at the Commands line, press the END key. Next, enter a space and enter []. Your screen should now look like the one in Figure 6-2. *Note:* You do not use the command separator (the vertical bars) between the name of the program and the brackets.

Once you have changed the Commands line, you should press F2 to install the changes. Now try the command. This time you are prompted for additional parameters. If no other parameters are specified, the CHKDSK command checks the currently logged-in drive. However, if you use a drive specifier (the drive letter followed by a colon) as a parameter, CHKDSK will check the disk in the drive you specify. Try this by specifying another drive on your system.

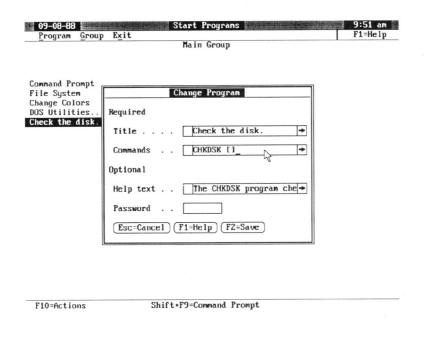

Figure 6-2   The Change Program window

Pausing the Program

Although you are now prompted for parameters, the Shell still overwrites the
screen before you can read all of the information. To prevent this you must
use the PAUSE command in the Commands line of the program. The PAUSE
command causes the line "Press any key to continue" to be displayed when
the program completes its execution.

To try this, activate the action bar and select **Program**. Select **Change**
from the menu. Using the TAB key, advance to the Commands line and press
the END key. Next, enter one space and press F4. Then enter **PAUSE**. Your
screen will look like the one shown in Figure 6-3. When you are done, press
F2. Try the CHKDSK command. Now it will display the prompt and wait for
a keypress before returning to the Shell.

Because **PAUSE** is another PSC, it is separated from the brackets by the
vertical bars.

```
 09-08-88                    Start Programs                    9:52 am
  Program  Group  Exit                                         F1=Help
                              Main Group

 Command Prompt
 File System       ╔══════════════ Change Program ══════════════╗
 Change Colors     ║                                            ║
 DOS Utilities..║  Required                                   ║
 Check the disk.   ║                                            ║
                   ║    Title . . . .  │Check the disk.   │ →  ║
                   ║                                            ║
                   ║    Commands  . .  │CHKDSK []│ PAUSE_  │ →  ║
                   ║                                            ║
                   ║  Optional                                  ║
                   ║                                            ║
                   ║    Help text . .  │The CHKDSK program che│→║
                   ║                                            ║
                   ║    Password  . .  │          │             ║
                   ║                                            ║
                   ║  ( Esc=Cancel ) ( F1=Help ) ( F2=Save )    ║
                   ╚════════════════════════════════════════════╝




 F10=Actions              Shift+F9=Command Prompt
```

Figure 6-3   Adding the PAUSE command

ADDING A GROUP

You can add a group to the Main Group by using the **Group** option. To see how this works, select **Group** at this time. You will see a window similar to that in Figure 6-4.

At the Title line enter **My Group**. This is the title that will be displayed on the screen. At the Filename prompt enter "**MYGROUP.**" This is the name of the file that the Shell will use to store information about the group. You should not enter any extension, because the Shell automatically appends the extension .MEU.

If you like, you can add help text about the group at the Help Text line. This text can be up to 478 characters long.

You can control access to a group by entering a password. If you do this, the user will be prompted for the password when the group is accessed. For now, just leave the Password line blank.

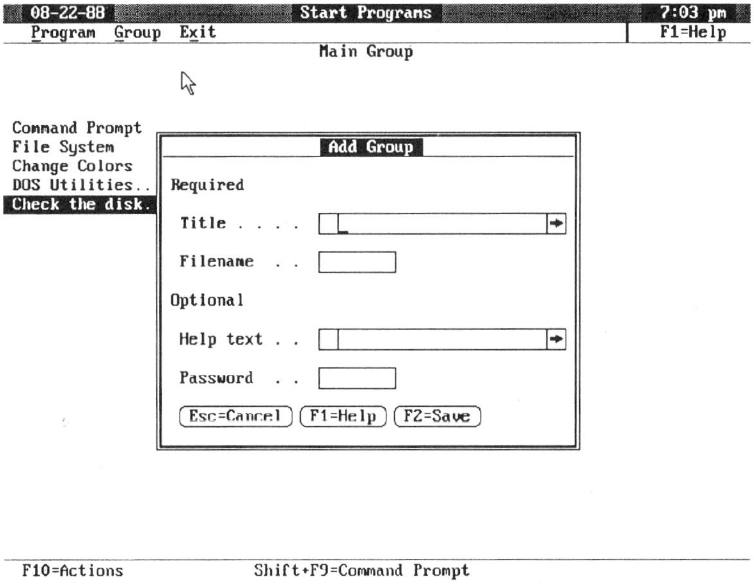

```
 08-22-88              Start Programs              7:03 pm
  Program  Group  Exit                             F1=Help
                           Main Group
              ⤴

Command Prompt
File System      ┌──────────────┤ Add Group ├──────────────┐
Change Colors    │
DOS Utilities..  │ Required
 Check the disk. │
                 │   Title . . . . ▐          ...          ►│
                 │
                 │   Filename  . . ▐          ▌
                 │
                 │ Optional
                 │
                 │   Help text . . ▐                        ►│
                 │
                 │   Password  . . ▐          ▌
                 │   ( Esc=Cancel ) ( F1=Help ) ( F2=Save )
                 └────────────────────────────────────────┘


  F10=Actions              Shift+F9=Command Prompt
```

Figure 6-4   The Add Group window

Once you have entered the information correctly, press F2 to install the group.

ADDING A PROGRAM TO A SUBGROUP

Adding a program to a subgroup is exactly like adding a program to the Main Group. First select the subgroup that you want to add the program to, and then activate the **Program** option. From this menu select **Add** to add the program.

For illustration, let's add one of DOS's external commands to the MYGROUP group. The command you will be adding is called MEM. It reports the amount of memory in the system, the amount that is free, and the largest program that can fit. This is an external command, so it must be on the currently logged-in disk.

Select MYGROUP at this time. As you can see, the message "Group is empty" is displayed because you have not yet put any programs into the group. Select the Program option, and activate the **Add** entry. For the title, enter "**Report system memory**." For the Commands line, enter

```
MEM || PAUSE
```

Notice that you must use the command separator (vertical bars) between the program name and the PAUSE command. The only time you do not need the command separator is between the program name and the brackets.

For most purposes, the MEM command does not require any options; the options available with the MEM command are primarily for programmers. Leaving out the brackets ensures that no Program Parameters window will be displayed. Try this command now.

COPYING PROGRAMS
BETWEEN GROUPS

You can copy a program's entry from one group to another by using the **Copy** option in the **Program** menu. First, highlight the program that you want to move inside its own group, and then select the Copy option. Next, select the group into which you want to copy the program. Finally, press F2 to actually copy the program entry. The copying operation does not erase the original entry for the program.

Try this by copying CHKDSK from the Main Group into MYGROUP. Activate the Main Group, and highlight the "Check the disk" title. Activate the **Program** option and select **Copy**. Next, select MYGROUP and press F2. As you can see, the information for the CHKDSK command has been copied into the MYGROUP group.

DELETING A PROGRAM
FROM A GROUP

To delete a program from a group, highlight the program you want to remove, and then activate the **Program** option. Next, select the **Delete** option. You will see a safety check window that gives you one last chance to change your mind before the program is deleted. Keep in mind that removing a program's entry from a group does not remove it from the disk.

To try a deletion, remove the copy of the CHKDSK program from the Main Group. Activate the Main Group, and highlight the "Check the disk" entry. Next, activate the **Program** option and choose **Delete**. When the safety check window appears, choose to delete the program.

DELETING A GROUP

From the Main Group you can remove a group by using the **Delete** option in the **Group** menu. Highlight the name of the group, and then activate the **Delete** option.

CUSTOMIZING THE PROGRAM STARTUP PROMPT WINDOW

Earlier you were introduced to two program startup commands. The Shell supports a wide variety of other program startup options. In this section you will learn to use three commands that let you control what the program start-up prompt window says.

The program startup prompt window is composed of four sections. The top line is the window title, and the next line is the instruction line. The third line is called the prompt line. Finally, the bottom line is the keys line. You can control the content of the first three of these four lines. A standard program startup prompt window is shown in Figure 6-5.

Before beginning, it is necessary for you to understand the general format of three commands you will be using.

Bracket Commands

There are two general types of program startup commands that can appear on the Commands line. Commands that affect the appearance or operation of the startup prompt window must go inside the square brackets that cause the startup prompt window to appear. These are commonly called *bracket commands*. Bracket commands *do not* need to be separated from each other by the F4 character. Most bracket commands begin with a slash (/).

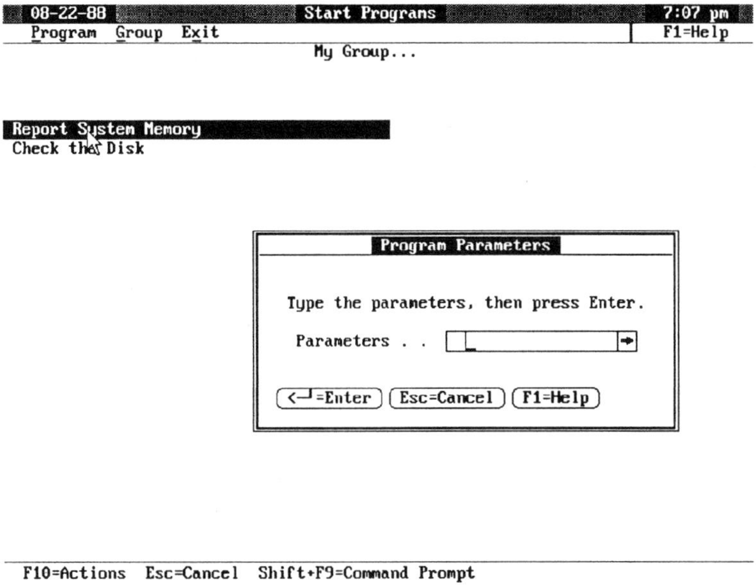

```
 08-22-88                    Start Programs                 7:07 pm
  Program  Group  Exit                                    | F1=Help
                          My Group...


 Report System Memory
  Check the Disk



                   ┌───────────────────────────────────┐
                   │        Program Parameters          │
                   │                                    │
                   │  Type the parameters, then press Enter. │
                   │                                    │
                   │  Parameters . .  [               →]│
                   │                                    │
                   │  (<─┘=Enter) (Esc=Cancel) (F1=Help)│
                   └───────────────────────────────────┘



  F10=Actions  Esc=Cancel  Shift+F9=Command Prompt
```

Figure 6-5   The default program startup window

The other type of commands allowed in the Commands line go outside of the square brackets. An example is the PAUSE command. Each of these commands must be separated by the F4 character.

Specifying a Title

You can specify the title of the program startup prompt window by using the /T command, which has this general form:

/T *"title—up to 40 characters"*

The title must be enclosed between double quotes and must not be longer than 40 characters in length.

To try this, select MYGROUP, highlight "Check the disk," and then activate the **Program** option. From this menu, select **Change**. Using the TAB key, advance the cursor to the Commands line. Move the cursor to the brackets ([]). If the Shell is not already in insert mode, press the INS key once. Now enter this title between the two brackets:

```
/T "Check the Disk"
```

After you have entered the title, the Commands line should look like this:

```
CHKDSK [/T "Check the Disk"] || PAUSE
```

Remember, you won't be able to see it all at once. Once you have entered it correctly, press F2 to install the change.

Try the CHKDSK command at this time. You will see that the title of the program startup prompt window is now "Check the Disk."

If an Error Occurs

If you accidentally enter something wrong on the Commands line, you will see an error message that tells you what the problem is when you try to run the program. For example, if you forget the closing square bracket, you will see this error message:

```
Brackets missing in Program Startup Command.
```

If you receive this type of error message, simply look for the error and correct it. After a while, you will have no trouble.

Changing the Instruction Line

To change the instruction line, use the /I command, which has this general form:

/I *"instructions—up to 40 characters"*

The instructions are enclosed between double quotes and must not exceed 40 characters.

To try this, add the following to the Commands line for the CHKDSK program. Add it inside the square brackets and after the closing quote from the title:

/I "Enter the drive you want to check."

The Commands line will now look like this:

CHKDSK [/T "Check the Disk" /I "Enter the drive you want to check. "] || PAUSE

Of course, there will be only one line, not two.

Install this change by pressing F2, and try the command again. This time, both the title and the instruction line will be different.

Changing the Prompt

To change the prompt that precedes the parameter entry area, use the /P command. It takes the general form

/P *"prompt—up to 20 characters"*

The prompt must be enclosed between double quotes and must not exceed 20 characters in length.

To see how this works, add the following prompt to the CHKDSK Commands line, inside the square brackets and after the closing quotes of the instruction command:

/P "Drive specifier: "

The Commands line will now look like this:

CHKDSK [/T "Check the Disk" /I "Enter the drive you want to check." /P "Drive specifier: "] || PAUSE

Install the change by pressing F2. Try the CHKDSK command. The program startup prompt window will now appear as shown in Figure 6-6.

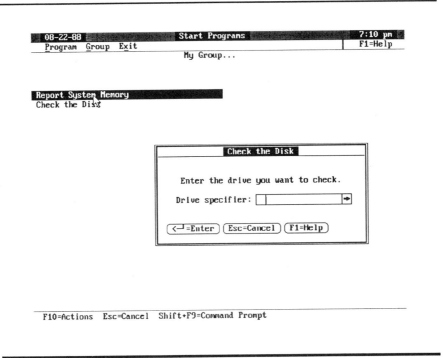

Figure 6-6   The customized CHKDSK startup window

REORDERING PROGRAMS
WITHIN A GROUP

You can change the order of items in a group by using the **Reorder** option
in the **Group** window. First, activate the group you want to reorder, and then
highlight the item whose position you want to change. Next, activate the
Group option and select the **Reorder** option. Move the highlight to the position where you want the item to be put, and press ENTER. The item will be
moved, and the list will reflect the new order. You might want to try this feature on your own.

USING A PASSWORD

You can restrict access to a program by giving it a password when you enter the program into a group. You can also control access to an entire group by giving the group a password when you define it. If you use a password, only people who know the password can activate the program or group from the Shell. (The program or group can still be executed from the command line.)

You can use any characters you like for a password, which can be up to eight characters in length. Be sure to remember the password, because you will also need it to activate the **Change** option in the **Program** menu.

Warning: The password only controls access to a program if that program is executed from the Shell; anyone who knows how to use the DOS command-line prompt will still be able to run the program. Therefore, at best, a password is a mild deterrent and is not real protection. At worst, password protection may tip someone off that a sensitive program is on your computer. A better approach to security is to lock up the computer when it is not in use.

THE SHELL'S EDITING KEYS

The Shell activates several special keys that can help you enter such information as program names or options. These keys are called *editing keys*. You have learned about one already: the BACKSPACE key. In this section you will learn about several others.

For this section you will need to enter and modify information. One of the best places to practice is in the Set Date and Time window, because even if you accidentally activate an option with invalid information, no harm can be done. Therefore, before continuing, select the **DOS Utilities** option from the Main Group and activate the **Set Date and Time** option.

The HOME and END Keys

At the Set Date and Time prompt for parameters, enter the word **TEST** but do not press the ENTER key. Now press the HOME key. You will see the cursor jump to the start of the field. Press the END key and the cursor will move to the end of the word "TEST." Whenever you are entering information in the Shell, pressing the HOME key moves the cursor to the start of the field; pressing the END key moves it to the end of whatever has been entered.

The Arrow Keys

Once you have entered something in a field, you can use the left and right arrow keys to move the cursor around in the text. For example, if you are not already there, move the cursor to the end of the word "TEST" by pressing END. Now press the left arrow key three times. The cursor will be under the "E." Press the right arrow once, and the cursor will be under the "S." As you can see, these operations have no effect on the text in the field; they simply reposition the cursor.

Insertion and Overwrite Modes

The Shell supports two input modes: insertion mode and overwrite mode. By default, the Shell is in overwrite mode. In this mode, whatever is at the current cursor position is overwritten by what you type. In insertion mode, whatever is at the current cursor position is moved to the right so that what you enter does not overwrite it.

You can toggle between insertion mode and overwrite mode by pressing the INS key. The shape of the cursor tells you which mode you are in. In overwrite mode the cursor is a short horizontal bar, similar in shape to an underscore. In insertion mode the cursor is a thin vertical bar if you are in graphics mode or a small solid box if you are in text mode.

To see the difference between the two modes, advance the cursor to the end of "TEST," pressing the END key if necessary. Next, press the left arrow twice. The cursor is under the "S." Make sure that the Shell is in overwrite mode (the cursor should look like an underscore). Now enter **AK**. The word will now be "TEAK."

Press the INS key to activate insert mode. Back the cursor up with the left arrow until it is on the "E" in "TEAK" and type **W**. As you can see, the "EAK" is moved right and the word becomes "TWEAK."

DEL and BACKSPACE

There are two ways to delete a single character in a field. Pressing the BACK-SPACE key will cause the character immediately to the left of the cursor to be deleted, and all text to the right of that character will move over one place to fill the void. You can also delete a character by pressing the DEL key. This deletes the character directly *under* the cursor, and all text to the right of the deleted character is moved to the left to fill the void.

Starting Over

Assume that you have entered some information, and then decide that it is wrong. You want to start over. Instead of repeatedly striking the BACKSPACE or DEL key, you can simply press the F9 key. Try this now. As you can see, the entire field is cleared and the cursor is positioned at the start of the line.

This concludes your practice with the Shell's editing keys. Press ESC at this time to cancel the command.

PRINTING THE SCREEN

This section assumes that you have a printer attached to your computer. If this is not the case, skip ahead to the next section. If you do not know how to attach your printer to your computer, refer to the installation guide that came with your computer.

It is sometimes very useful to print what is displayed on the screen. DOS lets you do this with the Print Screen command. Unlike most other DOS commands, you do not need to select a menu entry—you simply press the PRTSC key, which is activated with the help of the SHIFT key.

To try this, display a directory listing inside the File System. Hold down the SHIFT key and press PRTSC. As you can see, the information that is on the screen is printed at the printer.

SUMMARY

In this chapter you learned how to

- Add programs and groups
- Use some program startup commands
- Copy programs between groups
- Reorder a group
- Use the Shell's editing keys
- Use passwords
- Print the screen

In the next chapter you will begin to learn DOS commands in more detail.

7

USING THE COMMAND PROMPT

Activating the Command Prompt
Issuing Commands
Changing the Current Drive
A Closer Look at DIR
Clearing the Screen
The COPY Command
The TYPE Command
Command-Prompt Error Messages
The DOS Editing Keys
Summary

Earlier versions of DOS did not include the Shell. Instead of supplying menu options for common operations, these earlier versions displayed a command prompt and waited for the user to enter a command. Although DOS version 4 has supplied the Shell, it still allows you to activate the command prompt and operate DOS directly from it. In this chapter you will begin exploring the command prompt and its command-based interface.

You might wonder why you would want to use the command-prompt interface when the Shell is available. There are three main reasons. First, many computers will not be upgraded immediately to a version of DOS that supports the Shell. Therefore, if you will be working with a wide variety of computers, it is a good idea to know how to run DOS from the command prompt. Second, once you know how to use the command prompt, it is actually faster (and sometimes easier) than using the Shell. The Shell trades power and performance for ease of use. Third, a few commands cannot be activated easily from the Shell.

To follow along with the examples, you will need a blank, formatted disk.

ACTIVATING THE COMMAND PROMPT

There are three ways to activate the command prompt from within the Shell. The first two are identical in effect. First, you can choose the Command Prompt option in the Main Group. Second, you can press SHIFT-F9 while you are in the Start Programs window or the File System. With either of these methods, the Shell clears the screen and displays this message:

When ready to return to the DOS Shell, type EXIT then press enter.

When you use either of these methods to activate the command prompt, the DOS Shell stays in memory waiting for you to come back to it. To go back to the Shell, you must use the DOS EXIT command. It tells DOS to leave the command prompt and resume the Shell.

The third way to activate the command prompt is to press the F3 key while the Start Programs window is active. If you do this, the screen is cleared, but no message about returning to the Shell is displayed. Activating the command prompt in this way causes the Shell to be removed from memory, thus freeing this memory for other uses. There is nothing to exit to, so the EXIT command has no effect. To restart the Shell, you must use the DOSSHELL command.

Generally speaking, it is usually best to activate the command prompt by using one of the first two methods.

The Mouse and the Command Prompt

The mouse does not work with the command prompt. It may work with programs that you run from the command prompt, but there is no way to use the mouse to communicate with DOS.

The Sign-On Message and the DOS Prompt

Activate the command prompt by pressing SHIFT- F9 at this time. After the "When ready to return" message you will see the DOS sign-on message. It tells you the version number of the DOS program you are using. Some DOS commands work only with later versions of DOS, so it is a good idea to know what version you are running; make a mental note of it at this time.

Beneath and on the far left of the sign-on message, you will see either A> or C>. If you loaded DOS from a floppy disk, then you will see A>, and if you loaded it from a fixed disk, you will see C>. This is the DOS prompt. Whenever the cursor is positioned immediately after the prompt, DOS is ready to accept a command.

If your system has a fixed disk and has been in use for some time by other people, your DOS prompt may look different than is shown in the examples that follow. As you will see later in this book, you can tell DOS exactly what style of prompt you want. Thus, if your prompt differs, don't worry about it.

ISSUING COMMANDS

To run DOS from the command prompt, you tell DOS what you want it to do by giving it a command. Many of the commands have direct parallels in the Shell; a few do not. Before worrying too much about the theory of operation, let's try some commands.

One of the most useful commands is DIR, which displays the directory of the disk. At the prompt, type **DIR** and press ENTER. This displays the file directory on the screen.

Because there are more files on the disk than there are lines on the monitor, the first part of the list scrolls off the top of the screen. This is supposed to happen; later, you will learn how to control it. If you loaded DOS from a floppy disk, then your screen will be very similar to the screen shown in Figure 7-1. If you loaded DOS from a fixed disk, then you may see different file names.

Notice that once the directory has been listed, DOS returns the prompt to your screen. Whenever DOS finishes a command, it redisplays the prompt. This lets you know that it has completed the task. When DOS is accessing a disk, the drive's red in-use light comes on. Never remove a disk from the drive when this light is on; if you do, you might destroy some of the information on the disk.

The directory listing includes the following items from left to right: the name of the file, the size of the file (in bytes), and the date and time of file

NLSFUNC	EXE	6910	06-17-88	12:00p
RECOVER	COM	10732	06-17-88	12:00p
REPLACE	EXE	17199	06-17-88	12:00p
SORT	EXE	5914	06-17-88	12:00p
SUBST	EXE	18143	06-17-88	12:00p
TREE	COM	6334	06-17-88	12:00p
FILESYS	EXE	11125	06-17-88	12:00p
CHKDSK	COM	17771	06-17-88	12:00p
PCIBMDRV	MOS	295	06-17-88	12:00p
PCMSDRV	MOS	961	06-17-88	12:00p
PCMSPDRV	MOS	801	06-17-88	12:00p
SHELL	CLR	4438	08-11-88	2:24p
SHELL	HLP	66977	06-17-88	12:00p
SHELL	MEU	6660	08-22-88	7:04p
SHELLB	COM	3937	06-17-88	12:00p
SHELLC	EXE	153975	06-17-88	12:00p
DOSUTIL	MEU	8732	08-21-88	3:12p
PRINT	COM	14163	06-17-88	12:00p
DOSSHELL	BAT	185	08-04-88	2:42p
SHELL	ASC	1680	08-17-88	1:43a
MYGROUP	MEU	2516	08-22-88	7:09p
012345		678	109	08-22-88	5:11a

61 File(s) 471552 bytes free

Figure 7-1   The output of the DIR command

creation. The directory listing is similar to the one displayed in the Shell, except the Shell does not display a file's time of creation.

Besides listing the directory, the DIR command does two other things: it counts the number of files on the disk, and it tells you the amount of free space on the disk. The storage capacity of a floppy or fixed disk varies greatly; you should consult your owner's manual for specific information.

Let's try another command. One of the simplest is the VER command, which displays the version number of the DOS program you are using. To see how it works, type **VER** at the command prompt and press ENTER. You will see a message similar to this:

IBM DOS Version 4.00

As you learned while working with the Shell, DOS does not care whether you enter text in uppercase or lowercase letters. This book uses uppercase letters, but in actual practice you will probably usually use lowercase letters for your commands.

CHANGING THE CURRENT DRIVE

When you type the DIR command, you get a directory listing of the drive that corresponds to the letter in the prompt. If you have two floppy-disk drives or a fixed-disk drive and a floppy-disk drive, you can switch to the other drive by typing its drive specifier (the letter followed by a colon) and pressing ENTER. For example, to switch to drive B, you enter **B:** and press ENTER; try it now. Be sure that you have a formatted disk in the target drive. (If you loaded DOS from a fixed disk, then try switching to drive A.) As you can see, the DOS prompt has been changed to the new drive.

To switch back to either drive A or drive C, follow the same format and substitute the proper drive specifier. Switch back to drive A or drive C now. (If you have two floppy-disk drives, be sure that you put the DOS disk back in drive A.)

A CLOSER LOOK AT DIR

Earlier, you learned the simplest form of the DIR command. However, DIR is much more flexible than that. Two DIR options affect the display format so that you can vary the form in which you see your listings. In addition, you can use DIR to look for a specific file or a group of related files.

Two DIR Options

Many DOS commands allow you to use one or more options to alter the meaning or effect of the command. A DOS command option usually begins with a slash (/), which tells DOS that an option follows. The DIR command allows two options, / P and / W.

The / P option tells DOS to stop listing the directory temporarily when the screen is full. Remember, when you listed the directory, some file names

COMMAND	COM	37637	06-17-88	12:00p
CONFIG	SYS	114	08-04-88	1:31p
AUTOEXEC	BAT	99	08-04-88	2:40p
EGA	CPI	49052	06-17-88	12:00p
ANSI	SYS	9148	06-17-88	12:00p
COUNTRY	SYS	12838	06-17-88	12:00p
DISKCOPY	COM	10428	06-17-88	12:00p
DISPLAY	SYS	15741	06-17-88	12:00p
DRIVER	SYS	5274	06-17-88	12:00p
FFORMAT	COM	22923	06-17-88	12:00p
KEYB	COM	14759	06-17-88	12:00p
KEYBOARD	SYS	23360	06-17-88	12:00p
MODE	COM	23040	06-17-88	12:00p
PRINTER	SYS	18946	06-17-88	12:00p
VDISK	SYS	6376	06-17-88	12:00p
4201	CPI	6404	06-17-88	12:00p
5202	CPI	402	06-17-88	12:00p
4208	CPI	641	06-17-88	12:00p
SHARE	EXE	10285	06-17-88	12:00p
IFSFUNC	EXE	21637	06-17-88	12:00p
SYS	COM	11472	06-17-88	12:00p
XCOPY	EXE	17087	06-17-88	12:00p
LCD	CPI	10592	06-17-88	12:00p

Press any key to continue . . .

Figure 7-2   The first screen of the directory with the Pause option

scrolled off the top of the screen; the Pause option prevents this. At each pause, you will see the message

Press any key to continue . . .

This means that when you are ready for more of the directory, press any key.

To execute the DIR command with the Pause option, enter the command line like this:

DIR /P

The first screen should look like the one in Figure 7-2. Then press any key to continue until you return to the command prompt.

```
Volume in drive A is DOS400
Volume Serial Number is 340C-14E3
Directory of  A:\

COMMAND   COM  CONFIG    SYS  AUTOEXEC BAT  EGA       CPI  ANSI      SYS
COUNTRY   SYS  DISKCOPY  COM  DISPLAY  SYS  DRIVER    SYS  FFORMAT   COM
KEYB      COM  KEYBOARD  SYS  MODE     COM  PRINTER   SYS  VDISK     SYS
4201      CPI  5202      CPI  4208     CPI  SHARE     EXE  IFSFUNC   EXE
SYS       COM  XCOPY     EXE  LCD      CPI  APPEND    EXE  ASSIGN    COM
ATTRIB    EXE  BASICA    COM  COMP     COM  DEBUG     COM  DISKCOMP  COM
EDLIN     COM  FIND      EXE  GRAFTABL COM  GRAPHICS  COM  GRAPHICS  PRO
JOIN      EXE  LABEL     COM  MEM      EXE  MORE      COM  NLSFUNC   EXE
RECOVER   COM  REPLACE   EXE  SORT     EXE  SUBST     EXE  TREE      COM
FILESYS   EXE  CHKDSK    COM  PCIBMDRV MOS  PCMSDRV   MOS  PCMSPDRV  MOS
SHELL     CLR  SHELL     HLP  SHELL    MEU  SHELLB    COM  SHELLC    EXE
DOSUTIL   MEU  PRINT     COM  DOSSHELL BAT  SHELL     ASC  MYGROUP   MEU
012345    678
        61 File(s)    471552 bytes free
```

Figure 7-3   A wide directory listing

There are many times when all you want is a list of the files on a disk, and you are not interested in all the other information that DIR displays. When this is your goal, you can use the /W (wide) option, which causes DOS to display only the file names in the directory. The /W option displays file names in five columns across the screen, so many more file names than usual are visible at one time. To use this option, enter the command line like this:

DIR /W

The outcome of this command is shown in Figure 7-3.

Other Ways to Stop the Display

The /P option provides a convenient way to stop the directory display, but there is another way, which you will probably use more frequently. If you press CTRL-S, the display will stop until you press another key or press CTRL-S again. The CTRL-S key sequence acts as a toggle, which you can remember as stop/start. To try the CTRL-S command, list the directory and then stop the listing at various points.

DOS also lets you stop the display by pressing the CTRL- NUMLOCK key sequence on PC-type keyboards or PAUSE on AT or PS/2 keyboards. If you stop the display by using CTRL- NUMLOCK or PAUSE, you must restart it by pressing a different key—these commands are not toggles. (Some PC- compatible computers may behave slightly differently when these keys are pressed.)

Not all application programs that run under DOS recognize the CTRL-S or CTRL-NUMLOCK key combination. Therefore, it may not always be possible to use them to stop the display of some programs.

Looking for Specific Files

Until now, you have been using the DIR command to list the entire contents of the directory. However, you can use the DIR command to find a specific file, just as you did with the Shell. To do this, you specify the file's name after the command. This method allows you to quickly determine whether a file is in the directory or not.

Try this by entering

    DIR DISKCOPY.COM

DOS will display

    Volume in drive A is DOS400
    Volume Serial Number is 340C-14E3
    Directory of A:\

    DISKCOPY   COM   10428   06-17-88 12:00p
            1 File(s) 408576 bytes free

As you can see, DOS displays only information about the file you request, not the entire directory.

If you specify a file that is not in the directory, you will see this message:

    File not found

For example, see what happens when you enter

    DIR GARBAGE

Wild-card File Names

You can use the wild-card characters to list groups of related files with DIR. These characters work the same for the DIR command as they did in the File System.

Assume that you want to list the names of all files on a disk that share the .COM extension. To do this, enter the following:

    DIR *.COM

This causes DOS to display all files with a .COM extension.

Remember, when used in a file name that is part of a DOS command, the asterisk is a special character that tells DOS to match any sequence of characters. The filename and extension are separate, so the asterisk applies only to the part of the name in which it is used.

As another example, try this command:

    DIR SHELL?.*

As you can see, several files match this specification. The question mark matches any one character in its position; unlike the asterisk it does not match a sequence of characters.

Wild-card characters are very useful in commands other than DIR because they allow you to easily handle related groups of files. You will see more of them later.

CLEARING THE SCREEN

Let's look at another of DOS's simplest commands: CLS. CLS clears the monitor's screen. Enter the CLS command now. As you can see, the screen is cleared and the DOS prompt is redisplayed in the upper-left corner of the screen. The CLS command is not meaningful when the Shell is in use.

The CLS command is useful for three reasons. First, you may sometimes have sensitive information on the screen that you do not want everyone to see. When you are done with the information, executing the CLS command is an easy way to wipe it off the screen. Second, an application program will occasionally leave the screen looking "messy." Clearing the screen is a good way to remedy this situation. Finally, if you are not going to be using your computer for a while, you should clear the screen and thus save the phosphors in the picture tube from undue wear. These phosphors slowly burn out as they are used.

THE COPY COMMAND

The command-prompt version of COPY operates in essentially the same way as in the Shell's version. The only difference is that the command-prompt version is more powerful.

The basic form of the COPY command is

COPY *source_filename destination_filename*

You can remember this format as

COPY *from to*

The COPY command copies the contents of the first file (source) to the second file (destination). For example, this command copies the 012345.678 file into a file called TEST.TST:

COPY 012345.678 TEST.TST

Try this now. As the COPY command begins execution, the disk drive will start and its in-use light will be illuminated. When the DOS prompt returns, list the directory; you will see the TEST.TST file.

As is the case in the Shell, the only time that you will need to specify a name for the destination file is when it will not be the same as the source file name.

A COPY Option

The COPY command's /V option automatically verifies that the the destination file matches the original file exactly. On rare occasions, a file copy will not be successful; for example, a power fluctuation or loss can affect the data being written by the disk drive. The Verify option tells COPY to check the source and destination files against each other as the copying proceeds. Although this option makes the copying operation a little longer, the extra time is worthwhile to ensure the contents of very important files.

Enter the /V option after the rest of the COPY command. For example, to make a verified copy of a file named SORT.EXE from drive C to drive A, the command would be

```
COPY SORT.EXE A: /V
```

The Verify option is not available from the DOS Shell; it works only at the command prompt.

Using Wildcards with COPY

For this section you will need a blank formatted disk. If you have a fixed disk, then put this disk in drive A. If you have only floppy-disk drives, put the disk in drive B.

You will often want to copy several files from one disk to another. Although you could copy each file separately, you can instead use the DOS wild-card characters to copy several at once. To see how this works, try the following command, adjusting the drive specifiers to suit your system. (As the command is shown, it will work for fixed-disk systems.)

```
COPY *.EXE A:
```

This command tells DOS to copy to drive A all files with the .EXE extension. During the copying process, DOS prints on the screen the name of each file copied. A directory listing of the target disk will show that all the .EXE files have been copied.

One of the first things you should notice about the command you just gave is that the destination file name is missing—only the drive specifier is present. When you do not specify a destination file name, DOS assumes that you want the destination file to have the same name as the source file. This principle applies to wild-card copies as well; each file copied to the destination disk has the same name as it did on the source disk. It would be perfectly valid to use the command COPY *.EXE A:*.EXE, but it would be redundant.

You can use the question mark and asterisk wild-card characters with the COPY command just as you use them with the DIR command. If you are not sure which files will be copied with your wild-card file name, first execute the DIR command with the same wild-card characters and see what DOS reports.

Note: The Shell **Copy** option does not allow you to use wild-card characters. In this instance, the command-prompt version of DOS is more powerful than the Shell version.

If you wish to copy all of the files listed in the directory of one disk to another, use the wild-card characters *.*. For example, to copy the contents of the disk in drive A to the disk in drive B, issue the following command (assuming that A is the current drive):

    COPY *.* B:

Although this may seem obvious, it must be stated: you cannot copy a file onto itself. A command such as

    COPY SORT.EXE SORT.EXE

is therefore invalid. Also, if you try to copy a file that does not exist, DOS will display the message

    File not found

At this point, you should be able to copy files between disks without any trouble. If you do not feel confident, try some examples before continuing. Later in this book you will learn that the COPY command has several more features and options, making it one of the most powerful of DOS commands.

THE TYPE COMMAND

In the Shell, you used the **View** option in the **File** menu of the File System to see the contents of a file. The command prompt's similar command is TYPE, which displays the contents of a test file on the screen. For example, enter this command:

    TYPE 012345.678

It displays the contents of the 012345.678 file. You can use the TYPE command to list on the screen the contents of any text file. (TYPE can list any sort of file, but only text files will display meaningful information.)

The sample file that you just used is very short; longer text files will quickly scroll off the screen unless you stop them. You can freeze the display by using the control keys you used to stop the DIR command: either CTRL-S, CTRL-NUMLOCK or PAUSE.

Keep in mind that DOS has no way of knowing which files are text files. So far as it is concerned, a file is a file; and text, data, and program files all look pretty much alike to it. It is your responsibility to remember which files are which.

Although you will not be using TYPE again for awhile, you will find that in actual practice it is one of the most-used DOS commands because it lets you easily peek into a file to see what's in it.

COMMAND-PROMPT
ERROR MESSAGES

If you make a mistake and enter a command that DOS does not understand, DOS responds with an error message. Many error messages appear differently at the command prompt than they do in the Shell. As you continue to use DOS, you will probably see error messages. It is important to respond correctly when presented with an error, so let's take a look at some of the most common errors at this time.

You will find that many errors are followed by the prompt

Abort, Retry, Fail?

How you respond is in many ways determined by exactly what error has occurred. To see an example, let's generate the same type of error as we did in Chapter 3.

Open the door on drive A and enter the DIR command. (If you have a fixed disk, switch to drive A by typing **A:**.) Since the drive door is not latched, DOS cannot access the disk directory. In a few seconds you will see the message

Not ready reading drive A
Abort, Retry, Fail?

DOS is telling you that it cannot access (read) the disk in drive A. This is, of course, because the drive door is open. However, DOS does not know the exact cause of the problem; it only knows that the drive is not ready to be used. Several conditions could cause this error in addition to the drive door being open; for example, a faulty or unformatted disk could produce this error message.

As you learned in Chapter 3, DOS gives you three ways to respond to this error: you can abort the command, retry it, or ignore it. To abort the DIR command, type **A**. This causes DOS to stop trying to read the disk. You should use the Abort command when there is no way to remedy the condition causing the error. To retry the command, close the drive door and then type **R**. This lets you correct the condition causing the error. The disk directory will be displayed. Use Retry when you can eliminate the error.

The Fail command has limited applications. It tells DOS to ignore the immediate error and continue on with the command. Generally, once one error has occurred, more will follow. The Fail command usually is used only by programmers, because to use it successfully you need considerable knowledge about how the computer and DOS function.

If you have not done so, insert a disk in drive A, close the drive door now and press R for Retry. If you have a fixed disk, switch back to drive C by typing **C:**.

Bad Command or File Name

The "Bad command or file name" error message is the error message you will see most often. It tells you that DOS does not understand what you are asking it to do. This message does not ask for a response—you simply reenter the command properly.

This message usually results from a misspelled command. For example, if you type **DUR** instead of **DIR**, you will see this message.

General Failure

The "General failure" error message appears when you attempt to access a disk that has not been formatted, is damaged, or is not intended for the use of DOS or a DOS- compatible computer. To remedy the problem, either abort the operation or insert the correct disk and try again.

Insufficient Disk Space

A disk has only a finite amount of space on it. When you run out of space, you will see the "Insufficient disk space" message. To correct this error, either use a new disk or remove files from the existing disk.

Invalid Drive Specification

The "Invalid drive specification" message appears when you try to specify a drive that does not exist. For example, if you type Z: in an attempt to reach a nonexistent drive Z, you will see this message. Simply retry your command with the proper drive specifier.

Nonsystem Disk or Disk Error

The message "Nonsystem disk or disk error" appears when you try to load DOS from a disk that does not contain it. To correct this error, insert the DOS disk and strike any key.

Sector Not Found

The "Sector not found" error message is displayed when a sector that is part of a file cannot be found. Because the locations of sectors are stored in a file allocation table, if this table becomes damaged, DOS does not know where to find one or more sectors.

Generally, all you can do is try a different disk. If this error occurs on a fixed disk, you will have to use a new copy of the file.

Seek Error

The "Seek" error message indicates that the disk drive was unable to find a track. This problem can be caused by three errors. First, the disk drive may be out of alignment; this problem requires a professional technician to repair. Second, the disk may be improperly inserted in the drive. If it is, try inserting it again. Finally, the disk may be physically damaged. In this case, replace the disk.

THE DOS EDITING KEYS

Up to this point, when you made a mistake while typing a command you used the BACKSPACE key to back up to the error and then retyped the rest of the line. If you wished to reexecute a command, you retyped it. In this section you will learn how to use some special keys, called *editing keys*, that

Key	Function
F1	Redisplays one character from the input buffer each time it is pressed
F2	Redisplays all characters up to, but not including, a specified character in the input buffer
F3	Redisplays all characters in the input buffer
F4	Deletes all characters up to, but not including, a specified character from the input buffer
F5	Reedits the line you just typed
DEL	Deletes a character from the input buffer
ESC	Cancels the current line just typed prior to pressing ENTER
INS	Inserts the next character typed at the current location in the input buffer

TABLE 7-1   The DOS Editing Keys

will make the entry of DOS commands a little easier because they allow you to make changes to what you type on the command line.

Fundamental to using the editing keys is the concept of the *input buffer*, which is a small region of memory that is used by DOS to hold the commands that you enter from the keyboard. The input buffer contains the last command you typed until you enter a new one. This lets you reuse, alter, or fix the immediately preceding command by using the DOS editing keys. The DOS editing keys and their functions are listed in Table 7-1. Let's look at each in turn.

Note that in the remainder of this section you may disregard the "Bad command or file name" error message. Some of the examples in this section will send DOS unknown commands. This hurts nothing, but it does cause an error message to be displayed.

This discussion is accurate for the IBM PC, XT, AT, and PS/2 computers. Other types of computers may use somewhat different keys. You should refer to your user's manual.

The F1 Key

At the command prompt, enter **123456789**; then press ENTER. This loads 123456789 into the DOS input buffer. Once the command prompt returns, press the F1 key three times. Your command line will look like this:

```
C>123
```

As is obvious from this example, the F1 key redisplays one character at a time from the input buffer. Continue to press the F1 key until the 9 appears. At this point, pressing F1 again has no effect because you have reached the end of the buffer. (DOS does not store the ENTER key in the buffer.) Press ENTER now.

The F2 Key

The F2 key redisplays all characters in the input buffer up to the character that you specify. To use the F2 command, you first press F2 and then the character. For example, if you press F2 and then type **6**, the command line will look like this:

```
C>12345
```

Try this now. DOS redisplays all characters up to the 6. At this time press F1 until the 9 is redisplayed; then press ENTER.

The F3 Key

Probably the most useful editing key is F3, which redisplays the entire contents of the input buffer. This is especially useful because it lets you reexecute the previous command without retyping it. Press F3 at this time. The command line will look like this:

```
C>123456789
```

Do not press ENTER.

The ESC Key

The cursor currently should immediately follow the 9 on the command line. Press ESC now. As you can see, DOS prints a backslash (\ ) and positions the cursor directly under the 1. The command line will look like this:

```
C>123456789\
    _
```

The ESC key cancels whatever is on the command line. DOS uses the \ to indicate this cancellation. The command prompt is not redisplayed, but the cursor is placed directly under the location it occupied when the prompt was present.

After canceling a command with ESC, you can still use all of the editing keys to redisplay or change the previous command. For example, press F3 followed by ENTER.

The DEL Key

To delete a character from the input buffer, use the DEL key. Each time you press DEL, a character will be deleted. You will not see the characters you delete, so use this key with caution. For an example, press DEL three times and then press the F3 key. The command line will look like this:

```
C>456789
```

If you press ESC prior to pressing ENTER, you can cancel the effects of the DEL key. Press ESC followed by F3 and ENTER.

The F4 Key

To delete several characters, use the F4 key. It works like the F2 key in that you first press F4 and then a character. DOS then deletes all characters from the current position up to, but not including, the character you typed. For example, press F4, type **4**, and then press F3. The command line will look like this:

```
C>456789
```

Keep in mind that nothing is displayed when you use the F4 command, so it can be easy to forget what you have deleted. Use F4 with caution.

The INS Key

Enter **This a test** at the command prompt. Assume that you really wanted to enter **This is a test**. You can correct the command by first pressing F1 to position the cursor after the space that follows "This", pressing INS, typing **is**, and then pressing F3. When you press the INS key, DOS lets you insert any number of characters at that point without overwriting what is already in the buffer. You should try some examples.

The F5 Key

All the other editing keys let you manipulate the command that is already in the input buffer. Suppose, however, that you began typing a new command and made a mistake. Pressing the F5 key causes DOS to load the input buffer with what you just typed, giving you a chance to correct it without executing it.

SUMMARY

In this chapter you learned

- How to activate the command prompt
- How to use the DIR command
- About the VER command
- How to change the current drive
- How to freeze the display
- How to clear the screen
- How to copy files
- How to view a file with the TYPE command
- The meaning of several error messages
- The DOS editing keys

The next chapter will continue your exploration of DOS's command prompt.

8

EXPLORING THE DOS COMMAND PROMPT

The preceding chapter introduced the DOS command prompt. In this chapter, you will continue to explore the prompt as well as some commands that are specific to it.

Unless noted otherwise, this chapter assumes that if you are running DOS from a fixed disk, you are logged in to drive C and have selected the DOS directory. If you are running DOS from floppy disks, make sure that the DOS disk is in drive A.

PRINTING A TEXT FILE

This section assumes that you have a printer attached to your system and that it is attached in the standard fashion. If this is not the case, you should still read this section, but do not try the examples. If you have a specialized printer, contact a coworker or some other knowledgeable person to find out how to print files on it.

When you wish to make a hardcopy (printout on paper) of a text file, you can do so by using the PRINT command. PRINT cannot be used on nontext files. PRINT is an external command. Its simplest form is

PRINT *filename*

where *filename* is the name of the text file to be printed. The PRINT command is similar to the Print option in the File System's File menu, except that it is more flexible.

Let's begin with an example. Enter the command

PRINT 012345.678

When the PRINT command begins, you will see the message

C:\DOS\012345.678 is currently being printed

if you are using a fixed disk; if you are using a floppy disk, then the drive and path part of the message will be A:\ .

The command prompt will be redisplayed immediately, even though the printing is not yet complete. The PRINT command is one of a few DOS commands that operate in the background, allowing you to continue using the computer to do other things. A background task is a very simple form of *multitasking*, in which the computer performs two or more operations at the same time.

You can use a drive specifier in the file name to print a file that is not on the current disk. For example, to print a file called TEST.TST that is on drive B, you would use a command like this:

PRINT B:TEST.TST

Canceling a Printout

Suppose that you are in the middle of printing a long file and you decide that you don't need the printout. To cancel the PRINT command, enter

PRINT / T

The /T is a PRINT command option; it stands for "Terminate."

Printing Multiple Files

There are two ways to give PRINT a list of files to print. You can execute the PRINT command repeatedly, specifying one file at a time, or you can specify a list of files all at once. To see how this works, copy the 012345.678 file into the TEST1, TEST2, and TEST3 files. Now execute this PRINT command:

PRINT TEST1 TEST2 TEST3

PRINT will respond with

A:\TEST1 is currently being printed
A:\TEST2 is in queue
A:\TEST3 is in queue

PRINT creates a *queue* (a list) of the files you want to print and then prints them one at a time in the order in which they are specified. Using the DOS default setting, you can queue up to ten files. Later, you will learn how to set the queue size to fit your needs.

If you decide that you need to print a file called TEST4 while the other files are still being printed, you can add it to the print queue by entering

PRINT TEST4

This will add TEST4 to the list of files to be printed.

Removing Files from the Print Queue

Suppose that you have just specified a list of files to be printed, and you decide that one of the files doesn't need to be printed after all. You can remove a specific file from the queue by using the /C PRINT option in this general form:

PRINT *file name* /C

For example, to remove TEST2 from the print queue, enter

PRINT TEST2 /C

If you wish to cancel the printing of all files, the easiest way is simply to use the / T option. This terminates the PRINT command and removes all files from the queue.

You should experiment with the PRINT command at this time.

REMOVING FILES FROM A DISK

The ERASE command allows you to remove a file from a disk. Another DOS command, DEL, does the same thing, but this book will continue to use ERASE. Typing **ERASE** cannot be mistaken for typing any other command, whereas your fingers might slip up and enter **DEL** when you really meant **DIR**, destroying your hard-won efforts.

The general form of the ERASE command is

ERASE *filename*

where filename is the name of the file to be erased. The ERASE command is similar to the **Delete** option in the **File** menu.

For a first example, execute this command:

ERASE TEST1

TEST1 is the file you created in the previous section; you can verify that it is no longer present by listing the directory.

You can erase groups of files by using the DOS wild-card characters. For example, this command erases all files that share the .BAK extension.

ERASE *.BAK

Although you should not try this now, you can erase all files in the current directory with the command

ERASE *.*

DOS will prompt you with the message

All files in directory will be deleted! Are you sure (Y/N)?

If you do want to erase all the files, enter **Y**; otherwise enter **N**.

When using wild-card characters with the ERASE command it is a good idea to execute a DIR command with the same wild cards first, just to make sure that you know what you are erasing.

CHANGING FILE NAMES

You can change the name of a file by using the RENAME command. DOS allows a short form of this command, called REN, but this book will use RENAME to avoid confusion. The general form of this command is

RENAME *old_name new_name*

You can use RENAME to alter any part of a file's name, including the extension. The RENAME command is identical to the **Rename** option in the Shell's **File** menu.

For example, try the following command, which assumes that you have the TEST2 file on the current disk:

RENAME TEST2 RALPH

When the DOS prompt returns, execute the DIR command. You will see that the TEST2 file is no longer in the directory, but the one called RALPH is. By typing **RALPH** you can be assured that the contents of the file are the same; only the name has changed.

Since RALPH is a pretty silly name for a file, use RENAME to change it to SAMPLE.TXT by entering

RENAME RALPH SAMPLE.TXT

You can use drive specifiers with the RENAME command. For example, the following command changes the name of a file called TEST to OLDTEST on drive B:

RENAME B: TEST B: OLDTEST

If you try to give a file a name that already exists or if you try to rename a file that does not exist, DOS will respond with an error message.

CANCELING A COMMAND

Sometimes you will enter a command, change your mind, and want to cancel it. Many DOS commands can be canceled by pressing CTRL-C or CTRL-BREAK. For many purposes CTRL-C and CTRL-BREAK are equivalent, but in some situations CTRL-BREAK is more effective. For this reason, you should generally use CTRL-BREAK.

To try canceling a command, execute DIR and then press CTRL-BREAK before the directory listing has finished. As soon as you press CTRL- BREAK the screen displays "^C" (for Cancel), and the DOS prompt returns. Try this now.

Not all DOS commands can be canceled in this way. For example, because the PRINT command runs as a background task, you must use the / T option to stop it. Also, most commands cannot be canceled in the middle of their execution. Most DOS commands have a point of no return called the *critical section*; after this point, you cannot stop the command from proceeding because doing so would corrupt the structure of the disk. Once the RENAME command has begun to change a file's name for example, you cannot cancel it until it is done. You don't need to worry about destroying anything by trying to cancel a command, however, because DOS will not let you cancel at an inappropriate time.

WORKING WITH DIRECTORIES

Although the structure of the disk is unchanged, the way you work with directories in the Shell and the way you work with them at the command prompt are fairly different. As you saw when you worked with directories in the

Shell, directories can be quite valuable when organizing the files on your disk. In this section you will learn how to create, use, and delete directories from the command prompt.

You will need a blank formatted disk. Put this disk into drive A and log in to drive A at this time.

Creating a Directory

To create a directory from the command prompt, use the MKDIR command (MD, for short). The general form of this command is

MKDIR *directory_name*

A directory name must conform to the same conventions and restrictions as a file name, except that it may not have an extension. The name must not exceed eight characters.

In this example you will create the directory structure that is shown in Figure 8-1. To begin building the directories, enter the following command:

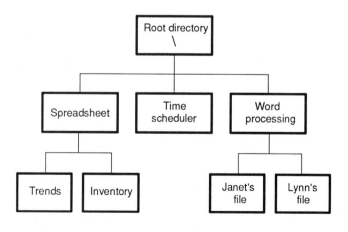

Figure 8-1   The example directory structure

```
MKDIR SPRDSHT
```

SPRDSHT is short for "Spredsheet," which is too long to be a directory name. Once the prompt returns, enter **DIR**. The only entry will look like this:

```
SPRDSHT        <DIR>    09-28-88 9:25a
```

The <DIR> signifies that SPRDSHT is a directory, rather than a file. Keep in mind that you are still in the root directory; so SPRDSHT is a subdirectory.

Before moving on, create the other two subdirectories that branch from the root. Enter these two commands:

```
MKDIR SCHEDULE
MKDIR WP
```

SCHEDULE is short for "Time scheduling," and WP is short for "Word processing." You can list the directory again to see the effect of these commands.

Changing Directories

Now that you have created three directories, it is time to see how to activate one of them. The CHDIR (or CD) command is used to change the current directory. The general form of CHDIR is

```
CHDIR new_directory
```

where *new_directory* is a valid path name for the new directory.

To make the WP directory current, enter

```
CD WP
```

Try it now. When a short form of a command exists, this book generally uses the long form to avoid confusion; however, since CD is almost universally used instead of CHDIR, it will be used in this book.

Once the prompt returns, list the directory. You will see the following display:

```
Volume in drive A has no label
Volume Serial Number is 4124-14CD
Directory of  A:\WP
.                 <DIR>     08-23-88  1:10p
..                <DIR>     08-23-88  1:10p
          2 File(s) 1456128 bytes free
```

Take a close look at this display. One of the first features you should notice is that the directory name is shown in the line that reads "Directory of A:\WP." If you recall, when you list the root directory, only the backslash is displayed. \WP specifies the path to the WP directory: it begins at the root and then goes to WP.

The two entries in this directory are in DOS shorthand. The single period is short for the current directory, and the two periods represent the parent directory, which in this case is the root directory. For example, if you enter

DIR ..

the root directory will be displayed. Entering

DIR .

lists the current subdirectory. Remember, to list the current directory (subdirectory or root), you need only enter **DIR**. The period is redundant.

Creating Subdirectories Within A Subdirectory

You create a subdirectory inside of a subdirectory in exactly the same way that you created a subdirectory from the root. Let's create the two subdirectories for WP at this time. Make sure that you are in the WP directory by typing **CD \WP**, and then enter

MKDIR JANET
MKDIR LYNN

A directory listing will now look like this:

```
Volume in drive A has no label
Volume Serial Number is 4124-14CD
Directory of  A:\WP
.                    <DIR>    08-23-88  1:10p
..                   <DIR>    08-23-88  1:10p
JANET                <DIR>    08-23-88  1:10p
LYNN                 <DIR>    08-23-88  1:10p
        4 File(s)   1455104 bytes free
```

Switch to the JANET directory by entering

```
CD  JANET
```

and list the directory. The "Directory of" line will now look like this:

```
Directory of  A:\WP\ JANET
```

\WP\JANET specifies the path to the JANET directory. It can be inter-preted as "Start at the root and go to the WP directory; from the WP direc-tory, go to the JANET directory."

Returning to the Parent Directory

There are two ways to move from a subdirectory to its parent. The first method—and by far the most common—is to issue this command:

```
CD  ..
```

Since the two periods are shorthand for the parent's directory name, this works no matter what the parent directory is called.

The second way to return to the parent directory is to specify its name ex-plicitly. For example, to go from the JANET directory to the WP directory, you can enter

```
CD  \WP
```

The backslash is necessary to indicate where to find the WP subdirectory.

Returning to the Root Directory

No matter how deep you are in subdirectories, you can always return to the root directory by entering this command:

```
CD \
```

Because the backslash represents the root directory, DOS makes the root directory active. Of course, you can always return to the root directory by entering repeated CD.. commands until you reach the root; but the CD\command is easier.

If you have not yet done so, return to the root directory, and switch to the SPRDSHT directory at this time. To continue setting up the directories on the disk, enter these commands:

```
MKDIR TRENDS
MKDIR INVNTRY
```

Moving Between Directories

There are several ways to move between directories. One way that will always work, no matter what directory is currently active, is to enter **CD** followed by the complete path name of the directory to which you wish to go. For example, return to the root directory by entering **CD **, and then move to the WP directory by entering **CD WP**. Now, to move from the WP directory to the TRENDS subdirectory of SPRDSHT, you can use this command:

```
CD \SPRDSHT\TRENDS
```

Return to the WP directory using

```
CD \WP
```

If you type an invalid path name or misspell a directory name, DOS will respond with the message "Invalid directory." In this case, enter the command again, correcting the error.

To move from the WP directory to the LYNN subdirectory, you *cannot* use this command:

```
CD \LYNN        (This is incorrect)
```

If you try this command, DOS will respond with the message "Invalid directory." The backslash preceding LYNN tells DOS to start at the root and to
then move to LYNN. However, LYNN is not a subdirectory of the root—it
is a subdirectory of WP.

To move from WP to LYNN you must use one of these commands:

```
CD  LYNN
CD  \WP\LYNN
```

The first command is a shorthand version of the second. Because the WP
directory is active and LYNN a subdirectory of WP, you can simply use CD
LYNN because DOS already knows the rest of the path. The second form
works, of course, because the entire path is explicitly stated. In general, any
time you move from a parent directory to a subdirectory, you only need to
specify the subdirectory name. However, the reverse is not true. To move
from a subdirectory back to the parent, you must use either the CD.. command or a complete path name.

Displaying the Current
Directory Name

The CD command not only allows you to change directories, it also displays
the current directory and path if it is executed with no arguments. If you ever
have any doubts about being in the proper directory, using this command is
the best way to find out.

For example, switch to the LYNN subdirectory of WP and enter **CD**. Your
display will look like this:

```
A:\WP\LYNN
```

Removing a Directory

Directories cannot be removed with the ERASE command. To remove a
directory, you must use the RMDIR (or RD) command. Its general form is

```
RMDIR directory_name
```

where *directory name* specifies a valid path to the directory you wish to remove. For example, you can remove the SCHEDULE directory with the command

```
RMDIR  SCHEDULE
```

(If you try this, be sure to recreate SCHEDULE before continuing.)

There are two restrictions on removing directories. First, the directory must be empty; it can contain no files or other subdirectories. When you list the directory, you should see only

```
.           <DIR>
..          <DIR>
```

Second, the directory cannot be the current directory; you cannot remove the directory that you are currently using.

If you try to remove the current directory or a nonexistent directory, you will see this message:

```
Invalid path, not directory,
or directory not empty
```

THE TREE COMMAND

You can display a directory tree that looks much like the one displayed in the File System by using the TREE command. TREE is an external command, which means that you must have it on your disk. The simplest form of this command is

```
TREE path
```

The path is unnecessary if you want to see the structure of the disk in the current drive beginning at the current directory.

To see how TREE works, copy the TREE.COM file into the root directory of the disk in the drive A, and enter **TREE**. (Make sure that drive A is active.) You will see output similar to that in Figure 8-2.

To display a subtree, you specify a starting point by passing TREE a path. For example, to have TREE display the WP subtree, you would use this command:

```
TREE \WP
```

```
Directory PATH listing
Volume Serial Number is 4124-14CD
A:.
|---SPRDSHT
| |---TRENDS
| |---INVNTRY
|---SCHEDULE
|---WP
|---JANET
|---LYNN
```

Figure 8-2   The output of the TREE command

TREE Options

The TREE command allows two options; /F and /A. The /F option gives you a list of the files in each directory. For example, the following command lists both the directory structure and the files in each directory:

```
TREE /F
```

On a full disk, the output from this command will be lengthy, but it will still be useful when you are trying to find a file on a disk.

By default, the TREE command uses text mode block-graphics characters. For English-speaking countries, a PC does provide a very limited set of simple graphics figures in standard text mode, including vertical and horizontal lines. If you live in an English-speaking country, these characters will be used by TREE. However, some foreign languages use an extended character set, which preempts these block graphics characters. For this reason TREE provides the /A option, which uses an alternate set of characters that will be valid in any language.

SUMMARY

In this chapter you learned how to do the following from the command prompt:

- Print a file
- Erase a file
- Rename a file
- Cancel a command
- Create, manage, and delete directories
- Use the TREE command

The next chapter will present more DOS commands. They can be used from either the Shell or the command prompt.

9

MORE DOS
COMMANDS

It's time for you to learn about more DOS commands that give you greater control over the computer. Some of these commands are fairly complicated, but they yield great returns for the time you invest learning them.

Many of the commands discussed here as command-prompt entries are also present as menu selections from within the Shell. When you execute a command from the command prompt, you enter its name followed by any options and parameters. When you execute a command from a Shell menu, you only specify the options and parameters—you do not enter the command name, but select it as a menu option.

From this point on, when new commands are discussed, their general forms and examples will be' shown in the command-prompt version. If you are using the Shell, you simply select the command name instead of entering it, and then enter whatever options or parameters you wish to use with the command.

Most of the commands you will be learning about are external. When an external command is not in a Shell menu, you can execute it from the File System as you did for the CHKDSK command. However, there are a few internal commands, such as the VER command, that are not represented in any Shell menu. To execute such a command, you must make an entry for it in the Start Programs window. The exact procedure for doing this will be described later in this chapter.

THE LABEL AND VOL COMMANDS

When you list the directory of the DOS disk from the command prompt, the first line looks something like this:

Volume in drive A is DOS400

Also, if you select the **Show Information** option in the File System's **Options** menu, you will see that a name is specified in the disk portion of the window. Until now, we have been ignoring the name of the disk. Here, you will learn to give a disk a volume label.

A volume label is essentially a name for either a floppy or fixed disk. It can be up to 11 characters long and can consist of any characters allowed in a file name. Note, however, that a period is not allowed in the volume label.

There are two reasons why you should give a disk a volume label. The first is that it helps you to positively identify the disk. This can be useful when you are trying to remember which disk is which. (The volume label, however, should never take the place of the external stick-on label.) The second reason is that in the future, new versions of DOS may allow you to access a disk by its volume label instead of by its drive letter.

Using LABEL

To change the name of a disk, use the external DOS LABEL command to give the disk a name. The general form of LABEL is

LABEL *name*

where *name* is the name that will be given to the disk.

To execute LABEL from the Shell, select LABEL.EXE in the File List window of the File System and press ENTER (or double-click on it with the mouse). When prompted for program parameters, enter MYDISK as the label and press ENTER. If you are using the command prompt, enter

LABEL MYDISK

This command changes the volume name of the disk to MYDISK. To confirm this, once again execute the LABEL command, but this time do not specify any additional parameters. You will see something similar to the following:

Volume in drive C is MYDISK
Volume serial number is 1250-2236
Volume label (11 characters, ENTER for none)?

When you execute LABEL without a volume name as a parameter, it first reports the existing volume name and serial number. It then gives the disk serial number that was assigned to the disk when it was formatted. This number allows DOS and other application programs to keep track of which disk is which. Finally, LABEL prompts you for a new name. If you just press ENTER, the existing name is kept. Press ENTER now. You will see this line:

Delete current volume label (Y/N)?

A disk does not have to have a volume name, so if you did not enter a new name, LABEL gives you a chance to delete the name. Type **N** now.

You can place a drive specifier in front of the label in the command-line version to change the volume label of a disk other than the current one. For example, the following command sets the volume label of the disk in drive B to SAMPLE:

LABEL B:SAMPLE

Using VOL

If you are using the command prompt and just want to see the volume label, enter **VOL**. VOL is an internal command.

For example, enter **VOL** now and you will see the following:

```
Volume in drive C is MYDISK
Volume serial number is 1250-2236
```

You can use a drive specifier with VOL to see the volume label of a disk in a drive other than the current one. For example, the following command displays the volume label for drive B:

```
VOL  B:
```

Remember, if you are using the Shell, you can view a disk's volume name by selecting the File System, selecting the desired drive, and, finally, selecting the **Show Information** option in the **File** menu.

THE DATE AND TIME COMMANDS

If you are using the Shell, then you can set the date and time by using the **Set Date and Time** option in the DOS Utilities group. However, if you are using the command prompt, you must use the DATE and TIME commands. To execute either command, simply enter its name.

The DATE command first displays the current system date and then prompts you for a new date. Enter it in the same format you used in the Shell version. You press ENTER if you do not wish to change the date after all.

The TIME command displays the current system time and then prompts you for a new time. Enter the time as you did for the Shell version.

Besides allowing you to change the current system date and time, the DATE and TIME commands are useful when you simply want to know the time of day.

FORMATTING FLOPPY DISKS

You have already seen how to format a floppy disk from the Shell. If you want to format a disk from the command prompt, use the FORMAT command. Its simplest form is

FORMAT *drive_specifier*

where *drive_specifier* determines which drive will be used to format the disk. FORMAT is an external command.

To format a disk in drive B, you would use a command like this:

FORMAT B:

Some FORMAT Options

All FORMAT options use the same form—a slash followed by the option character. All options follow the drive specifier. There can be more than one option present. You use the same options when you execute the FORMAT command from the Shell or from the command prompt. Remember, the FORMAT command can be executed from either the File System or from the DOS Utilities group in the Shell.

SPECIFYING A VOLUME LABEL   You can specify a volume label for a disk when you format it by using the /V option. For example, if you are formatting a disk in drive B and want to give it a volume label, use this command;

FORMAT /V

When the disk has been formatted, you will see this prompt:

Volume label (11 characters, ENTER for none)?

The same prompt is used by the LABEL command. Enter the name you want to use, and press ENTER.

Putting System Files on a Disk

A disk cannot load DOS unless at least three files are present on the disk. These files are

COMMAND.COM
IBMBIO.COM
IBMDOS.COM

(On some systems these files may have slightly different names.) These files are called *DOS system files*, or just *the system* for short. They form different parts of the DOS program. Only COMMAND.COM will show up when the directory is listed; the other two will be hidden.

IBMBIO.COM and IBMDOS.COM must be the first files on a disk, so DOS offers the FORMAT /S option to copy them onto the newly formatted disk. Once the formatting has been completed, the message "System transferred" will be displayed in addition to the other messages.

FORMAT must have access to the system files in order to transfer them to the new disk. If they are not on the current disk, you will be prompted to insert a system disk so that the system files can be copied.

Although a disk formatted with the /S option can start the computer and load DOS, you will have access only to DOS's internal commands—the external commands are not transferred to the new disk. However, you can copy the external commands to the disk.

LEAVING ROOM FOR THE SYSTEM FILES   DOS is a copyrighted program that you can use but cannot give or sell to anyone else except as described in the DOS license agreement. Therefore, you may need to create a disk that reserves room for the DOS system files but does not actually contain a copy of them. For example, you might wish to prepare a disk for a friend that contains several of your files, but you want to make sure that he or she can put a system on it if necessary. (This is done with the SYS command, which will be discussed next.) If you don't reserve room, the system cannot be put on the disk.

Using the /B option during formatting reserves storage space for the system. No additional messages will be displayed, but room will be set aside for the system files.

Transferring the System with SYS

If a disk has been formatted with the /B option or if no files are on the disk, you can copy the system files to it by using the SYS command. SYS has the general form

SYS *drive_specifier*

where *drive_specifier* determines the drive that will receive the system files. SYS is an external command. You can also execute it from the File System by selecting it from the File List window.

To see how SYS works, format a fresh disk using no options whatsoever. If you do not have a fixed disk, make sure that A is the current drive and that your DOS disk is in it. Put the blank formatted disk into B. (If you only have one disk drive, you will need to swap disks.) If you have a fixed disk, put the freshly formatted disk in drive A and make sure that C is the current drive.

Now, execute SYS using A: as a drive specifier if you have a fixed disk and B: if you do not. Once the system files have been transferred, you will see the message

System transferred

There is one little wrinkle in how SYS works. As stated previously, there are three system files—IBMDOS.COM, IBMBIO.COM, and COM-MAND.COM. For some reason, COMMAND.COM is not transferred by the SYS command. Fortunately, COMMAND.COM can go anywhere on the disk, so its position is not important, but you do need it on any disk that will be used to start the computer and load DOS.

COMMAND.COM is the part of DOS that interprets your commands. Without it, you cannot communicate with DOS. If you try to use a disk without COMMAND.COM to load DOS, you will see this message:

Bad or missing Command Interpreter

To install COMMAND.COM on the disk, simply copy it there by using the COPY command. It must go in the root directory.

THE VERIFY COMMAND

Disk write operations are usually successful. However, rare problems (such as a power surge) can cause an error, and the contents of the disk file will not be exactly what they are supposed to be.

DOS can verify for you that the data has been written correctly by reading the section of the file just written and comparing it to what is in memory. If a discrepancy is found, a write error is reported. The VERIFY command turns this verification process on and off. It takes this general form:

VERIFY on/off

VERIFY is an internal command. It is not found in any Shell menu. Let's learn to use it from the command prompt first, and then see how to access it by customizing the Shell.

By default, VERIFY is off. To turn it on, enter

VERIFY ON

You might think it a good idea to always have VERIFY turned on, but it isn't. Each write operation takes about twice as long with VERIFY on because of the extra work that DOS must do, so turn it on only when you are working with very important files. You can turn off VERIFY by typing **VERIFY OFF**. Remember, disk errors are quite rare. If you are experiencing frequent errors, your computer should probably be checked by a qualified service technician.

You can see if VERIFY is on or off by entering **VERIFY** with no argument. It will produce the appropriate message for the current status:

VERIFY is on

If you are using the Shell you will find that VERIFY, as an internal command, is not in any menu. If it were an external command, you could just select from the File List window, but since it is internal, it is not a file. The only way to execute VERIFY from within the Shell is to create a new program entry in a group in the Start Programs window.

To see how this is done, first select DOS Utilities from the Main Group. Next, activate the action bar and select **Add**. At the Add Program Title prompt enter

Execute VERIFY

At the Commands prompt, enter

VERIFY [\l "ON or OFF"]

You may also enter any help text you like. Press F2 to save. To execute VERIFY, simply select it and enter the correct parameter.

In general, you can add any DOS command—internal or external—to a group and execute it from the Start Programs window.

XCOPY: AN EXPANDED COPY COMMAND

Assume that you have a floppy disk containing directories that are organized as shown in Figure 9-1. How can you copy the entire contents of the WP directory, including the contents of the ANN and MARY subdirectories and ANN's subdirectory FORMS, and still maintain the directory structure?

With the standard COPY command, you must copy each directory individually, making sure that all files are copied into the correct destination directory. This approach is clearly error-prone and tedious. For this reason,

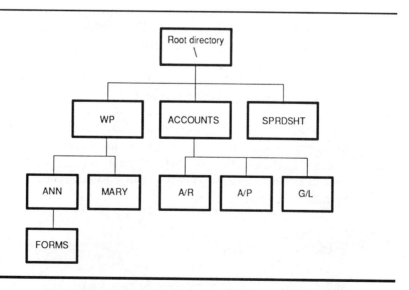

Figure 9-1 A sample disk directory structure

DOS includes the XCOPY command, which, in addition to having many other useful features, lets you copy complete sets of directories and subdirectories automatically.

XCOPY is an external command. To execute it from the Shell, you must select it in the File List window; it is not found in any other menu.

In its simplest form XCOPY works much like COPY. For example, to copy a file called SAMPLE from drive A to drive B, you could use the following command:

    XCOPY A:SAMPLE B:

However, XCOPY goes far beyond this. Its general form is

    XCOPY *source destination options*

where *source* and *destination* may be a drive specifier, a file name, a directory name, or any combination of the three. The options let you control exactly what and how XCOPY copies.

Let's look at how XCOPY functions with its various options.

Copying Files

Although it is faster to copy files with the internal COPY command, you can copy files by using XCOPY. The wild-card characters * and ? are allowed. Also, the /V (Verify) option is supported.

Copying Groups of Directories

You can use XCOPY to copy the contents of the current directory plus the contents of any subdirectories. To see how this works, format two floppy disks and label them ONE and TWO. (Fixed-disk users should not use their fixed disks for this example.) On disk ONE, create two subdirectories using the following commands:

    MKDIR WP
    MKDIR ACCOUNTS

Switch to the WP directory and issue the command

MKDIR LETTERS

The directory structure of disk ONE should now look like this:

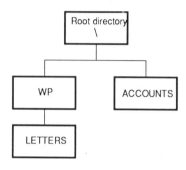

Copy the 012345.678 file into the root directory of this disk, but call the destination file SAMPLE.TXT. To do this, use a command similar to

COPY 012345.678 A:SAMPLE.TXT

Then create another file called SAMPLE2.TXT in the WP directory. Next, create a file called SAMPLE3.TXT in the WP\LETTERS directory. Finally, copy XCOPY.EXE into the root directory of disk ONE. Put disk ONE in drive A. If you have a dual-floppy system, put disk TWO into drive B. Otherwise, you will need to swap it in and out of drive A as prompted by DOS.

As an example, first try the following command:

XCOPY A: B:

If you have only one floppy-disk drive, DOS will alternately call it A and B, allowing you to swap the correct disk. After the command is finished, only the SAMPLE.TXT and XCOPY.EXE files from the root directory will have been copied to disk TWO; you can confirm this by displaying its directory.

In order for XCOPY to copy the contents of a group of directories, you must use the /S option. Try the following command:

XCOPY A: B: /S

When the command has finished, list the directory of disk TWO. As you can see, the WP directory has been created. If you change to WP, you will see that SAMPLE2.TXT has been copied to that directory and that the LETTERS subdirectory has been created. SAMPLE3.TXT will be found in WP/LET-TERS.

The /S option tells XCOPY to copy the contents of the current directory plus all subdirectories. If necessary, it will create the subdirectories on the destination disk.

You might wonder why the ACCOUNTS directory was not found on disk TWO. This is because ACCOUNTS had no files in it. If a directory contains no entries, XCOPY will not create it on the destination disk. If you want all directories created, whether empty or not, you must specify the /E option. For example, the following command will cause the ACCOUNTS directory to be created on disk TWO:

```
XCOPY A: B: /S /E
```

You can copy less than the entire disk by specifying the directory to begin with. For example,

```
XCOPY A:\WP B: /S
```

will copy only the contents of the WP directory plus its subdirectory.

Using the Archive Attribute

You can use XCOPY to copy only files that have the archive attribute turned on by using either the /A or the /M option. The archive attribute is turned on whenever a file is created or changed. The difference between the two options is what happens to the archive attribute on the source files.

If you use /A, the archive attribute is not changed on the source file, which means that you can make repeated copies of those files with the archive attribute turned on. However, /M causes the archive attribute of the source files to be turned off after they are copied. This gives you an easy way to copy only those files that have changed since the last time a copy was made.

DOS provides a better command, called BACKUP, which also uses the archive attribute to perform backup operations. It is best to leave this sort of backing up to BACKUP, which is designed expressly for this purpose.

Using the Date Option

You can use XCOPY to copy all files created on or since a certain date by using the /D option, which takes the general form

/D:*mm-dd-yy*

Only files with creation dates the same as or later than the specified date will be copied. For example,

XCOPY A: B: /S /D:12-12-88

will copy all files with creation dates beginning with 12-12-88 to the current date of the system.

The /D option applies only to files. Directories will be established on the destination disk without regard to their creation dates.

Query Before Copy

The /P option causes XCOPY to prompt you before each file is copied. Its message takes the form

filename (Y/N)?

If you type **Y**, the file is copied. Typing **N** causes the file to be skipped.

The Wait Option

As you have noticed, XCOPY begins to copy files immediately. If you need to switch disks before the copying takes place, specify /W, which causes XCOPY to issue the following prompt before it starts the copying process:

Press any key to begin copying file(s)

After switching disks, press a key.

REPLACING FILES

As you continue to use DOS, you will find that there are two very common situations that involve copying files that neither COPY nor XCOPY can handle. The first is when you want to replace the files on the destination disk with files of the same name from the source disk. For example, a work disk may contain several files for which a new version exists. The second situation is the opposite of the first; you will sometimes want to add files to a disk without overwriting any file already on the disk. You can accomplish both of these activities with REPLACE.

The general form of REPLACE is

REPLACE *source destination options*

where *source* and *destination* specify the source and destination file names, directories, or drives, which may include the * and ? wild-card characters. REPLACE is an external command that can be executed from the File System by selecting it from the File List window, but it is not found in any other menu.

In its simplest form, REPLACE behaves much like COPY. For example,

REPLACE A:SAMPLE.TXT B:

copies the SAMPLE.TXT file from A to B. However, REPLACE really shines when wild cards are used.

Using the two floppy disks that you created for the XCOPY examples, copy the REPLACE.EXE file to disk ONE. Now insert disk ONE in drive A and, if you have two floppies, disk TWO in drive B. If you only have one floppy disk, DOS will alternate the drive A and B messages and you will be prompted to swap the two disks. Now enter

REPLACE A:*.* B:

Your screen will look like this:

A> REPLACE A:*.* B:

Replacing B:SAMPLE.TXT

Replacing B:XCOPY.EXE

2 File(s) replaced

As you can see, REPLACE copied SAMPLE.TXT and XCOPY.EXE, but not REPLACE.EXE. This is because REPLACE.EXE did not exist on the destination disk. Remember, REPLACE will copy only those files that it finds on the destination disk.

In this example only the files in the root directory were replaced. However, if you specify the /S option, DOS will also examine and replace all files in all subdirectories if possible. For example, enter

```
REPLACE A:*.* B: /S
```

As you can see, this replaces all files on the destination disk in all directories.

You can use REPLACE to add to a disk only those files that are not currently on the destination disk. This prevents existing files from being overwritten. To do this, you use the /A option. Try this command:

```
REPLACE A:*.* B: /A
```

You will see the following:

```
Adding B:REPLACE.EXE
1 File(s) added
```

This time, the only file copied is the one that did not already exist on disk TWO.

If you need to insert a different disk before REPLACE begins, use /W, which causes REPLACE to wait until you press a key before beginning.

The /P option causes REPLACE to prompt you before a file is replaced. For example, if you enter

```
REPLACE A:*.* B: /P
```

you will see the following prompt:

```
Replace B:\SAMPLE.TXT (Y/N)
```

If you type **Y**, the file will be replaced; otherwise, it will not.

REPLACE offers two other valuable options. You can replace just the read-only files on the target disk by using the /R option. If you want to replace only those files on the target disk that are older than the ones on the source disk you can use the /U option.

When you are using REPLACE, keep these points in mind:

- You cannot use the /A and /S options together

- You cannot use the /A and /U options together

- The source and destination need not be on different disks—they can simply be different directories on the same disk

CHECKING A DISK USING CHKDSK

Whether you are using a floppy disk or a fixed disk, the state of the magnetic media that holds your information is of crucial importance. Unless physical damage is obvious, it is impossible to determine whether the information on a disk is valid or not simply by looking at it. To verify that the magnetic information on a disk is correct requires the use of the CHKDSK command.

You have used CHKDSK in several earlier examples in this book; now it is time to take a closer look at it. CHKDSK is an external command, so you will need to have a copy of it on the disk that is in the current drive. To execute CHKDSK from the Shell, use the File System.

The general form of CHKDSK is

CHKDSK *drive_specifier options*

where *drive_specifier* is the drive to be checked. Both the drive specifier and the options are optional; if no drive specifier is used, the current drive is checked.

To execute the simplest form CHKDSK, run it with no options. For example, assuming that the DOS disk is in drive A, the output of the CHKDSK command is

```
Volume DOS400     created 08-04-1988 1:31p
Volume Serial Number is 340C -14E3
      1457664 bytes total disk space
      69632 bytes in 3 hidden files
      916480 bytes in 61 user files
      471552 bytes available on disk

      512 bytes in each allocation unit
      2847 total allocation units on disk
      921 available allocation units on disk

      655360 total bytes memory
      558688 bytes free
```

As you can see, the CHKDSK command reports the number of bytes of total disk space, the number of bytes used by DOS's hidden files, the number of bytes used by user-accessible files, the amount of space used by directories, and the amount of storage space still available on the disk. The hidden files are part of DOS and do not show up in the directory listing. "User files" refers to a file that the user can display and manipulate.

CHKDSK also reports the number of bytes in each allocation unit (sector), the total number of units on disk, and the number of units available. It reports both the total system memory and the amount of free memory. (The difference between the total free memory and the total system memory is the amount of memory used by DOS itself.) CHKDSK also gives the disk volume label, if one is defined, and the serial number. It also shows the amount of disk space used by bad sectors.

Disk Errors

Aside from actual physical damage, a disk can become partially unusable for two reasons. First, an application program could have an error in it that causes that part of the disk to become detached from the directory. Second, a system fault or an unplanned power loss may cause the links between the sectors that make up the disk to contain incorrect values.

In most cases, these types of errors can be detected and corrected by CHKDSK, although information may be lost. In CHKDSK's default mode, errors are detected but not corrected. To make CHKDSK correct errors, you need to specify the /F (Fix) option after the CHKDSK command. For example,

```
CHKDSK /F
```

causes any detected error to be fixed if possible.

One of the most common errors you will encounter is reported with this message:

```
X lost clusters found in Y chains.
Convert lost chains to files (Y/N)?
```

where X is the number of lost clusters and Y is the number of chains. Recall from Chapter 2 that DOS organizes files into sectors. A *cluster* is a group of sectors that are all in one track, and a *chain* is a group of clusters. If a cluster becomes disassociated from the directory, then it is said to be lost because DOS no longer knows what file it belongs to.

What CHKDSK does with the lost space is up to you. If you answer yes to the question in the error message, then new files composed of the lost clusters will be created. They will be called by file names in the form FILE*num*.CHK, where *num* is the number of the file. The files will be numbered 0 through 999. In theory, you can examine these files to determine whether they contain useful information; if they do not, you can erase them. In practice, however, these files seldom contain information that is usable, and even if they do, in most cases you will not be able to tell simply by looking at the file. For these reasons, you should generally answer no to the prompt. CHKDSK will then free the space for future use.

You should run CHKDSK frequently to make sure that your disk is in good working condition. Once a day is normally sufficient unless you have reason to suspect that an error has occurred.

Remember, CHKDSK can clean up certain types of disk errors, but it can do nothing to help a disk that has been physically damaged.

BACKING UP A DISK

Just as you made a backup copy of the DOS master disk in Chapter 2, you can make backup copies of any floppy disk with DISKCOPY. You can execute this command from the Shell by using the File System or by selecting Disk Copy in the DOS Utilities group.

The general form of the DISKCOPY command is

DISKCOPY *source destination*

For example, to copy the contents of the disk in drive A to the one in drive B, enter

DISKCOPY A: B:

If the destination disk is not formatted, DISKCOPY will format it before it copies the source disk. The formatting process does increase the time it takes to copy a disk, so it is often helpful to have a number of formatted disks on hand.

If you have only one floppy-disk drive, use this form of the DISKCOPY command:

DISKCOPY A: A:

Technically, you can omit either the destination drive specifier or both drive specifiers, because DISKCOPY will use the current drive by default. However, it is safer to specify the drive specifiers fully to avoid any misunderstanding.

DISKCOPY may not be used to copy to or from a fixed disk. However, you can still use floppy disks created by DISKCOPY on a system that has a fixed disk.

As you learned earlier in this book, several different types of floppy disks and disk drives are in use, and these all have different storage capacities. The general rule for applying DISKCOPY is this: the capacity of the source disk must be smaller than or equal to the capacity of the destination disk. If this is not the case, DOS will issue a warning message. You do not need to worry about this when you are simply backing up a disk that was created on the system that is performing the backup.

DISKCOPY creates an *exact* copy of the source disk: sector by sector, the source disk and the destination disk are exactly the same. In contrast, executing a COPY *.* command will copy all of the user files, but the resulting destination disk, although containing the same files, will not be an exact duplicate of the original.

Most of the time this difference does not matter. However, there are some special situations in which one method of copying the contents of a disk is more desirable than the other. For now, however, when you want to copy an entire disk, you should use DISKCOPY.

Although several things can go wrong during the disk-copy process, fortunately, they seldom do. If an error does occur, your course of action is determined by the nature of the error. If DISKCOPY reports an error in reading the source disk, you should abort the DISKCOPY command and try a different disk, if a duplicate is available. If a duplicate disk is not available, try removing the source disk from the drive and reinserting it. Sometimes a disk is not aligned correctly in the drive. As a last resort, tell DOS to ignore the error and continue; however, this may lead to the loss of data. If DISKCOPY reports an error in formatting or writing to the destination disk, start over again with a new disk.

DISKCOPY offers the /1 option, which causes it to copy only one side of a disk, even if it is a double-sided disk. Using both sides of a disk doubles the storage capacity. Virtually all disk drives in service today are double-sided, but the original drives issued when the first IBM PCs came out were single-sided. You will use the /1 option only when you need to copy a single-sided disk to a double-sided disk. You will probably never need this option.

If you purchase a program, the disk it comes on may be copy protected to prevent unauthorized duplication. In general, you cannot use DISKCOPY to copy a copy-protected disk.

When to Back Up Disks

Although you are new to DOS, it is never too early to learn about the importance of backing up disks. When you made the backup copy of a DOS master disk in Chapter 2, you did so to protect the original from harm. This concept can be generalized. Whenever you have valuable data on a disk, you should make one or more copies in case the original disk is lost, destroyed, or accidentally erased.

Most computer professionals (programmers, systems analysts, maintenance personnel, and so on) recommend a system of *rotating backups*. In this method, you create one master disk and two backup disks, a primary and a secondary disk. At the end of each work period in which the master disk is altered, the master disk is copied to the primary backup disk. Periodically—weekly, for example—the master disk is copied to the secondary backup disk. Occasionally—monthly, for example—the secondary disk is "retired" and put in a safe place. A new secondary backup disk is then created. This method reduces the risk of losing important information. Later in this book, you will look at the backup and protection of disks in greater detail.

Comparing Two Files

From time to time you may be unsure if two files with the same names on different disks are really the same file. For example, imagine you have an inventory program that creates and maintains a file called INV.DAT. If you have two copies of this file, you may not know if they both contain the same information. Another related situation arises when you suspect that two files with different names may actually be the same file. Finally, you will sometimes want to be sure that a file has, indeed, been accurately copied and is exactly the same as the source file.

Although you can type or print text files and visually compare them, some types of files do not lend themselves to visual inspection. The only way to be sure that two files are the same—or different—is to use the DOS COMP (Comparison) command. COMP is an external command, so you will need a copy of it on your work disk.

So that you can work along with the examples in this chapter, execute the following command with your work disk in the current drive (or use drive C if you have a fixed disk):

```
COPY 012345.678 TEST
```

There are two ways to execute COMP. The first is to execute it with no options. You will then be prompted for the two files to be compared. As a first example, compare the 012345.678 file with TEST. The first prompt is

Enter primary filename

Respond by entering **012345.678**. Next, you will see the prompt

Enter 2nd filename or drive id

Here, "drive id" refers to a file specifier. Respond with **TEST**.

COMP will then compare the files. Upon completion, your screen will look like this (assuming that you are using the fixed disk):

Enter primary filename
012345.678

Enter 2nd filename or drive id
TEST

C:012345.678 and C:TEST

Eof mark not found

Files compare ok
Compare more files (Y/N)?

Answer **N** to the prompt. You should give no special significance to the term "primary file"—it really just refers to the first file.

As you would expect, since the two files are identical, COMP finds them to be the same. It reports this by printing the message "Files compare ok." You will soon see what happens when the files differ.

You are probably wondering about the message "Eof mark not found." The *EOF* marker is used to signal the end of the file. However, not all files have EOF markers. When the EOF marker is not present, DOS uses the length of the file to determine the end of the file. Many times, it doesn't matter whether an EOF marker is found or not, but in some special cases it can make a difference. Here's why.

As you learned in Chapter 3, the smallest amount of disk space that DOS can allocate is one sector, which is usually 512 bytes. Even though a file can be as short as one character, it will still require an entire sector to hold it, because a sector cannot be subdivided.

Some application programs will pad their files to completely fill the last sector. If this occurs, and if the characters used to pad the last sector differ, then COMP could find differences between the two files, even though they contain the same actual, relevant data. Thus, if you see the "Eof mark not found" message, the rule of thumb is not to worry about differences between the two files if they only occur at the very end.

An easier way to invoke the COMP command is by specifying the two files when you execute COMP. For example, to compare 012345.678 and TEST, use this command:

```
COMP 012345.678 TEST
```

This form of the command does not prompt you for the file names; it simply performs the comparison.

Keep in mind that when you use the command-line form of the COMP, the files you are comparing must be on disks that are already mounted in the drives, because the comparison operation begins immediately. If you must switch disks, then use the form of COMP that prompts you for the file names. This will allow you to insert the proper disks.

Finding Differences

Enter this command:

```
COMP 012345.678 SORT.EXE
```

You will see the message "Files are different sizes," and no comparison will be performed. The COMP command will not compare files that have different sizes because it assumes (rightfully) that different-sized files cannot be the same.

To see what happens when two files of the same length differ, assume that there are two files, called TEST and TEST2, and the contents of TEST is

```
This  is  a  sample
text  file.
```

and TEST2 contains

```
This  is  a  simple
test  file.
```

TEST2 differs from TEST by the "i" in "simple" and by the "s" in "test".
However, the length of the files is identical. If you were to compare the two
files, you would see this output:

```
Compare error at OFFSET B
File 1 = 61
File 2 = 69
Compare error at OFFSET 14
File 1 = 78
File 2 = 73
```

This rather odd-looking output tells you that the two files differ in byte numbers 11 and 20. Although this is not immediately obvious, it further reports
that TEST has an "a" where TEST2 has an "i" and that TEST has an "x" where
TEST2 has an "s". The COMP command reports the position and contents
of bytes that differ in *hexadecimal* code, which is a number system based on
16 (a number that computers like). The commonly used decimal number system is based on 10. Hexadecimal digits are the standard digits 0 through 9
plus the letters A through F, which correspond to the numbers 10 through 15.
Therefore, the number 10 in hexadecimal format is 16 in decimal format; the
number 1A in hexadecimal format is 26 in decimal format. Therefore, the
message "Compare error at OFFSET B" means that there was a difference
between the two files at character number 11.

COMP reports the characters at the point of difference by using the internal code that the computer uses to represent the character set. For example,
hexidecimal 61 (97 in decimal format) is the code for the letter "a", and
hexidecimal 69 (105 in decimal format) is the code for the letter "i". Unless
you intend to become a programmer, you need not worry about hexadecimal
format or character codes. What you do need to understand is that the two
files differ; it usually does not matter how they differ.

Although the COMP command uses the term "error" when two files differ, this is really not a proper usage of the word. Remember, just because two
files are not the same does not mean that one is in error—it just means that
they are different. The files may differ because of an error, but that is not the
only—nor the most likely—reason.

Comparing Files on Different Disks

It is very easy to compare a file on one disk to a file of the same name on
another disk. For example, to compare the TEST file on a fixed disk to the
TEST file on a floppy disk in drive A, you would enter

COMP C:TEST A:TEST

Because both file names are the same except for the drive specifier, you can shorten this command to

COMP C:TEST A:

Of course, when the two files have different names, you must fully specify both.

COMPARING DISKS

In some situations it may be easier to compare entire floppy disks than to compare individual files. For example, if you back up your data disks with DISKCOPY, you must compare all of the files on the disks to determine whether the backup disk is current. This can be tedious if there are several files.

To solve this problem, DOS provides the DISKCOMP command, which compares two floppy disks. DISKCOMP is an external command. If you are using the Shell, you may execute it by using the File System or by selecting **Disk Compare** in the DOS Utilities group.

The general form of the DISKCOMP command is

DISKCOMP *source destination*

where *source* and *destination* are the drive specifiers for the disks to be compared.

It is not possible to compare the fixed disk. Even if you have two fixed disks in your system, they cannot be compared.

If you have two floppy-disk drives, you can easily compare two floppy disks by using this form of the DISKCOMP command:

DISKCOMP A: B:

You will then be prompted to insert the two disks you wish to compare into the drives.

If you have only one floppy-disk drive, use this form of the command:

DISKCOMP A: A:

You will then be prompted to insert the first disk into drive A. As DISK-COMP runs, it will prompt you to swap disks.

If the two disks are identical, DISKCOMP displays the message "Compare OK." If there are differences, DISKCOMP reports the sides and tracks in which these differences occur. Knowing the side and track is not very meaningful (except to programmers); usually you only need to know if the disks are the same.

Just as two files of different sizes cannot be compared with the COMP command, two disks of different capacities cannot be compared with DISK-COMP. The smallest-capacity disk currently available holds about 160,000 bytes, and the largest holds about 1,440,000 bytes. Generally, disks that are formatted and used on the same computer will be of the same size, so size is not often a problem when comparing disks. However, be prepared for this problem if you are comparing disks that were created on different computers.

DISKCOMP is especially useful for verifying that DISKCOPY successfully copied the contents of an important disk. Although DISKCOPY performs its own error-checking operation, if the data on a backup disk is extremely important, executing the DISKCOMP command to compare the original and the copy is a very good idea—even if for nothing else than peace of mind.

THE ATTRIB COMMAND

You learned about file attributes when you studied the File System. Recall that DOS associates a set of file attributes with each file on disk. Most of these attributes are for DOS's internal use and cannot be examined or modified. However, you can examine and change some of them from within the File System.

DOS also provides a command-prompt version of this operation. The AT-TRIB command allows you to examine and set the archive and read-only attributes. (The command-line version does not let you make a file hidden.)

ATTRIB is an external command. Its general form of the ATTRIB command is

ATTRIB *attribute filename*

where *attribute* is either not present or is one of the following:

+R\   Turn on read-only attribute
-R\   Turn off read/write attribute
+A\   Turn on archive attribute
-A\   Turn off archive attribute

The *filename* parameter is the name, including drive and path specifiers, of the file that will have its attributes changed or examined.

You can examine the attribute setting of a file with the ATTRIB command by not specifying an attribute. For example, if you enter

ATTRIB ATTRIB.EXE

DOS will respond with

A   C:\DOS\ATTRIB.EXE

if you are running DOS from a fixed disk. The "A" signifies that the archive attribute is turned on. When an attribute is turned on, its first letter is displayed; when it is turned off, nothing is displayed.

To set a file to read-only mode, use the +R argument. For example, enter the following command:

ATTRIB +R ATTRIB.EXE

Examine the attribute settings of ATTRIB.EXE again by using ATTRIB without any attribute arguments. You will now see this display:

A R   C:\DOS\ATTRIB.EXE

which tells you that TEST is now in read-only mode.

To see the effect of the read-only attribute, try to erase ATTRIB.EXE. DOS will respond with "Access denied." DOS will not let you erase a read-only file.

To turn off the read-only attribute, use the following command:

ATTRIB -R ATTRIB.EXE

You can use DOS wild-card characters in the file name, but you should do so with caution: you will be setting the attributes of all the files specified.

You can change the attributes of all files in a directory, plus those in any subdirectories, by placing the /S qualifier after the end of the file name. (Be sure to leave a space between the file name and the /S.) For example, the following command will set the archive attribute of all files with the .TXT extension on a disk in drive A (do not try this example):

ATTRIB +A *.TXT /S

PRINTING GRAPHICS IMAGES

When you press the PRTSC key, whatever is on the screen is printed on the printer. However, this works correctly only for screens that contain text and no *graphics*. Graphics are such things as lines, circles, boxes, and charts.

Except for the Shell, DOS does not generate graphics displays, but many application programs do. To print a screen that contains graphics, you must first execute the GRAPHICS command. GRAPHICS is an external command. When you are in the DOS Shell, you can execute it from the File System.

The GRAPHICS command has the general form

GRAPHICS *printer_name option*

The name of the printer is determined according to the following list:

Printer Type	Name
IBM Personal Graphics Printer	GRAPHICS
IBM Proprinter	GRAPHICS
IBM PC Convertible Printer	THERMAL
IBM Compact Printer	COMPACT
IBM Color Printer with black ribbon	COLOR1
IBM Color Printer with red, green, and blue ribbon	COLOR4
IBM Color Printer with black, cyan, magenta, and yellow ribbon	COLOR8
Printers that use 11-inch-wide paper	GRAPHICSWIDE

If no printer name is specified, the IBM Personal Graphics Printer is the assumed printer. The Epson MX-70, MX-80, and MX-100 printers are quite commonly used with microcomputers and also work with the default setting.

Let's try an example. To allow graphics to be printed on a color printer with a red, green, and blue ribbon, enter

GRAPHICS COLOR4

By default, white on the screen is printed as black on the printer, and black on the screen is printed as white. The /R option causes black to print as black and white to print as white. This option is seldom used.

The background color of the screen is usually not printed. However, if you have a color printer, you can print the background by specifying the /B option.

Finally, the /LCD option should be specified for computers using the IBM PC Convertible Liquid Crystal Display.

SUMMARY

This chapter introduced a number of powerful DOS commands that expand the control you have over the system. These commands are

- LABEL
- VOL
- DATE
- TIME
- SYS
- VERIFY
- XCOPY
- REPLACE
- GRAPHICS
- ATTRIB
- COMP
- DISKCOMP

You also learned how to install the DOS system files on a disk by using the FORMAT command and how to check the condition of your disks with CHKDSK.

In the next chapter you will learn how to operate EDLIN, the DOS text editor.

10

EDLIN: THE DOS TEXT EDITOR

What EDLIN Is and Isn't
EDLIN Basics
Using EDLIN's Commands
Summary

DOS provides a text editor, called EDLIN, that you can use to create and modify text files. For the remainder of this book, you will need to be able to create and modify text files, so you should pay special attention to this chapter if you do not have your own text editor or word processor.

If you do have a different text editor or word processor and know how to use it, you may want to skip this chapter. There is little point in learning to use EDLIN if you already have and use a different editor.

You will need your work copy of the DOS disk to follow the examples in this chapter unless you are a fixed-disk user.

WHAT EDLIN IS AND ISN'T

EDLIN is a *line-oriented* text editor. It is neither a screen-based editor nor, in the proper definition of the term, a word processor. Its sole function is to allow the creation and modification of text files on a line-by-line basis. As text editors go, EDLIN is rather old-style and contains no flashy features. However, it is sufficient for our purposes.

If you are new to microcomputers, be aware that EDLIN is not representative of the types of text editors in general use. It is a simple editor supplied by DOS to allow you to create and modify short text files that will help you customize and tailor DOS to your needs. It is not intended to take the place of either a full-featured, screen-oriented text editor or a word processor. If you need to perform extensive editing or word processing, you should invest in a high-performance package.

Most current editors use the WYSIWYG ("wiz-ee-wig") approach: "What You See Is What You Get." This means that the way a file appears on the screen is the way it will look when printed. EDLIN, however, does not completely follow this principle; the file will look somewhat different in the editor than it will when printed.

Another difference between EDLIN and most modern-style editors is that you do not use the arrow keys to move around on the screen. EDLIN is not screen oriented; instead, it is line oriented, which means that it can only deal with one line of text at a time. Also, EDLIN does not work with the mouse.

EDLIN BASICS

In this section you will learn some of the essentials of EDLIN's operation, including entering text, listing the file, saving the file, and exiting EDLIN. EDLIN's commands will be discussed in detail later in this chapter.

Executing EDLIN

EDLIN is an external command, so you will need a copy of EDLIN.COM on your work disk. To execute EDLIN from the Shell, select it from the File List window and enter the name of the file you want to edit when you see the Options prompt.

From the command prompt, use this general form:

EDLIN *filename*

where *filename* is the name of the text file you wish to edit. If filename does not exist, EDLIN will create it. If you do not specify a file name, DOS tells you that you must do so. Remember that the filename may include a drive specifier and a path name.

Creating a Text File

Execute EDLIN by entering

```
EDLIN EDTEST.TXT
```

from the command prompt or by selecting EDLIN in the File System and specifying EDTEST.TXT as the option. (From now on, only the command-prompt version will be shown. If you are using the Shell, simply use the options.)

When EDLIN begins executing, you will see the following:

```
New file
*
```

The "New file" message simply means that the specified file did not exist and EDLIN has created it. The asterisk is EDLIN's prompt. Whenever you see it, you know that EDLIN is ready to accept a command.

EDLIN operates a little like DOS itself by displaying its prompt and then waiting for commands. Each time you give EDLIN a command, it does what it is told.

Entering Text

When EDLIN displays its prompt, it is in command mode; it is *not* ready to accept text. To make EDLIN accept text, you must enter the I (Insert) command. (Like DOS commands, all EDLIN commands can be entered in upper- or lowercase, as you like.) For example, type **I**, press ENTER, and type these lines of text:

```
Now is the time
for all good men
to come to the aid of their country.
```

Your screen will look like this:

```
*I

                    1:*Now is the time
                    2:*for all good men
                    3:*to come to the aid of their country.
                    4:*
```

In insert mode, EDLIN tabs in, displays the current line number and an asterisk (which in insert mode indicates the currently active line), and waits for input. Each time you press ENTER, a new line number is displayed. Keep in mind that when the asterisk follows the line number, it is not a command prompt—it is simply an indicator of the active line. (This is one of the most confusing aspects of EDLIN.)

Line numbers are not part of your file and will not be on the disk when the file is saved. EDLIN supplies them as both a convenience and a means of referring to a line.

If you make a mistake while typing, you can use the same commands, functions keys, and control keys that you use to correct your mistakes in DOS. However, once you have pressed ENTER, you must use a special EDLIN command to make corrections.

To stop entering text, you must press the CTRL-BREAK or CTRL-C key sequence. Try this now. As you can see, a "^C" is displayed, and EDLIN's prompt returns once more.

Listing the File

To list the contents of the file currently being edited, you use the L (List) command. To execute its simplest form, simply type L and press ENTER. The text you just entered will be displayed like this:

```
                    1: Now is the time
                    2: for all good men
                    3: to come to the aid of their country.
```

Terminating EDLIN

There are two ways to terminate EDLIN. The one that you will use most often is the E (End) command, which causes EDLIN to save the contents of the file and then terminate. The other is the Q (Quit) command, which causes EDLIN to abort without saving the file to disk.

Exit EDLIN by using the E command at this time.

Reediting a File

When you are editing a preexisting file, EDLIN behaves a little differently than it does when you are editing a new file. To begin editing EDTEST.TXT again, enter

```
EDLINE EDTEST.TXT
```

When EDLIN begins execution, you will see the following:

```
End of input file
*
```

This is EDLIN's way of telling you that it has loaded the entire file into memory. The only time you will not see this message is when (and if) you edit a file that is too large to fit into memory. In such a case EDLIN will read the file until 75 percent of the memory is used, leaving 25 percent for working spaces. To edit the remainder of a large file, you will need to use some special commands (discussed later) that write part of the file back to disk and read more of the file from disk. However, you will probably never have a file that is larger than your memory space.

List the file at this time by using the L command. The file will look like this:

```
1:*Now is the time
2: for all good men
3: to come to the aid of their country.
```

Notice that the asterisk is at the start of line 1. This is how EDLIN tells you which line is current. The *current line* determines where certain editor commands will take place. You can think of the current line as being the line you are "on" or "at." When you first begin editing a file, line 1 is current. As you will see shortly, a number of EDLIN commands change the current line. When you insert text, it is placed before the current line, and the rest of the existing text is moved down. For example, if you enter the I command and begin inserting text, the text that you enter will be inserted *before* line 1. Try this now by entering insert mode and then typing

    This is before line one

Press ENTER and then CTRL-BREAK (or CTRL-C). List the file. Your screen will look like this:

    1: This is before line one
    2:*Now is the time
    3: for all good men
    4: to come to the aid of their country.

Notice that line 2 is now current.

Now enter the E command, which saves the file to disk and exits the editor. If you are in the Shell, examine the directory by using EDTEST.* for the Name line in the Display Options window. If you are using the command prompt, enter

    DIR EDTEST.*.

Two files will be displayed. One is EDTEST.TXT, as you would expect. The other is called EDTEST.BAK. It contains the previous version of ED-TEST.TXT. The .BAK extension stands for "backup."

Each time EDLIN saves text to an already existing file, it first renames the extension of the existing file to .BAK and then writes the text to disk with the actual file name. In this way you always have the old version of your file to fall back on if you accidentally corrupt the current version. Periodically, you may want to erase backup files that you no longer need in order to free disk space.

USING EDLIN'S COMMANDS

Now that you know the basics of EDLIN's operation, it is time to study its commands in greater detail. EDLIN has 14 commands, which are summarized in Table 10-1. You will see each of these commands in turn.

Command	Meaning
A	Append lines (from disk file)
C	Copy lines
D	Delete lines
E	End edit and save file
I	Insert lines
L	List lines
M	Move lines
P	Display a page (23 lines)
Q	Quit (do not save file)
R	Replace text
S	Search text
T	Transfer lines (merge one file into another)
W	Write lines (to file)
line_num	Intraline edit on *line_num* line

Table 10-1   The EDLIN Commands

Inserting Text

At this point let's edit EDTEST.TXT. Type **2I** and press ENTER. Type

    this is new line two

and press ENTER and CTRL-BREAK.

Use the L command to list the file. It will look like this:

    1: This is before line one
    2: this is new line two
    3:*Now is the time
    4: for all good men
    5: to come to the aid of their country.

By placing a line number in front of the I command, you told EDLIN to begin inserting text immediately before that line.

The general form of the I command is

line_num I

where *line_num* is the number of the line you wish to begin adding text in front of. If you do not specify the line number, text is inserted before the current line.

To add text to the end of a file, simply specify a line number that is greater than the last line number of the file.

For example, to add lines to the end of the EDTEST.TXT file, you enter **6I**. Try this now. Add the lines

```
Text editors
are fun to use
as long as you know the
right commands.
```

and then press CTRL-BREAK. If you list the file, you will see that the lines have indeed been added to the end.

Deleting Lines

To delete lines of text, use the D (Delete) command. The Delete command takes the general form

*start_line, end_line*D

Start_line and *end_line* are line numbers. The Delete command will delete all lines from *start_line* to *end_line*.

For example, using the EDTEST.TXT file, enter the command

3,5D

and then list the file. Your screen will look like this:

```
1: This  is  before  line  one
2: this  is  new  line  two
3:*Text  editors
4: are  fun  to  use
5: as  long  as  you  know  the
6: right  commands.
```

If you do not specify the starting line number, the Delete command will delete all lines from the current line to the ending line. However, you must start this form of the command with the comma. For example, this command would delete lines 3 and 4 in our example; the current line is line 3, and you are telling EDLIN to delete from the current line to line 4:

```
,4D
```

You can delete any one line simply by specifying its line number. For example, this would delete line 2:

```
2D
```

Notice that no comma precedes this form of the command.

Finally, if no line number is specified, the current line is deleted.

Listing the File

So far, you have seen only the simplest form of the L command. Its general form is

```
start_line, end_lineL
```

where *start_line* and *end_line* specify a range of lines to list on the screen. For example, to list lines 3 through 5, enter

```
3,5L
```

This will display

```
3:*Text editors
4: are fun to use
5: as long as you know the
```

If you omit the starting line number, EDLIN will display 11 lines before the current line and stop at the specified ending line. You must start this form of the command with a comma.

Omitting the ending line causes EDLIN to display 11 lines before and after the specified line. If fewer than 23 lines remain, EDLIN will display lines until the end is reached. For example, still using EDTEST.TXT, the command

```
4L
```

causes the following display:

```
4: are fun to use
5: as long as you know the
6: right commands
```

If no line numbers are specified, then up to 11 lines before and after the current line are displayed. This makes a total of 23 lines (if there are that many in the file).

Editing Lines

You can edit (modify) an existing line in a file by first entering its line number. The specified line will be displayed, and the cursor will be positioned beneath the first character in the line.

You can use any of the DOS editing keys to make changes to the line. The process of editing an existing line is called *intraline editing*.

For example, enter **2** now. You will see the following:

```
2:*this is new line two
2:
```

You may now edit this line exactly as you would the DOS command line. First, press F1 until the cursor is positioned past the space following the word "is." Now press INS, enter

a new addition to

and then press F3 followed by ENTER. When you list the file, line 2 will look like this:

2:*this is a new addition to new line two

Once you press ENTER, any changes you have made to the line will be part of the file. You can cancel the edit at any time by pressing either ESC or CTRL-BREAK. If you have not moved the cursor from the start of the line, then pressing ENTER will also cancel the intraline editing process. You may edit the current line by entering a period instead of its line number.

Try some examples of intraline editing now.

Copying Lines

The C (Copy) command is used to copy a range of lines. It has the general form

*start_line, end_line, dest_line, count*C

The lines between *start_line* and *end_line,* inclusive, are copied *count* number of times before *dest_line.* If *count* is not specified, the default is 1.

For example, once again using the EDTEST.TXT file, enter the following command:

1,3,6C

The file will now look like this:

```
1: This is before line one
2: this is a new addition to line two
3:*Text editors
4: are fun to use
5: as long as you know the
6: This is before line one
7: this is new line two
8: Text editors
9: right commands.
```

Remember that the Copy command duplicates lines, which means that the lines copied are still in their original place as well as in the new location. The Move command (discussed next) is used to move lines from one spot to another.

If you specify a *count* value, the specified lines will be duplicated that many times. For example, try the following command:

```
1,1,4,3C
```

Your file will now look like this:

```
1: This is before line one
2: this is a new addition to line two
3:*Text editors
4:*This is before line one
5: This is before line one
6: This is before line one
7: are fun to use
8: as long as you know the
9: This is before line one
10: this is a new addition to line two
11: Text editors
12: right commands.
```

Keep in mind that the destination line must be outside of the range of the lines to be copied.

Moving Lines

The M (Move) command is similar to the Copy command except that it moves the specified range of lines from one spot in the file to another. Its general form is *start_line, end_line, dest_line*M

Before proceeding, let's clean up the EDTEST.TXT file. First, delete all existing lines by entering **1,100D**. Then, insert the following lines:

```
one
two
three
four
five
six
seven
eight
nine
ten
```

Then press CTRL-C. Once you have done this, try the following command:

```
2,5,8M
```

List the file; it will look like this:

```
1: one
2: six
3: seven
4:*two
5: three
6: four
7: five
8: eight
9: nine
10: ten
```

As you can see, the original lines 2 through 5 have been relocated to the position immediately before line 8.

If you leave off the starting or ending line (or both), the current line is used by default. For example, executing this command would move line 4 to the top of the file:

```
,,1M
```

As with the Copy command, the destination must not be within the range to be moved.

Searching

To find a specific string in the file, use the S (Search) command. A *string* is simply a sequence of characters. The Search command takes the general form

start_line, end_line, ? Sstring

It searches the file between *start_line* and *end_line,* looking for an occurrence of *string.* The question mark (?) is optional and is used to find multiple occurrences.

To begin, delete all the lines in the file and enter the following:

This is a test
of the Search command.
From time to time,
you will find this command useful--
especially when the file is very large.

Once you have entered these lines, try the following command:

1,5Stime

EDLIN will display

3: From time to time

The line in which a match is found is also made current.

If you want to search for a specific occurrence of a string that appears more than once in the file, use the question-mark option. For example, enter the following command:

1,5?Sthe

You will first see

```
                       2: of the search command.
          O.K.?
```

The question mark causes EDLIN to ask you whether the proper occurrence of the string has been found. If it has, type **Y** or press ENTER; otherwise, press any other key. Type **N** at this time. EDLIN will find the second "the" in line 5 and will once again prompt you. Type **N** again. Because "the" does not occur again in the file, EDLIN prints the message "Not found."

The Search command is case-sensitive, which means that upper- and lowercase versions of the same character are considered to be different. For example, try

```
          1,5?SThis
```

EDLIN finds the match with "This" in the first line but does not report any other matches; the word "this" in line 4 begins with a lowercase "t."

If you omit the first line number, the Search command begins with the line immediately following the current line. Omitting the second line number causes the search to continue to the last line in the file. If you omit the search string, the previous string is used.

Try some examples of searching at this time.

Replacing Text

To replace one string with another, use the R (Replace) command. The general form of this command is

```
          start_line, end_line ?Rold- string<F6>new-string
```

The first two line numbers define the range over which the replacement will take place. The question mark (?) is optional. If it is used, you are prompted before each replacement. The old string is the one to be replaced by the new string. You separate the old and new strings by pressing the F6 key.

Using the file developed in the section on searching, try the following command:

```
          1,5Rtime<F6>day
```

Note that the F6 key (denoted by <F6>) displays as "^Z." This command will change line 3 from

From time to time

to the following:

From day to day

If you do not want to change all occurrences of a string, use the question-mark option. You will then be asked at each occurrence whether you want to change it or not. For example, to change the sentences to past tense, use the following command:

1,5?Ris<F6>was

The first thing you will see is

                    1: Thwas is a test
O.K.?

As you can see, EDLIN found the "is" in "This." Because you do not want to change this "is" to "was," type **N**. EDLIN will then look for other occurrences. The next one is the one that you want to change:

                    1: This was a test
O.K.?

Because you want to change this "is," type **Y**. This process will continue until all five lines have been searched.

   You can use the Replace command to remove unwanted text by leaving the new string blank. For example, try the following command:

1,5Ra<F6>

As you can see, all occurrences of the letter "a" have been removed from the file. Pressing F6 is technically unnecessary in this case.

   As with the Search Text command, omitting the first line number causes the replacements to begin with the line immediately following the current line. If the ending line number is not present, the replacement process ends with the last line in the file. If no strings are specified, the strings from the previous R command are used.

Try some examples at this time.

The Page Command

The P (Page) command is used to list a block of lines on the display. It differs from the List command in that it resets the current line so that it is the last line displayed. In its simplest form, the P command pages through a file 23 lines at a time. This is done by simply entering **P** repeatedly. Its general form is

*start_line, end_line*P

If present, *start_line* and *end_line* specify the range of lines to display. If *start_line* is omitted, the line following the current line is used. If *end_line* is not specified, then 23 lines are listed.

End Edit and Quit

The E (End) command terminates the editing process and saves the file as described earlier. The Q (Quit) command terminates the editor but does not save what has been edited.

Transferring Text Between Files

EDLIN allows you to read the contents of a file on disk into the file you are currently editing by using the T (Transfer) command. To follow along, create two files called TEST1.TXT and TEST2.TXT with EDLIN. Enter these lines into TEST1.TXT:

one
two
three
four

Into TEST2.TXT, enter

This is a test

Now edit TEST1. Try the following command:

3TTEST2.TXT

List the file; it will look like this:

one
two
This is a test
three
four

As you can see, the contents of TEST2 were read into TEST1 immediately before line 3.

The Transfer command takes the general form

line_numTfilename

where *line_num* is the number of the line before which the text from the disk file will be placed. The *filename* parameter is the name of the file to read in. If no line number is specified, the text is placed before the current line.

There are three things to remember about the Transfer command. First, the text is read in immediately before the specified line. Second, if the file is not in the current directory, you will receive the message "File not found." Finally, the entire contents of the disk file are read in; it is not possible to read in just part of a file.

Append and Write

When you are editing a file that is too large to fit in memory, EDLIN reads the file until 75 percent of free memory is used. You can tell EDLIN to read more lines by using the A (Append) command. This command has the general form

num_linesA

where *num_lines* is the number of lines to read in; for example, **45A** reads in 45 more lines. If no number is specified, then one line is read.

To edit the end of a large file, you must write part of it out to disk in order to free memory before issuing the Append command. To do this, you use the W (Write) command, which has the general form

*num_lines*W

Here *num_lines* refers to the number of lines to write to the disk. If a number is not specified, text is written until 75 percent of memory is free. The Write command writes lines from the top of the file starting with line 1.

SUMMARY

In this chapter you learned to use the DOS editor, EDLIN. You learned to

- Insert, edit, and delete text
- List the file
- Move and copy text
- Search for and replace character sequences
- Read the contents of one file into another

In the next chapter you will learn how to create your own DOS commands.

11

BATCH FILES

There are times when you will want to give the computer a list of commands all at once and then have the computer whir away on its own without further interaction from you until the list of commands has been executed. For example, you might want to tell the computer to prepare payroll information, print checks, and create weekly backup files without having to wait for each task to be completed before you give the next command. The creation of lists of commands, called *batch files*, is the subject of this chapter.

This chapter assumes that you have your DOS work disk in drive A or are using a fixed disk.

WHAT ARE BATCH FILES?

A batch file is a text file that contains one or more DOS commands. All batch-file names must have the extension .BAT. Once you have created a batch file, DOS will execute the commands in it as it would execute any other external command. You can think of batch files as custom commands that you create.

To execute a batch file from the command prompt, simply enter its name. For example, to execute a batch file called MYBATCH.BAT, you would enter **MYBATCH** at the prompt. From the Shell, you either select the file by using the File System or put it in a menu in the Start Programs window.

For now, if you are using the Shell, execute the batch files from the File System. You will need to know more about batch files before you can add them to a group in the Start Programs window.

TWO SIMPLE BATCH FILES

For your first example, use EDLIN (or another text editor) to create a file called TEST.BAT that contains the following lines:

```
DIR
CHKDSK
```

Now execute TEST. As you can see, DOS first lists the directory and then executes CHKDSK. Note that you do not need to use the extension when you enter a batch file's name at the prompt.

How Batch Files Work

When you execute a command, a sequence of events begins. First, DOS checks to see if the string of characters that you entered matches one of DOS's internal commands. If it does, then the command is executed. Otherwise, DOS checks the current disk to see if what you executed matches one of DOS's external commands or an application program. (Remember, all DOS external commands and programs end with the .EXE or .COM extension.) If the command or program is found, it is executed. Otherwise, DOS sees if there is a batch file that matches. If one exists, DOS executes the commands in the batch file sequentially, starting with the first and finishing with the last.

A batch file must not have the same name as any other DOS command or application program that you are using. If you accidentally create a batch file with the same name as a DOS command and then enter that name as the batch-file command, DOS will always execute the DOS command—never the batch file.

A Second Example

You will find that you often execute the same sequence of commands over and over again. For example, if you are using an accounting program, you may make copies of all of your data files at the end of each day. Assume your data files are called REC.DAT, EMP.DAT, INV.UPD, WITHHOLD.TAX, and PAYABLE.DAT. To copy these files from drive C to A, you would enter the following commands:

```
COPY *.DAT A:
COPY INV.UPD A:
COPY WITHHOLD.TAX A:
```

However, if you create a batch file that contains these commands and call it BKUP.BAT, you can just enter **BKUP** to copy the files.

To see how such a command works, use EDLIN to create three files: SAMPLE1.TXT, SAMPLE2.TXT, and SAMPLE3.TXT. Enter a few characters of your own choosing into each. Now create the BKUP.BAT file, which contains the following commands:

```
COPY SAMPLE1.TXT A:
COPY SAMPLE2.TXT A:
COPY SAMPLE3.TXT A:
```

(If you have two floppy-disk drives, use B as the destination drive.) Place a disk into drive A (or B for two-floppy systems) and enter **BKUP**. You will see DOS copy the files.

Although creating a batch file certainly saves some typing, its main advantage is reliability. Once you have created a batch file, the batch-file command you enter (the batch file's name) will always do exactly what you want it to do. You need not worry about it accidentally forgetting to copy a file, for example.

CANCELING A BATCH COMMAND

The easiest way to cancel a batch command once it begins is to press the CTRL-BREAK key. (The CTRL-C key sequence also works.) Depending on what commands make up the batch file, DOS may wait until the current command finishes before stopping the batch file. DOS will prompt you with the following message:

Terminate batch job (Y/N)?

If you really want to stop execution of the batch command, type **Y**; otherwise, type **N**, and the command will continue to run.

If any of the commands that make up the batch file have already been executed by DOS, their effects will not be nullified. For example, if the first command erases some file, subsequently stopping the batch command will not prevent the file from being erased.

ADDING PARAMETERS

You will often want to create a batch command that will operate in different ways depending on how it is used. For example, consider these two batch files:

Batch File 1   Batch File 2

COPY SAMPLE1.TXT A: COPY SAMPLE2.TXT A:
COMP SAMPLE1.TXT A: COMP SAMPLE2.TXT A:

As you can see, the only difference between file 1 and file 2 is the file name used in the COPY and COMP commands. In this section you will learn how to create one batch file that can replace these two batch files by using placeholders instead of actual file names.

Replaceable Parameters

DOS allows you to use up to ten *replaceable parameters* (sometimes called *dummy parameters*) as placeholders in a batch file. These replaceable parameters are %0 through %9. Each piece of information that you pass to the batch file is placed on the command line immediately after the batch-file name, or as an option when you start the batch file with the Shell. For this reason, they are called *command arguments.*

Each replaceable parameter in a batch file is replaced by its corresponding argument. Parameter %0 will be replaced by the name of the batch file; parameter %1 will be replaced by the first argument; %2 will be replaced by the second argument, and so on.

To see how this works, create a batch file called CPYFILE.BAT that contains the following line:

```
COPY %1 %2
```

When you execute this command

```
CPYFILE SAMPLE1.TXT TEMP
```

parameter %1 will be replaced by SAMPLE1.TXT and %2 will be replaced by TEMP. (In this and the rest of the examples in this book, the %0 parameter is not needed and is not used.)

The most important thing to remember about the command arguments used in a batch command is that they must be separated by spaces. DOS does not recognize any other character as a separator. Thus, the string

```
this,is,a,test
```

will be seen by DOS as one argument, not four.

This line will be seen as four separate arguments by DOS:

```
this is a test
```

Also, because the space character is used as a separator, you cannot use an argument that contains spaces.

A Practical Example of Parameterized Batch Files

As you learned in Chapter 10, each time you reedit a file with EDLIN, it creates a backup copy that contains the previous version of the file. Assume for the moment that the disk you are using is nearly full and does not have enough room for such backup copies. This means that each time you finish editing a file, you will also want to erase its backup.

You could manually erase the file, but a better way is to create a batch-file command that automatically erases the backup when you are done editing. To accomplish this, create a file called ED.BAT and put the following commands in it:

```
EDLIN %1
ERASE *.BAK
```

Now, each time you want to edit a file, use the ED batch command, like this:

ED *filename*

If the file that you wish to edit does not have an extension, do not specify one. After the editing session ends, the ERASE command will be executed, removing the backup file from the disk. (Remember, when you first create a file, there will be no backup. Thus, there will be no file to erase.) You might want to try this batch command now.

SPECIAL BATCH-FILE COMMANDS

DOS allows you to use special batch-file commands that give you greater control over how a batch file is interpreted or operates. These special commands let you create batch files that are actually very much like programs.

The ECHO Command

The ECHO command has two uses. First, it is used to control whether DOS displays the commands in a batch file. By default, ECHO is on, which means that DOS displays each command in the batch file as it is executed. If ECHO is turned off, the batch commands will not be displayed, but any output produced by them will still be shown. The second use of the ECHO command is to print messages on the screen.

The ECHO batch command takes the general form

ECHO on/off/*message*

To turn ECHO off, enter

    ECHO OFF

To turn it on, enter

    ECHO ON

For example, create a file called E.BAT and enter these lines into it:

    ECHO OFF
    VER

When you execute this batch file, you will see the output of the VER command, but you will not see DOS actually execute the command. The output displayed by this batch file looks like this:

    C>ECHO OFF
    IBM Personal Computer DOS 3.30
    C>

For comparison, remove the ECHO command and try the batch command again. This time, each command is displayed as it is executed. The output now looks like this:

    C> VER
    IBM Personal Computer DOS 3.30

In short, when ECHO is off, only the output of the commands is displayed on the screen. When ECHO is on, DOS also displays the execution of each command.

When a batch-file command sequence concludes, ECHO is turned on automatically.

You can also use ECHO to display a message on the screen. To do this, simply place the message after the ECHO command. For example, the following batch file tells the user what to do if errors are found in a file-comparison operation:

    ECHO OFF
    COMP %1 %2
    ECHO If errors have been reported, call the office manager.

Keep in mind that the message will be displayed whether ECHO is on or off.

SUPPRESSING ECHO ONE LINE AT A TIME   If you wish to suppress the display of only certain batch commands, it is easiest to accomplish this on a line-by-line basis. To prevent a batch command from displaying, place the @ character in front of the command. For example, DOS will echo all commands except the second one in this batch file.

```
DIR
@COPY %1 %2
CHKDSK
COMP %1 %2
```

The PAUSE Command

You can temporarily stop a batch command by using the PAUSE command, which takes the general form

PAUSE *message*

The message is optional. When a PAUSE is encountered, DOS displays the message (if present) and then displays its own message, which is

Strike a key when ready . . .

DOS will now wait until any key is pressed on the keyboard. You can cancel the batch command by pressing CTRL-BREAK.

The PAUSE command is very useful when a condition must be met before processing can continue. For example, the following batch file can be used to copy the files on the disk in drive A to the one in drive B. It first prompts you to place the proper disks in the drives:

```
ECHO OFF
PAUSE Put source diskette in A and destination diskette in B
COPY A:*.* B:
```

Your screen will look like this:

```
Put source diskette in A and destination diskette in B
Strike a key when ready . . .
```

The REM Command

Sometimes you may want to embed messages or notes to yourself (or others) in a batch file to help you remember precisely what the file does. You can do this with the REM command, which has the general form

REM *remark*

The remark can be any string from 0 to 123 characters in length. No matter what the remark contains, it will be completely ignored by DOS.

The following batch file contains remarks to show who created the file and what it is used for:

```
REM Purpose: weekly accounting back-up batch file
REM Author: Herbert Schildt
REM Date of creation: 8/31/88
COPY *.DAT B:
COPY *.INV B:
COPY *.BAK B:
```

It is a good idea to identify your more important batch-file commands, especially when several people will be sharing the same system. As you begin to write larger batch-file sequences, you will find that remarks help you remember what is behind them. It is sometimes useful to provide remarks that give a "play-by-play" description of what a batch file is doing.

The IF Command

It is often useful to create a batch command that will do different things depending on certain conditions. To accomplish this, DOS supports the IF batch-file command, which takes the general form

IF *condition command*

Here, *condition* is one of three possible types of conditions and *command* is any other DOS command. If the condition evaluates as true, the command following the condition is executed. Otherwise, DOS skips the rest of the line and moves on to the next line (if there is one) in the batch file.

You can use the IF command for three different types of conditional expressions. First, you can test two strings for equality. Second, you can check to see if a file exists. Finally, you can see if the previously executed program (or command) terminated because of an error.

CHECKING STRINGS FOR EQUALITY   You can use IF to check two strings for equality by using the general form

IF *string1* == *string2 command*

If *string1* equals *string2*, the condition is true; otherwise, it is false. To see a simple example, create a file called CHKSTR.BAT that contains the following lines:

```
IF RED == YELLOW ECHO This will not be printed.
IF RED == RED ECHO This you will see.
```

Try this batch command now. As you can see, only the second ECHO statement is executed.

Comparing two strings as shown in the previous example is of little practical value. However, you can use this feature to compare command arguments. For example, change the CHKSTR.BAT file like this:

```
IF %1 == YELLOW ECHO The color is yellow.
IF %1 == RED ECHO The color is red.
```

Now try executing CHKSTR with an argument of RED. As you can probably guess, it reports that the color is red.

For a more useful example, imagine that a computer in a small office is used by George, Fred, and Mary. Assume further that Mary does word processing, George is in charge of accounting, and Fred uses a spreadsheet. You could write one backup batch file that will back up the files in the proper directory, given the name of the person. This batch file might look like this:

```
IF %1 == MARY COPY \WP\*.* A:
IF %1 == FRED COPY \SPSHEET\*.* A:
IF %1 == GEORGE COPY \ACC\*.* A:
```

Assuming that this file is called BK.BAT, then to back up her files, Mary only needs to place a disk into drive A and enter **BK MARY**.

CHECKING FOR A FILE   You can check to see if a file or set of files exists by using the EXIST condition of IF, which takes the general form

   IF EXIST *file_name command*

where *file_name* is the name of the file that you are checking for. The name may include both a drive specifier and a path name. You may also use the question-mark and asterisk wild cards if you wish.

   For example, enter the following lines into a file called EXTEST.BAT.

```
IF EXIST GARBAGE.FIL ECHO This should not be found.
IF EXIST SORT.EXE ECHO SORT.EXE is on the disk.
```

Run it now. As you can see, only the message "SORT.EXE is on the disk" is displayed.

   You can also use the EXIST condition to double-check the copying of files. If the file already exists on the destination disk, the batch file will allow the user to cancel the command if the file should not be overwritten:

```
IF EXIST B:%1 PAUSE B:%1 exists - press control-Break to
cancel
COPY %1 B:
```

CHECKING FOR ERRORS   An application program can set an internal DOS variable that indicates whether the program terminated normally or because of an error. For the sake of discussion, call this variable the *error variable*. If a program terminates normally, it sets the error variable to 0, indicating that everything went all right. If it terminates because of an error, it sets the error variable to a number greater than 0. If a program does not actually set the value of the error variable, it is 0 by default.

   DOS lets you check this variable through the use of the ERRORLEVEL condition in the IF command, which takes the general form

   IF ERRORLEVEL *n command*

where *n* is a number greater than or equal to 0 and represents the error number set by the application program. If the value of the error variable is equal to or greater than *n*, the condition is true.

The use of ERRORLEVEL is somewhat complicated and is used most frequently by programmers. However, all programs will set ERRORLEVEL to 0 if they terminate normally. Therefore, you can use the following form of the IF command in any batch file you create to check for normal program termination before proceeding:

```
REM Check to see that the previous program terminated
REM normally.
IF ERRORLEVEL 1 PAUSE Abnormal program termination.
```

Keep in mind that not all application programs will set this variable when they terminate because of an error, so some errors could be missed.

The NOT Command

You can precede the IF condition with the word NOT, which will then reverse the outcome of the condition. For example, if

```
EXIST TEST.DAT
```

is true, then the following is false:

```
NOT EXIST TEST.DAT
```

To understand how NOT works, assume that you have an application program that requires the INFO.DAT file to be present on the current disk. You could use the following batch command to check for the file before the program is run:

```
IF NOT EXIST INFO.DAT PAUSE Insert the program disk.
```

The GOTO Command

The GOTO batch command directs DOS to execute the commands in a batch file in a nonsequential order. The general form of GOTO is

GOTO *label*

where *label* is a label defined elsewhere in the batch file. When GOTO is executed, DOS goes to the specified label and begins executing commands from that point. Using GOTO, you can cause execution to jump forward or backward in the file.

For example, create a file called GOTOTEST.BAT and enter the following lines:

```
IF %1 == RED GOTO RED
IF %1 == BLUE GOTO BLUE
:RED
ECHO You chose the color red.
DIR
GOTO DONE
:BLUE
ECHO You like blue.
CHKDSK
:DONE
REM The batch file is now finished.
```

Now try this batch file with BLUE and RED as arguments.

All labels must begin with a colon. Though a label can be up to 125 characters long, DOS will use only the first 8 characters because in the language of computers, only those characters are significant. This means that the following labels will appear the same to DOS.

```
:longlabel1
:longlabel2
```

You may not use a period in a label name.

As the example illustrated, you can use GOTO in conjunction with IF to create *blocks* of commands that will be executed only if the condition controlling the IF is true. Notice that you must provide a GOTO around other blocks of commands (as in GOTO DONE in the RED block) if you do not want execution to "fall through" into the next block.

You can use GOTO and a label to create a loop. For example, the following batch file continues to list the directory until you press CTRL-BREAK, which cancels the command:

```
:ONE
DIR
GOTO ONE
```

The CALL Command

Sometimes you will want to execute another batch-file command from within a batch file. The best way to do this is with the CALL command. Its general form is

CALL *batch_file*

where *batch_file* is the name of the batch-file command that you wish to execute.

As a first simple example, create a file called ONE.BAT that contains the following lines:

```
ECHO OFF
ECHO This is in batch file ONE
CALL TWO
ECHO This is back in batch file ONE
```

Now create the TWO.BAT file, which contains the following line:

```
ECHO This is in batch file TWO
```

Now execute batch file ONE. After it has run, your display will look like this:

```
This is in batch file ONE
This is in batch file TWO
This is back in batch file ONE
```

The CALL command works like this. When it is encountered, it suspends the execution of the current batch file. When the called batch file terminates, the first batch file resumes its execution at the next line following the CALL command.

A batch file can call itself, but you must make certain that some terminating condition eventually stops the process.

A good use for CALL is to allow the creation of *master batch files* that simply consist of CALLs to other batch files. Such a master file looks somewhat like an outline and provides a quick way for you to see what is actually happening; as you create your own batch files, you will be surprised at how long and complicated they can become. For example, a master batch file for word processing might look like this:

```
REM First create the document
CALL WORDPROC
REM Next, check it for spelling
CALL SPELL
REM Now, print it
CALL PRNT
```

You can pass command arguments to the called batch file by specifying them after the name of the batch file. For example, the following CALL statement passes the arguments "one" and "two".

```
CALL MYBATCH one two
```

One final point about calling other batch-file commands: canceling a called command cancels all batch files, including both the one currently executing and the one that called it.

The FOR Command

You can repeat a series of commands with different arguments through the use of the FOR command. It takes the general form

FOR *%%var* IN (*argument list*) DO *command*

where *var* is a single-letter variable that will take on the values of the arguments. The arguments must be separated by spaces. The FOR will repeat the specified command as many times as there are arguments. Each time the FOR repeats, *var* will be replaced by an argument, moving from left to right.

For a first example, create a file called SIMPFOR.BAT that contains the following commands:

```
ECHO OFF
FOR %%I IN (%1 %2 %3) DO ECHO %%I
```

This batch file will print the first three command arguments with which it is called. For example, execute it with the arguments ONE TWO THREE. The output produced by FOR will look like this:

```
ONE
TWO
THREE
```

As a second example, create a file called FORTEST.BAT that contains the following commands:

```
ECHO OFF
FOR %%H IN (FORTEST.BAT ONE.BAT TWO.BAT) DO DIR
%%H
```

Run FORTEST now. As you can see, the DIR command is executed three times, each time with a different file name. Each time the FOR command repeats, %%H is replaced by the next argument in the list; the first %%H equals FORTEST.BAT, the second %%H equals ONE.BAT, and so on. FOR continues to repeat until the last argument is used.

You can use FOR to execute a list of commands by placing the commands in the argument list. For example, the following command will clear the screen, list the directory, and finally, check the disk.

```
FOR %%C IN (CLS DIR CHKDSK) DO %%C
```

You may not use a FOR command as the object of DO. That is, FOR cannot be used to execute another FOR command.

The SHIFT Command

As you know, there are only ten replaceable parameters, %0 through %9. You can use the SHIFT command to gain access to more command arguments than ten. Each time SHIFT is executed, the contents of the replaceable parameters are shifted down one position—with whatever was in %0 is lost, and %9 contains a new argument if one exists. For example, after one SHIFT, the beginning values shown here

Replaceable Parameter	Value
%0	TEST
%1	A
%2	B
%3	C
%4	(empty)

will have the following values:

Replaceable Parameter	Value
%0	A
%1	B
%2	C
%3	(empty)

For an example, create a file called SHFT.BAT containing the following commands:

```
ECHO OFF
ECHO %0 %1 %2 %3
SHIFT
ECHO %0 %1 %2 %3
```

Execute the following command as shown here:

```
SHFT ONE TWO THREE
```

You will see this output:

```
SHFT ONE TWO THREE
ONE TWO THREE
```

Using a loop makes it easier to access a large number of arguments. For example, change the SHFT.BAT file so that it contains the following commands:

```
ECHO OFF
:LOOP
ECHO %1
```

```
SHIFT
IF NOT %1 == END GOTO LOOP
REM This will loop until an argument containing
REM the word END is reached.
```

Now execute the batch file as shown here:

```
SHFT THIS IS A TEST THAT ACCESSES EACH ARGUMENT
END
```

This will display the following:

```
THIS
IS
A
TEST
THAT
ACCESSES
EACH
ARGUMENT
```

EXECUTING A BATCH FILE
FROM WITHIN A BATCH FILE

You can start another batch file from within a batch file without using the
CALL command. However, executing a batch-file command without using
CALL produces different results than when CALL is used. To cause one
batch file to execute another, simply use the name of the batch file like any
other command. When the batch file's name is encountered, DOS will
automatically stop executing the first batch file and begin executing the
second. However, when that file terminates, control returns to DOS and the
prompt is displayed—DOS does not return to the original batch file.

For example, assume that BKUP is the name of a batch file. Given the
batch file

```
CLS
CHKDSK
BKUP
DISKCOMP A: B:
```

the final line will never be executed. If you want control to return to the original batch file, use the CALL command.

AUTOEXEC.BAT

There is one very special batch file, AUTOEXEC.BAT, that you will probably want to create. This is the batch file that DOS automatically executes at startup. You will often want DOS to perform one or more tasks when the computer is first started; you can place these tasks in the AUTOEXEC.BAT file.

If DOS was installed with the IBM-recommended procedure, then an AUTOEXEC.BAT file already exists. You are free to add to this file, but you should *not* delete anything in it. Also, anything you add must go before the line that reads "DOSSHELL." DOSSHELL is the batch file that starts the execution of the DOS Shell.

You can use the AUTOEXEC.BAT file to create a "custom look" to your system. For example, for a computer dedicated to word processing you might add these lines to the AUTOEXEC.BAT file:

```
CLS
ECHO WELCOME TO WORD PROCESSING
ECHO             AT WIDGET CORP.
PAUSE
```

You can also use the AUTOEXEC.BAT file to confirm that the proper programs are available for use. For example, assume that the AC-COUNT.EXE program is required for the operation of the computer and that it must be located on drive A. The following will cause the computer to wait until you put a disk containing ACCOUNT.EXE into drive A:

```
:LOOP
IF EXIST A:ACCOUNT.EXE GOTO OK
ECHO Insert program diskette into drive A
PAUSE
GOTO LOOP
:OK
```

Later in this book you will learn that there are several ways to customize DOS. Some of these customization commands are perfect candidates for inclusion in the AUTOEXEC.BAT file.

ADDING A BATCH FILE TO THE START PROGRAMS WINDOW

You can add a batch file to a group in the Start Programs window just as you can any other program—by using the **Add** option—with this single exception. When you enter the name of the batch file at the Commands line of the Add Program window, it must be preceded by the CALL command. Thus, if the name of the batch file is MYBATCH.BAT, you must use this line to execute it:

```
CALL MYBATCH
```

If you do not use CALL, the DOS Shell will not reappear when the batch file terminates.

Batch Commands as Program Startup Commands

You should recall that when you add a program to a group in the Start Programs window, you not only specify the name of the program at the Commands line but also specify any startup options or commands required by the program. Along with the program startup commands (PSCs) that you have already learned, you can also use any batch command with the single exception of GOTO.

THE SHELL'S OWN BATCH FILES

Now that you have learned about batch files, you might be interested to know that the DOS Shell generates a batch file for each command or program you execute. It then passes control to the DOS prompt, which then executes your command. Once the command has finished, control is passed back to the Shell.

The fact that the Shell uses batch files is strong testimony to their power and effectiveness.

SUMMARY

In this chapter you learned how to create custom DOS commands through the use of batch files. You learned

- How to parameterize a batch file
- About the special batch commands

  ECHO
  PAUSE
  CALL
  REM
  IF
  FOR
  GOTO
  SHIFT

- About the AUTOEXEC.BAT file and its special purpose in DOS

In the next chapter you will learn about filters and pipes for redirecting input and output. These elements give you control over how information is moved around inside the computer.

12

REDIRECTING I/O

Data goes into the computer through input devices and leaves by way of output devices. The transfer of information to or from these devices is called an *input/output operation,* or an *I/O operation* for short. The computer has several I/O devices, including the keyboard, monitor, printer, and disk drives. By using special DOS commands, you can reroute the flow of data. This is called *redirected I/O*.

STANDARD INPUT
AND STANDARD OUTPUT

You might be surprised to learn that DOS does not "know" where its commands come from or where its output is sent. For example, DOS does not know that you use a keyboard to enter commands and that you see DOS's reponse on a monitor. This is because DOS does not deal directly with the I/O devices. Instead, it works through two special internal pseudodevices, called *standard input* and *standard output,* often abbreviated as *stdin* and *stdout.* These pseudodevices provide the programming support for the various I/O devices in the computer.

When DOS begins execution, standard input is linked to the keyboard and standard output is linked to the monitor. However, you can change which device is linked with which pseudodevice. Figure 12-1 shows how you can think of standard input and standard output in terms of your devices and files.

In this chapter, you will first look at the redirection of I/O to and from a disk file. Later, you will learn to redirect I/O to other devices supported by the computer. For the examples shown in this chapter, make sure that your DOS disk is in drive A and that A is the current drive (unless you are using a fixed disk, in which case you may use drive C).

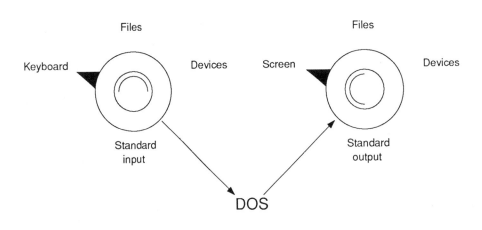

FIGURE 12-1.   A depiction of standard input and standard output

REDIRECTING OUTPUT TO A FILE

DOS uses the > and >> operators to redirect the output generated by a DOS command or an application program that would normally be shown on the screen. The general format of these operators with files is

command > *filename*
command >> *filename*

where *command* is either a DOS command or an application program, and *filename* is the name of the file that will receive the output generated by *command*.

For example, execute the CHKDSK command with this command line:

CHKDSK > OUT

If you are using the Shell instead, select CHKDSK with the File System and enter this at the **Options** prompt:

OUT

When the command executes, nothing is displayed on the screen.

Now examine the OUT file using **TYPE** at the command prompt or selecting the **View** option in the File System. You will see that the output of the CHKDSK command is contained in this file. The OUT file can be edited with EDLIN and is normal in every way.

The difference between the > and >> operators lies in how the output file is handled. The > operator always creates a new, empty file to hold the output information. If a file by the specified name already exists on the disk, it is erased, and then a new one is created. Thus, if OUT had already existed on your work disk, the example you just performed would have erased it, destroying its contents, and then recreated it and put the new information into it.

The >> operator does not destroy an already existing file. If the specified file already exists, the >> operator causes the output to be placed on the end of the file. If the file does not exist, however, it will still be created.

To understand the difference between these operators, try the following command:

MEM > OUT

Recall that MEM is the command that displays information about your computer's memory. If you examine the OUT file now, you will see the following (the exact information may vary slightly):

```
655360 bytes total memory
654336 bytes available
558688 largest executable program size
2490368 bytes total extended memory
2490368 bytes available extended memory
```

As you can see, the old contents of OUT are no longer present.

Now try the following command:

```
CHKDSK >> OUT
```

OUT will now contain this:

```
655360 bytes total memory
654336 bytes available
558688 largest executable program size

2490368 bytes total extended memory
2490368 bytes available extended memory

Volume DOS400     created 08-04-1988 1:31p
Volume Serial Number is 340C-14E3

1457664 bytes total disk space
  69632 bytes in 3 hidden files
 918528 bytes in 66 user files
 469504 bytes available on disk

   512 bytes in each allocation unit
  2847 total allocation units on disk
   917 available allocation units on disk

655360 total bytes memory
558688 bytes free
```

As you can see, the previous contents of the file were preserved and the new output was placed on the end.

Only the output that would normally go to the screen is being redirected. Other I/O operations performed by the command are not affected. For example, try the following COPY command at the command prompt (you cannot redirect the Shell's Copy command):

```
COPY OUT TEST > OUT2
```

This command correctly copies the contents of OUT into TEST. Only the information that COPY sends to standard output will be placed into the OUT2 file. In this case, OUT2 will only contain the message "1 File(s) copied."

One of the most common uses of redirected output is to create a *log file* that records the activity of the computer when you are not physically present. For example, the end-of-month phase of an accounting package might include several lengthy operations that are best run overnight. If you place all of the commands in a batch file with output redirected into a log file by means of the >> operator, you can check to see that all went well when you come in the next morning.

REDIRECTING INPUT TO A FILE

You can redirect standard input with the < operator. It is used in the same manner as the > operator, but instead of causing the command to send its output to a file, < causes a command to use the contents of a file as input. When input is redirected, information that is normally entered at the keyboard is read from the specified file.

Although you will seldom need to redirect the input to a command to a file, it is easy enough to do if you are careful. As a simple example, first create a file called INPUT.DAT that contains the word "SAMPLE" followed by a blank line. Now execute the following command:

```
LABEL < INPUT.DAT
```

Recall that LABEL sets the volume label name of the disk. As you can see, DOS no longer pauses and waits for you to enter the label name. Instead, it reads the name from the INPUT.DAT file. To confirm that this actually happened, use VOL to display the volume label. (You can change the label back to what it was previously if you like.)

You must be very careful when redirecting input to a file. If the file fails to contain sufficient input to satisfy the command, the computer will stop running and lock up. If this happens, the only thing that you can do is restart the system.

REDIRECTING I/O TO APPLICATION PROGRAMS

All of DOS's commands allow their input and output to be redirected, but some application programs do not. Certain programs bypass DOS's standard I/O routines and communicate directly with the hardware—usually to achieve improved performance. In this situation the redirection operators will not be effective. If you attempt to redirect I/O to an application program and it doesn't work right, this is probably the reason.

REDIRECTING I/O TO OTHER DEVICES

You can redirect I/O operations to devices other than disk drives by using their DOS *device names*. These names, and what they refer to, are shown in Table 12-1. You cannot create a disk file with the same name as any device

Name	Device
CON	The console, either keyboard or screen
AUX	The first asynchronous serial port
COM1	The same as AUX
COM2	The second asynchronous serial port
COM3	The third asynchronous serial port
COM4	The fourth asynchronous serial port
PRN	The first printer—output only
LPT1	The same as PRN
LPT2	The second printer—output only
LPT3	The third printer—output only
NUL	A nonexistent device; used by programers for testing software

TABLE 12-1   The DOS Device Names

name. For traditional reasons, you may place a colon after the device name; however, this will not be done in this book because it is superfluous.

For the most part, you can use device names anywhere you would use a file name. For an example, create a short text file called MYNAME that contains your name. Now try the following command from the command prompt (if you have a printer):

```
COPY MYNAME PRN
```

As you can see, your name is printed by the printer, as long as your printer is configured in the standard manner.

Because of what must surely have been an oversight by IBM, the Copy option in the File System will not accept DOS device names. This is why you had to execute the previous example from the command prompt. Later versions of the Shell will probably correct this deficiency. For now, execute the next few examples from the command prompt.

An alternative to using the TYPE command to display the contents of a text file on the screen is to simply copy it to CON with the COPY command. For example, the following command prints your name on the screen:

```
COPY MYNAME CON
```

The following command acts as a clever trick that allows you to use your computer like a very expensive typewriter:

```
COPY CON PRN
```

To cancel this command, press CTRL-Z and then ENTER. Using this command, whatever you type will be printed on the printer. However, COPY will wait until you enter a CTRL-Z and press ENTER before printing begins.

You can use the I/O redirection operators on device names as well as file names. For example, this command routes the output of the CHKDSK command to the printer. (This command can be executed from the Shell using the File System.)

```
CHKDSK > PRN
```

Using CTTY

DOS allows you to redirect both input and output to a different device by means of the CTTY command. The command name is short for "Change

TeleType" and is derived from the early days of computing, when teletype machines were used instead of terminals.

CTTY allows you to hook up a remote terminal to a DOS-based computer and then switch control of the computer to that terminal. For example, if the terminal were connected to the COM1 serial port, you would enter

CTTY COM1

to switch control to it. Don't try this, however, unless you know that the device you are switching to can actually control the computer; a printer, for example, cannot.

To switch control back to the console, enter

CTTY CON

Unless you have a remote terminal attached to your computer, do not use the CTTY command.

FILTERS

DOS has three special commands, called *filters,* that read standard input, perform manipulations on the information, and write it to standard output.The three filter commands are MORE, FIND, and SORT. They are external commands that you can execute from the Shell by means of the File System or from the command prompt.

MORE

The MORE filter command reads standard input, displays 24 lines at a time on the screen, and waits for you to press a key before displaying the next screenful of information. To see how MORE works, create a text file called BIG.TXT that is 50 lines long, with each line containing its line number. The first 10 lines of the file will look like this:

```
 1
 2
 3
 4
 5
 6
 7
 8
 9
10
```

Now try the following command:

```
MORE < BIG.TXT
```

As you can see, the first 24 lines of the file are displayed. The twenty-fifth line contains the prompt

```
— More —
```

To see more of the file, press any key.

The general form of MORE is

MORE < *file_name/device_name*

The < operator and the file or device name are optional. However, if you leave them off, MORE will simply read characters from the keyboard and display them on the screen, which is not very useful.

If you use the command prompt, MORE is better than TYPE at browsing through large text files because it automatically pages through them 24 lines at a time. If you use the Shell, the **View** option in the File System may be more to your liking for simply viewing a file, but as you will see, MORE is more flexible.

FIND

The FIND filter command searches a list of files for occurrences of a specified string and displays each line in which a match occurs. FIND has the general form

FIND *options "string" file_list*

The *string* parameter is the sequence of characters that you are looking for and must be enclosed between double quotes, and *file_list* is the list of files that FIND will search. You may not use wild-card characters in the file names.

Before you can try the examples, you must create a file that is called SAMPLE.TXT and enter the following lines into it:

```
This is a sample text
file that illustrates
the use of the FIND filter command.
Notice that upperCASE
and lowercase
are considered separately by FIND.
```

Now try the following command:

```
FIND "that" SAMPLE.TXT
```

FIND will respond with

```
---------- SAMPLE.TXT
file that illustrates
Notice that upperCASE
```

Each time that an occurrence of the search string is found, FIND will respond by printing the line in which the match occurs.

As the contents of the file suggest, FIND treats upper- and lowercase letters separately. For example, try the following command:

```
FIND "CASE" sample.txt
```

FIND will only report a match in the line "Notice that upperCASE"; it will not find the lowercase version.

You can specify more than one file to search. To see how this works, copy SAMPLE.TXT to SAMPLE2.TXT and change the first line so that it reads as follows:

```
This  is  a  second  sample  text
```

Now try the following command:

```
FIND  "second"  SMPLE.TXT  SAMPLE2.TXT
```

FIND will respond with:

```
--------  SAMPLE.TXT
--------  SAMPLE2.TXT
This  is  a  second  sample  text
```

Notice that the files are searched in the order in which they appear on the command line. In this case, the word "sample" occurs only in the file SAMPLE2.TXT. However, in response to the command

```
FIND  "text"  SAMPLE.TXT  SAMPLE2.TXT
```

FIND will display

```
--------  SAMPLE.TXT
This  is  a  sample text
--------  SAMPLE2.TXT
This  is  a  second  sample  text
```

You may have any number of files in the list, as long as the total length of the command line does not exceed 128 characters.

If you only want to know if there are any occurrences of the string and how many occurrences there are, use the /C option. For example, try the following command:

```
FIND  /C  "that"  SAMPLE.TXT
```

FIND will respond with:

-------- SAMPLE.TXT: 2

As you can see, only the number of occurrences is reported—the line containing the string is not shown.

You can use the /N option to show the relative line number of each occurrence. Try the following:

FIND /N "that" SAMPLE.TXT

The output will now look like this:

-------- SAMPLE.TXT
[2]file that illustrates
[4]Notice that upperCASE

The line numbers are shown between angle brackets. Keep in mind that you cannot use the /N and /C options together.

Finally, you can have FIND report all lines that do *not* contain the string by using the /V option. For example, the command

FIND /V "that" SAMPLE.TXT

produces this output:

This is a sample text
the use of the FIND filter command.
and lowercase
are considered separately by FIND.

SORT

The SORT filter command sorts information read from standard input and writes the sorted version to standard output. SORT has the general form

SORT *option* < *input* > *output*

where *input* and *output* are either file or device names. If they are not specified, the screen is used for output and the keyboard for input. It is not uncommon to have SORT display its output on the screen.

SORT works by sorting information on a line-by-line basis. It makes no distinction between upper- and lowercase characters. Unless you specify otherwise, SORT arranges the information in ascending alphabetical order.

As a first example, create a file called SORTTEST.TXT and enter the following lines:

```
one
two
three
four
five
six
seven
eight
nine
ten
```

Now try the following command:

```
SORT < SORTTEST.TXT
```

This causes SORT to display the sorted file on the screen. The sorted output will look like this:

```
eight
five
four
nine
one
seven
six
ten
three
two
```

You can have the sorted information placed in a file by specifying it. For example, the following command places the information in the TEMP file:

```
SORT < SORTTEST.TXT > TEMP
```

You can sort in reverse order by specifying the /R option. The following command displays the SORTTEST.TXT file in reverse alphabetical order:

```
SORT /R < SORTTEST.TXT
```

If you are using the command prompt, not the Shell, SORT is very useful for sorting the directory. To do this, first create a file called OUT that contains the directory listing using this command:

```
DIR > OUT
```

Now try the following command:

```
SORT < OUT
```

As you can see, a sorted directory is displayed.

SORTING ON A SPECIFIC COLUMN   Tables of information are very common. Sometimes it is useful to sort a table by the information contained in columns other than the first column. Unless directed otherwise, SORT begins sorting with the first character of each line. However, you can tell SORT what character to begin sorting on with the /+ n option, where n is the column to begin with.

For example, a hardware store might keep its inventory in a file similar to the one shown here:

```
item        cost    on hand
pliers       10      10
hammers       8       3
nails         1      100
screws        1       0
```

The store manager could use SORT to sort the data based on the "on hand" column, which would make it easy to see which items were out of stock or running low. Assuming the file is called INVENT.DAT; the manager would use this command

```
SORT /+13 < INVENT.DAT
```

The output would be

screws	1	0
hammers	8	3
pliers	10	10
nails	1	100
item	cost	on hand

The number "13" in the manager's command is the character position that starts the "on hand" column. If you try this example, do not use any tabs in the file.

PIPES

The process called *piping* allows you to route the output of one command into the input of another. You can think of the information flowing from one command to the next through a pipe. To create a pipe between two programs, you use the I operator, which has the general form

command1 I command2

where the output of *command1* is redirected automatically to the input of *command2*. For an example, try the following command from the command prompt (or put it in a menu in the Start Programs window):

DIR | MORE

This sends the directory listing as input to MORE instead of to the screen. MORE then displays the directory 24 lines at a time.

In the previous section you saw one way to produce a sorted directory listing. However, there is an easier way, as the following command illustrates

DIR | SORT | MORE

Try this from the command prompt, or put it in a Start Programs menu. As you can see, the directory is displayed in sorted order. In this case two pipes were used. The output of DIR was used as input by SORT, whose output was in turn used as input by MORE. Figure 12-2 should help you visualize how

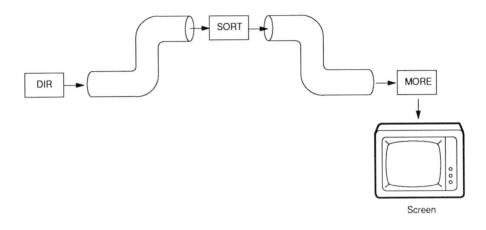

FIGURE 12-2.   A visualization of the DIR I SORT I MORE command

this command operates. You can have as many pipes as can fit on the command line.

When a pipe is created, so, too, is a temporary disk file that will be erased automatically when the commands are completed. There must be room on your disk for this temporary file. The size of the file is governed by the amount of output generated by the command that is putting data into the pipe. A few thousand free bytes are usually sufficient.

A pipe is very useful for finding a "lost" file. From time to time, a file will be placed accidentally into the wrong directory of a disk. If there are a great many subdirectories, it can take you a long time to find the file by searching each directory manually. However, the following command will search all directories on a disk and report the path to the file. The file is called TEST here, but you should substitute the name of the file for which you are looking.

    CHKDSK /V | FIND "TEST"

Remember, when CHKDSK is used with the /V option, it displays all of the files on the disk in the basic form *drive:path\file_name*. Thus, when a match is reported, the path to the file is shown. You can execute this command from the File System or from the command prompt.

PUTTING IT ALL TOGETHER— CREATING SIMPLE DATABASES

With I/O redirection and pipes, you can create simple but effective databases. You can use the FIND command to locate information, the SORT command to sort the database, and the MORE command to browse through it. You will use EDLIN (or any other editor) to enter information into the database; the only restriction is that each entry in the database must be on one line.

As a simple example, let's develop a quick- reference telephone directory database containing frequently called numbers. The database will use the basic format

Last_name, First_name area_code number

as in this example:

```
Bell, Alexander 222 555-2222
```

Enter the following information into PHONE.DAT:

```
Washington, George 111 555-1111
Bell, Alexander 222 555-2222
Newton, Isaac 333 555-3333
Nietzsche, Friedrich 444 555-4444
```

Then, to find Newton's telephone number, you use the command:

```
TYPE PHONE.DAT | FIND "Newton"
```

A second or so later, Newton's phone number appears.

You can sort your phone list by using the following series of commands:

```
SORT < PHONE.DAT > TEMP
COPY TEMP PHONE.DATA
ERASE TEMP
```

You can also list the numbers for groups of people based on the beginning letters in their names. For example, the following command lists the telephone numbers for both Newton and Nietzsche:

```
TYPE PHONE.DAT | FIND "N"
```

You can expand this telephone directory to include addresses or perhaps remarks, as long as everything fits on one line. Use the same basic approach to create databases for other items. The possibilities are limited only by your imagination.

SUMMARY

In this chapter you learned about the following:

- Standard input and output
- Redirecting I/O
- DOS devices
- The SORT, FIND, and MORE filter commands
- Pipes
- Creating simple databases with DOS

In the next chapter you will learn how to configure DOS to best suit your needs.

13

CONFIGURING DOS

Using the MODE Command
Changing the DOS Prompt
Using the CONFIG.SYS File
PATH
APPEND
ASSIGN
SUBST
JOIN
Shell Startup Options
International Configurations
Summary

There are several things about DOS that you can change. Some affect the way DOS operates or appears, and others alter the way DOS accesses disk drives or defines devices. You can also configure DOS for use in a foreign country. In this chapter you will learn about the commands that let you configure DOS to best meet your needs.

Unless stated otherwise, the configuration options in this chapter are applicable to both the Shell and the command prompt.

USING THE MODE COMMAND

As you know, DOS controls the devices that constitute your computer. Some of these devices have various modes of operation. When DOS starts, these devices are set to operate in a way that applies to the widest range of situations. However, you can change the way some of them operate to take advantage of how your system is configured. You can use MODE to change the operation of the video adapter, the keyboard, the serial communication ports, and the printer. MODE is an external command that you can execute from the command prompt or from the Shell using the File System.

Controlling the Video Adapter

The *video adapter* is a circuit card inside the computer that controls the monitor. It generates and maintains the text and graphics that you see on the screen. There are two basic types of video adapters: monochrome adapters, which can only display text characters in a single color, and color/graphics adapters, which can display text and graphics in multiple colors. Though uncommon, it is possible for both types of adapters to be in your computer.

You can use the MODE command to select a video adapter or to set the way that it displays information. To do so, you use this form of MODE:

MODE *video_mode*

where *video_mode* is one of the adapter codes shown in Table 13-1.

If you have a color/graphics adapter, you can set it to display in either 40- or 80-column mode and to display in either color or black and white. For example, if you have a color/graphics adapter, enter

MODE CO40

The screen will clear, and the DOS prompt will be displayed at twice its usual size. In 40-column mode the letters are twice as big, so only 40 can fit from side to side. For this reason, 40-column mode is almost never used. To reset the display to the normal 80-column mode, enter

MODE CO80

Code	Effect
40	Sets a color/graphics adapter display width to 40 columns
80	Sets a color/graphics adapter display width to 80 columns
BW40	Activates the color/graphics adapter, sets the width to 40 columns, and sets the display mode to black and white
BW80	Activates the color/graphics adapter, sets the width to 80 columns, and sets the display mode to black and white
CO40	Activates the color/graphics adapter, sets the width to 40 columns, and sets the display mode to color
CO80	Activates the color/graphics adapter, sets the width to 80 columns, and sets the display mode to color
MONO	Activates the monochrome adapter; the display width is always 80 columns

TABLE 13-1 The Video Adapter Codes

If you have a monochrome adapter, you cannot change its mode of operation. However, if you have two adapters in your system, you can enter

```
MODE MONO
```

to switch to the monochrome adapter.

On rare occasions a mismatch between the color/graphics video adapter and the monitor can occur, which causes the image to be off-centered (shifted left or right) on the screen. You can shift the display left or right to center it by using the following form of MODE:

```
MODE video_adapter, R/L, T
```

Enter **R** to shift the display to the right or **L** to shift it to the left. The display is shifted two spaces in 80-column mode and one space in 40-column mode.

The T parameter is optional; when present, DOS displays a test pattern and asks you whether the screen is correct. For example, the command

```
MODE CO80, L, T
```

produces this display:

```
012345678901234567890/.../012345678901234567890
Do you see the rightmost 9 (Y/N)?
```

If you type **N**, the display is shifted again and you are reprompted.

Setting the Autorepeat Rate and Delay

You can control the rate at which characters are automatically repeated when you hold a key down and set the delay before the autorepeat begins with this form of MODE:

MODE CON RATE=*rate* DELAY=*delay*

Here, *rate* is the number of characters generated per second and *delay* is the number of quarter seconds before the autorepeat begins. The maximum value for *rate* is 32, and the maximum value for *delay* is 4. You must always specify both the rate and the delay value—you cannot leave one off.

The following command sets the autorepeat feature to 25 repetitions per second with a delay of 1/4 second:

```
MODE CON RATE=25 DELAY=1
```

This use of the MODE command will not be applicable to all computers. It will work with the PS/2 line and some compatibles.

Setting the Printer

You can set the maximum number of characters per line and the number of lines per vertical inch that the printer will produce with the following form of MODE:

```
MODE LPT# COLS=length LINES=lines_per_inch
```

The # must be printer number 1, 2, or 3 (there can be up to three printers on the system). The *length* parameter must be either 80 or 132, and *lines_per_inch* must be either 6 or 8. When DOS begins, the line length is 80 with 6 lines per inch.

When you select a value like 132, the printer automatically makes each character smaller so that 132 characters can fit on one line. Selecting 8 lines per vertical inch simply puts the lines closer together. For example, this configures the first printer for 132 columns and 8 lines per inch:

```
MODE LPT1 COLS=132 LINES=8
```

You can also use MODE to change the way DOS handles a printer status check. However, this is generally set by your programs, so you will not usually have to worry about it.

Configuring the Serial Port

To transfer data to external devices, a computer can use two types of ports: *parallel* and *serial*. Parallel ports are usually used for printers, and serial ports are used for modems, plotters, and other special devices, although a printer can be connected to a serial port. The full name for the serial port—and the way it is referred to in IBM user manuals—is the "asynchronous serial communications adapter," but "serial port" is much shorter and is the commonly used term.

The most important difference between the two types of ports is that a parallel port transmits eight bits of data (one byte) at a time, while the serial port transmits data one bit at a time. The rate at which the bits are transmitted is measured in *bits per second,* abbreviated as *baud*. In order for a serial port to communicate with an external device, the bauds of the device and the serial port must match. This is usually taken care of automatically by the application programs you are using, but you may occasionally be told to set the baud manually. You can do so by using this form of MODE:

```
MODE COM# baud
```

where # is the adapter number 1 through 4 and *baud* is the baud setting, which must be one of the following numbers:

110
150
300
600
1200
2400
4800
9600
19200

The larger the baud value, the faster the transfer rate. Although only the first two digits are actually necessary, you can use the whole number if you like. For example, to set COM1 to 9600 baud, enter

```
MODE COM1 9600
```

The default setting for the serial ports is 1200 baud.

Serial ports have several other attributes that may need to be set to something other than their default values. It is beyond the scope of this book to explain the technical details of these attributes, but a brief overview will be helpful.

- A serial port uses *even, odd,* or *no parity.* The parity setting determines if and how error checking will be performed. The parity of the serial port and the external device communicated with must be the same. No parity means that no error checking occurs. The default setting is even.

- The number of *data bits* determines how many bits are used to transfer information. This number can be 7 or 8; the default is 7.

- The number of *stop bits* determines how many nondata bits occur between the data bits. This can be either 1 or 2; the default is 2 for 110 baud and 1 for the other baud rates.

The general form of MODE used to set all the information for the port is

MODE COM# *baud, parity, data_bits, stop_bits*

where *parity* is E for even, O for odd, or N for none. The *data_bits* and *stop_bits* values are numbers. For example, to set the COM1 port to 300 baud, even parity, 8 data bits, and 2 stop bits, you would enter

```
MODE COM1 300, E, 8, 2
```

Finally, if the serial port is to be used with a printer, you should specify the P option. For example, if you have a printer that runs at 9600 baud and uses even parity, 7 data bits, and 1 stop bit, you should enter

```
MODE COM1 9600, E, 7, 1, P
```

Redirecting Printer Output

If you have a serial printer, you can redirect all printer output to it by using this form of MODE:

```
MODE LPT#=COM#
```

where # is a number from 1 to 3 for LPT or 1 to 4 for COM. For example, the following command switches the default printer to COM1:

```
MODE LPT1=COM1
```

Now all printer output, including that produced by the PRINT command, the **Print** option in the Shell, or the PRINT SCREEN command, will be directed to COM1.

CHANGING THE DOS PROMPT

By default, the DOS system prompt is the current drive followed by the greater-than symbol. However, you can change this prompt practically anything you want by using the PROMPT command. Its general form is

```
PROMPT message
```

where *message* is a string that will become the new system prompt. This command has no effect on the Shell; it can only be used from the command-prompt version of DOS.

To see how PROMPT works, enter

PROMPT My Computer:

DOS will now display the prompt as

My Computer:

To return the DOS prompt to its default message, enter **PROMPT** without a message.

Although short prompts are usually best, a prompting message can be up to 128 characters long. For example, you might use a prompt like the following to discourage unauthorized use:

PROMPT Warning: authorized users only!

You can include special characters and other information in the prompt by using one or more of the codes shown in Table 13-2. All PROMPT codes begin with a dollar sign. Because the >, <, |, and = characters have special meanings when they appear on a DOS command line, you must use the proper code if you want one of these characters to appear in the prompt.

One of the most useful of customized prompts is created with the following command:

PROMPT PG

This causes the current directory path name to be displayed in the DOS prompt. For example, if the current path is C:\ACCOUNTS\AP, the DOS prompt will look like this:

C:\ACCOUNTS\AP>

Code	Meaning
$$	Dollar sign
$b	I character
$d	System date
$e	Escape character
$g	> character
$h	Backspace
$l	< character
$n	Current drive letter
$p	Current directory path
$q	= character
$t	Current time
$v	DOS version number
$_	Carriage return/linefeed sequence

TABLE 13-2   The PROMPT Codes

This prompt is popular because it makes it easy to tell what directory you are in. You might want to put this PROMPT command into the AUTO-EXEC.BAT file so that it executes automatically upon startup.

Another popular prompt is formed with the following command:

```
PROMPT $D $T $P$G
```

This causes the current system date and time to be displayed along with the directory path. For example, if the date is 12/2/88, the time is 12:00 noon, and the root directory is current, the prompt will look like this:

```
Fri 12-02-88 12:00:00:00 C:\ >
```

Experiment to see what sort of prompt you like best. Then place the appropriate PROMPT command in the AUTOEXEC.BAT file.

USING THE CONFIG.SYS FILE

DOS has a number of features that can only be set when it begins execution; that is, some aspects of DOS cannot be changed once the DOS prompt or the Shell is first displayed, because they affect the fundamental operation of the system. To alter these types of attributes, you must use a special configuration file, called CONFIG.SYS, and some special DOS configuration commands.

When DOS begins execution, it looks for the CONFIG.SYS file in the root directory of the disk from which it was loaded. If CONFIG.SYS is present, DOS reads the given configuration commands and sets the specified parameters accordingly. If CONFIG.SYS is not present, DOS uses its own default settings. When you create or alter the CONFIG.SYS file, none of the changes will take effect until you restart DOS.

Some configuration commands are intended only for programmers or for people specifically in charge of configuring a system; these will not be examined here. Instead, you will learn about the configuration commands that you may want or need to use.

If DOS was installed on your computer in accordance with IBM's instructions, you will already have a CONFIG.SYS file. In general, you will not want to remove anything from the file; the instructions contained in it are necessary to support the Shell. However, you may want to make a few commands work differently, as you will see in the next few sections.

BREAK

As you know, the CTRL-BREAK key combination is used to cancel a command or application program and return to DOS. However, DOS's default method of operation only checks for CTRL-BREAK when I/O operations involve the standard input or output device, the printer, or a serial port. Some programs may not perform any of these operations for quite some time and therefore may not respond quickly to a CTRL-BREAK command. For example, a database program that is doing a sort operation on a very large file may not perform I/O operations for several minutes.

You can instruct DOS to check for a CTRL-BREAK more frequently by placing the following command in the CONFIG.SYS file:

```
BREAK = ON
```

Keep in mind, however, that this will cause all commands and programs to run more slowly than usual, because DOS spends more time checking to see if you have pressed CTRL-BREAK.

COUNTRY

Different countries and different languages vary in the display and definition of time, date, and currency symbols. In addition, collating sequences and certain capitalization conventions sometimes differ. In Europe, for example, the comma—not the period—is used as a decimal separator. If you live in a country other than the United States, your computer will usually, by default, be configured to that country's standards. However, should you need to change DOS to conform to the conventions of a different country, you can use the COUNTRY command. It takes the general form

```
COUNTRY = code
```

where *code* is one of the codes listed in Table 13-3. For example, the following command configures DOS for Spain:

```
COUNTRY = 034
```

If the country you want is not listed, you must choose the one whose conventions are the closest to what you need.

DOS contains extended support for countries with special character requirements, and you can specify a character-set definition with the COUNTRY command. You will learn more about this at the end of this chapter when you will explore foreign-language versions of DOS.

Country or Language	Code
Arabic	785
Australia	061
Belgium	032
Canada—English	001
Canada—French	002
Denmark	045
Finland	358
France	033
Germany	049
Israel—Hebrew	972
Italy	039
Japan	081
Korea	082
Netherlands	031
Norway	047
Portugal	351
Simplified Chinese	086
South America	003
Spain	034
Sweden	046
Switzerland	041
Traditional Chinese	088
United Kingdom	044
United States	001

TABLE 13-3   The DOS Country Codes

DEVICE

The parts of DOS that control the various devices of the computer are called *device drivers*. All the drivers necessary for the operation of a standard configuration of the computer are included in DOS when it begins execution. However, some special device drivers are optional, and you must tell DOS to load them if you want to use them. DOS 4 supplies these device drivers:

ANSI.SYS
DISPLAY.SYS
DRIVER.SYS
PRINTER.SYS
VDISK.SYS
XMAEM.SYS
XMA2EMS.SYS

You may also have special hardware that requires special device drivers (for example, a mouse requires a special device driver). These are usually supplied with the equipment.

To tell DOS to load a device driver, use the DEVICE command, which takes the general form

DEVICE = *device_driver*

Let's examine the function and use of the DOS device drivers in turn.

ANSI.SYS   Occasionally, an application program will instruct you to load the ANSI.SYS device driver, which allows DOS to understand an additional method of controlling the cursor's position on the screen. It does not give you any more control or command over the screen, but it does make it easier for some types of application programs to use the screen. If you need to load this driver, use the following command in the CONFIG.SYS file:

DEVICE = ANSI.SYS

DRIVER.SYS   DRIVER.SYS is a complicated device driver that alters the way DOS accesses the disk drives of your system. Although most of what the command can do is of interest only to programmers, it can be used to solve a common—and very perplexing—problem.

If you have an AT-type computer, the first floppy-disk drive will probably be a 1.2-megabyte drive. The second floppy, if it exists, can be either a 1.2M or a 360K drive. If your second drive is 360K, how can you copy a 1.2M disk? The answer is to tell DOS to assign drive A a second drive designation, such as D, and then use a command like the following:

COPY A:*.* D:

Each time the name of the drive is changed, DOS prompts you to strike a key. For example, before switching to D, you will see the following:

```
Insert diskette for drive D: and strike
any key when ready
```

This allows you to switch disks and thus to copy a disk using only one drive. If you have only one floppy-disk drive, DOS automatically assigns the drive two names, A and B; however, when the second drive exists, DOS does not do this.

To allow drive A to be called by another name, place the following command in your CONFIG.SYS file:

```
DEVICE = DRIVER.SYS /D:C /F:1
```

Depending on how your system is set up, the second drive name will be the next letter in the alphabet that is not currently assigned. The number after the /F is determined by the following table:

Value	Floppy Drive Type
0	160/180K
0	320/360K
1	1.2M
2	720K
7	1.44M

Select the value that suits your needs.

PRINTER.SYS AND DISPLAY.SYS   The PRINTER.SYS and DIS-PLAY.SYS drivers form part of DOS's increased support of language environments other than English. If you speak English, you will not need to use these drivers. Also, if you live in a non-English-speaking country, your computer is probably already configured for you. Generally, then, you won't have to worry about these device drivers.

VDISK.SYS   The one device driver that you will really want to use is VDISK.SYS, which is used to create a *virtual disk* in RAM (sometimes referred to as a "RAM disk"). A virtual disk holds files by simulating the operation of a disk drive in RAM rather than on the magnetic surface of the disk. As far as your programs are concerned, a virtual disk looks and acts just like a regular disk drive.

There is one difference between virtual disks and real disks that you will appreciate: virtual disks are much faster than standard disk drives. They run at the speed of the computer's memory, which is always faster than the transfer rate of a disk drive. However, this speed has its price. A virtual disk reduces the amount of available system memory. Although this is not often a problem, some application programs may require so much memory that a virtual disk cannot be used. You should also be aware that when the power is turned off, or if the computer is restarted, the contents of what is stored on the virtual disk are lost. Be sure to copy files that you wish to save to a physical disk before concluding a session at the computer.

The basic form of the VDISK.SYS command is

DEVICE = VDISK.SYS *total_size sector_size entries*

where *total-size* is the size of the virtual disk in kilobytes. The default value is 64K, but this is usually too small to be of any value. If you specify a value larger than can be allocated, VDISK adjusts it to the largest amount that will fit in memory. The *sector_size* specifies how large the sector size should be; it must be 128, 256, or 512 bytes. Real disks use large sector sizes to achieve faster performance, but there is little or no advantage to this on a virtual disk. Therefore, it is best to use the default value of 128 because it makes the most efficient use of memory. The *entries* argument specifies the number of directory entries to be allowed by the virtual disk. This value is 64 by default and is usually a good choice, although you can specify any number between 2 and 512.

The following command in CONFIG.SYS creates a virtual disk that is 384K in size, uses 128- byte sectors, and has 64 directory entries:

DEVICE = VDISK.SYS 384 128 64

Many computers have *extended memory,* which is memory that is not directly usable by DOS but may be used by programs running under DOS. If you have extended memory, you can use it for the virtual disk by placing the /E option at the end of the VDISK command. For example, the following command tells VDISK to use the extended memory of the computer:

DEVICE = VDISK.SYS 384 128 64 /E

Also, some computers have what is referred to as *expanded memory,* which is another form of memory that is not usually available to DOS, but which VDISK can use. To specify expanded memory, use the /X option.

When VDISK.SYS is installed during startup, you will see

IBM DOS Version 4.00, VDISK virtual disk *X:*

where *X* will be the letter of the virtual disk.

Using a virtual disk is highly recommended because it increases speed dramatically.

XMAEM.SYS and XMA2EMS.SYS

The XMAEM.SYS and XMA2EMS.SYS device drivers are used to support expanded memory. If you have an application program that requires these drivers, you will be given instructions on their installation and use. They require a computer that has an 80386 CPU.

FILES and FCBs

You can specify the number of files that can be open concurrently and the number of *file control blocks* (FCBs) that can be in use concurrently. (A file control block is a region of memory used by DOS to store information about an open file.) The default values given to these items are acceptable in most cases, but some application programs may require you to change them in order to run correctly.

The number of concurrently open files is eight by default. If you need to change this, use the FILES command, which has the general form

FILES = *number*

where *number* is a number from 8 to 255. For example, the following command sets the number of files to 10:

FILES = 10

To change the number of file control blocks, use the FCBS = command, which has the general form

FCBS *total, permanent*

where *total* is the total number of file control blocks. It must be from 1 to 255; the default is 4. The number of file control blocks that DOS may not automatically close is determined by *permanent*. The default value is 0, but it may be from 0 to 255. For example, the following command tells DOS to allow 12 file control blocks and not to close any of them automatically:

FCBS=12, 12

INSTALL

The INSTALL command is used to install the following DOS commands:

FASTOPEN.EXE
KEYB.COM
NLSFUNC.EXE
SHARE.EXE

SHARE is used in networking, and NLSFUNC provides extended foreign-language support. You will look at KEYB later in this chapter and FAST-OPEN in Chapter 15. The general form of the INSTALL command is

INSTALL *filename*

where *filename* is the name of the file to be installed.

LASTDRIVE

By default, DOS assumes that the last drive in the system will be drive E. However, because it is possible to have more drives— especially with virtual disks—you can use the LASTDRIVE command to increase the number of drives allowed. The general form of LASTDRIVE is

LASTDRIVE = *letter*

where *letter* is the drive letter, which must be between A and Z.

PATH

Until now, whenever you needed to execute a command or program, the file had to be in the current working directory. However, if you are using the command prompt, you can tell DOS to look in other directories for external commands, programs, and batch files by using the PATH command. The general form of PATH is

PATH *path_list*

where *path_list* is a list of paths, separated by a semicolon, that will be searched. You cannot use spaces in the path list. Keep in mind that the PATH command has no effect on the Shell.

To understand how PATH works, assume that a disk has the directory structure shown here:

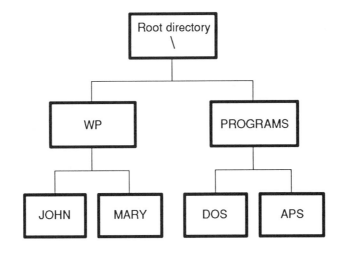

Further assume that all DOS external commands are in the DOS directory and all application programs are in the APS directory. To allow the access of any DOS external command or application program from any directory, enter

PATH \PROGRAMS\DOS;\PROGRAMS\APS

Now, whenever a command is given to DOS that is not internal, DOS will first check the current directory. If it is not found, DOS then will begin checking, in order, the directories specified in the PATH command, beginning with the \PROGRAMS\DOS directory. If the command is not found there, DOS then searches the \PROGRAMS\APS directory.

To see what the current path is, simply enter **PATH** with no arguments. To reset the path to its default, enter

```
PATH ;
```

Remember, setting a search path with PATH causes DOS to search the specified directories only for .EXE, .COM, and .BAT files. You cannot access data files with the PATH command.

APPEND

The APPEND command gives you access to files in other directories and operates much like PATH, except that it can work with any type of file. The general form of APPEND is

APPEND *path_list*

where *path_list* is a list of path names separated by semicolons. APPEND is both an internal and external command. The first time that APPEND is executed, it is loaded from disk. Afterward, however, it becomes part of DOS's internal commands. As with PATH, there can be no spaces in the path list.

Assume the same directory structure that you used with the PATH command. APPEND allows you to access data files in the JOHN and MARY directories in this manner:

```
APPEND \WP\JOHN;\WP\MARY
```

The data files in these directories can now be accessed from any other directory. However, they will not show up in a directory listing of any other directory. In addition, you cannot execute commands or programs in the appended directory.

To see which directories are currently appended to the current one, enter **APPEND** with no arguments. To cancel an APPEND command, enter

```
APPEND ;
```

The APPEND command has several options. APPEND will ignore program files if you specify the /X:OFF option. To allow APPEND to access these files, specify the /X:ON option, which is the default. The /PATH:ON option allows APPEND to search the specified directories even if an application program specifies a directory. This option is on by default. /PATH:OFF suspends search when a full path is specified. Finally, the /E option allows APPEND to access the DOS environmental parameters, which you will learn more about shortly.

At this point you might be tempted to simply append all directories together so that you can reach any file in any directory at any time. This is a bad idea for two reasons. First, it negates the basic philosphy of tree-structured directories and can easily make it impossible for you to correctly manage your files. Second, although you can read a file from any directory, if an application program writes a file, it will be written in the current directory. This means that if you edit a file in the JOHN directory while the current directory is MARY, saving that file writes it to MARY, leaving the original version in JOHN unchanged.

ASSIGN

You can make DOS reroute an I/O request from one drive to another by using the ASSIGN command. This is most useful for allowing applications designed for two-floppy systems to take advantage of a hard disk, which otherwise would be ignored.

The general form of ASSIGN is

ASSIGN *old_drive = new_drive*

ASSIGN is an external command.

If you have two floppy-disk drives, try the following command:

```
ASSIGN A = B
```

Now put your DOS disk in B and enter

```
DIR A:
```

As you can see, drive B is activated.

If you have a fixed disk, put a DOS disk in A and try this sequence of commands:

```
ASSIGN C = A
DIR C:
```

This activates drive A.

You can specify more than one drive reassignment at a time. For example, the following command switches drives A and B:

```
ASSIGN A = B  B = A
```

To reset drive assignments to their original values, enter **ASSIGN** with no arguments.

SUBST

The SUBST commmand lets you use a drive specifier that can refer either to another drive or to a directory. You can think of this drive specifier as a nickname.

SUBST is an external command that has the general form

SUBST *nickname: drive_name:\path*

where *nickname* is the new drive letter that can be used to refer to *drive_name\path*. The drive letter that you select as a nickname can only be selected from the letters A to E unless you have used a LASTDRIVE command to change this requirement in your CONFIG.SYS file.

The following command allows you to refer to drive A as drive E (as well as A):

```
SUBST E: A:\
```

You can also substitute a drive specifier for a subdirectory that is on the same disk. For example, assume that this directory structure is on drive C:

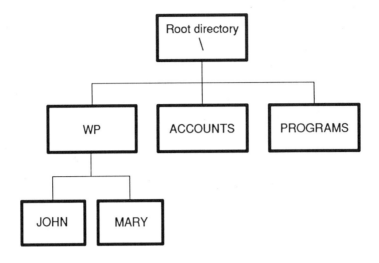

After executing the command

    SUBST E: C:\WP\MARY

you can refer to the \WP\MARY directory as if it were drive E.

You can display the current substitutions by entering **SUBST** with no arguments. If drive E has been substituted for \WP\MARY, for example, SUBST will display the following:

    E: => C:\WP\MARY

To remove a substitution, use the general form

    SUBST *nickname* /D

The SUBST command allows application programs that do not recognize path names to be used. Although most programs available today recognize the full DOS path name, early programs do not. However, they do recognize drive specifiers, so you can use SUBST as a way of making a program work correctly with directories. The likelihood of your coming across a program that does not recognize path names is becoming increasingly low.

JOIN

The JOIN command allows the directory of one disk to be connected to a directory on a different disk, so that the second directory can access the first disk's files. JOIN is an external command with the general form

JOIN *first_drive joined_drive:directory*

where *first_drive* is the drive specifier of the drive that will be joined to *joined_drive* as directory *directory*.

The following command joins drive A to drive B in the B:ADRIVE directory:

JOIN A: B:ADRIVE

If drive B is made current, a directory listing will show the ADRIVE directory. You can switch to this directory in the same way you switch to other directories—by using the CD command. In short, after the preceding JOIN command has executed, all references to files on A will be made as if they are in the ADRIVE directory of B.

You can see what is joined to what by entering **JOIN** with no arguments. To cancel a joining, use the general form

JOIN *first_drive* /D

JOIN has a number of restrictions. The directory you specify for the joined drive, must be empty or nonexistent. Also, you cannot join the currently selected drive, because the drive name for the joining drive becomes invalid immediately following the JOIN command. Furthermore, you cannot use JOIN if SUBST or ASSIGN has been used on either of the drives specified in the command. Finally, do not use the BACKUP, DISKCOPY, FORMAT, RESTORE, and DISKCOMP commands when one drive has been joined to another.

SHELL STARTUP OPTIONS

The Shell is activated by the DOSSHELL.BAT batch file, which is the last entry in the AUTOEXEC.BAT file. If you look at the contents of DOS-SHELL.BAT, you will see one line that begins with

    SHELLC

Following this command is a long list of options, each begining with a slash. These options determine how the Shell is configured and behaves. By editing DOSSHELL.BAT, you can add to or delete from the list of options (remember, you can use EDLIN to edit a file). Let's begin by examining the standard options and end with a look at some of the more exotic ones.

Standard Startup Options

If you install DOS in the standard way, then several options will be included automatically in the DOSSHELL.BAT file. These are called the *standard options*.

/DOS   The inclusion of this option causes the File System to be included in the Shell. Without it, only the Start Programs screen will be present.

/DATE   This option displays the time and date in the Start Programs screen.

/PROMPT   This option causes the Command Prompt entry to appear in the Start Programs screen.

/EXIT   This option activates the Exit Shell option. You might want to leave this option out if the computer is going to be used for only a few specific tasks; you do not want users to activate the command prompt accidentally.

/MAINT   The inclusion of this option allows you to add, change, and delete programs and groups in the Start Programs screen.

/MEU:SHELL.MEU   This option specifies the name of the Main Group's menu file.

/MUL   This option allows multiple directories in the File System.

/MENU   This option activates the Start Programs screen. Without it, only the File System is displayed.

/COLOR   This option puts the Change Colors entry in the Main Group. If you do not want to change colors, you can leave it out.

/TRAN   When this option is present, the Shell can swap part of itself out of memory (and onto disk) when a program has begun to run. This allows an application program to access more memory than it could if all of the Shell were resident. When the program ends, the part of the Shell that was swapped out is brought back in.

/CLR:SHELL.CLR   This option specifies the name of the file that determines the colors used by the Shell.

/SND   This option makes the Shell beep when an error occurs. If you do not like this sort of feedback, remove the /SND option from the DOS-SHELL.BAT file.

/SWAP   This option allows the File System to swap information to and from disk whenever a program is run, which means the File System can respond faster when it is reactivated. However, /SWAP does generate temporary files that are not erased by DOS. These files begin with 0.

/MOS:DRIVER   This option specifies the mouse device driver. If you do not have a mouse, take this option out of the list.

Nonstandard Startup Options

In addition to the standard options normally included in DOSSHELL.BAT, several other startup options can be added to customize the Shell to your needs.

/LF   Use this option if you want to run the mouse with your left hand.

/TEXT   Use this option to force the Shell to run in text mode.

/CO1   This option causes the Shell to use 640x350 16-color graphics mode, if possible.

/CO2   This option causes the Shell to use 640x480 2-color graphics mode, if possible.

/CO3   This option causes the Shell to use 640X480 16-color graphics mode, if possible.

/B:*size* KB   This option specifies the amount of memory (*size*) allocated to the file system. The defaults used by the Shell are usually sufficient. The value of *size* is in kilobytes.

/COM2   This option tells the Shell that a serial mouse is plugged into the second serial port.

INTERNATIONAL CONFIGURATIONS

As you learned earlier in this chapter, several conventions concerning time, date, and currency symbols differ among countries. In addition, some non-English languages require additional characters, accented characters, or both, as well as a different keyboard layout to accommodate these characters. (Your DOS manual illustrates keyboard layouts for other countries and languages.)

DOS allows you to change the configuration of the keyboard and to change which characters are actually displayed through the use of the KEYB command. Keep in mind that configuring DOS for a language other than English does not cause DOS to translate any messages—all DOS prompts and commands remain in English.

The KEYB Command

When DOS receives signals from the keyboard, it translates them into the appropriate letters and symbols. With the KEYB command you can change the translation of these signals, allowing you to use another keyboard layout for a foreign country. If you live in the country in which the computer was purchased, the proper keyboard layout has probably already been configured by the dealer, so you will not need to do it. This section presents a brief overview so that you will know something about the KEYB command even if you do not need to use it.

DOS supplies several files with the extension .CPI. These are *code-page information files,* which hold the codes for the various keyboard and printer character sets. Table 13-4 shows the countries supported by these files, as well as their keyboard and code-page codes.

If you live in a country that uses code page 437, you do not need to worry about code-page switching. If you do not, refer to your DOS manual for explicit instructions on how to switch to the proper code page if your computer is not already configured for you.

The general form of the external KEYB command is

KEYB *keyboard code_page path*

Country	Keyboard Code	Code-Page Code
Australia	US	437
Belgium	BE	437
Canada—English	US	437
Canada—French	CF	863
Denmark	DK	865
Finland	SU	437
France	FR	437
Germany	GR	437
Italy	IT	437
Latin America	LA	437
Netherlands	NL	437
Norway	NO	865
Portugal	PO	860
Spain	SP	437
Sweden	SV	437
Switzerland—French	SF	437
Switzerland—German	SG	437
United Kingdom	UK	437
United States	US	437

TABLE 13-4   Keyboard and Code-Page Codes for DOS-Supported Countries

where *keyboard* is a keyboard code for the country desired, *code_page* is the proper code page, and *path* is the path to the KEYBOARD.SYS file. You do not usually specify the last two arguments, allowing them to default to the current code page and the root directory.

For an example, switch to a French-speaking Swiss keyboard by entering the following command:

    KEYB SF

Notice that the positions of the "Y" and the "Z" are reversed on the French keyboard. You can switch back to the U.S. keyboard at any time by pressing the CTRL-ALT-F1 key combination. To return to the other language, press CTRL-ALT-F2.

You can also specify a *keyboard ID code* with the KEYB command. Some countries use more than one keyboard, so you must use the appropriate code for the one you want. However, these codes (shown in table 13-5) are seldom needed.

To specify a keyboard ID code, use the /ID option, which takes this general form:

    /ID:*nnn*

where *nnn* is the keyboard ID. For example, this specifies the French keyboard, with 120 as the keyboard code:

    KEYB FR /ID:120

Using SELECT to Prepare
Foreign Versions of DOS

When you install DOS, you begin the installation process with the Install disk. It contains a command called SELECT, which performs the installation. It is possible to use SELECT to specify the keyboard layout and other

Country	Keyboard ID
Australia	103
Belgium	120
Canada—English	103
Canada—French	058
Denmark	159
Finland	153
France	120 and 189
Germany	129
Italy	141 and 142
Latin America	171
Netherlands	143
Norway	155
Portugal	163
Spain	172
Sweden	153
Switzerland—French	150
Switzerland—German	000
United Kingdom	168 and 166
United States	103

TABLE 13-5   Keyboard ID Codes

country-related parameters; refer to the DOS installation instructions that accompanied your computer for details.

SUMMARY

In this chapter you learned a number of ways to configure your system, including how to

- Change the DOS prompt
- Use the MODE command
- Create a CONFIG.SYS file
- Set up a virtual disk
- Use PATH and APPEND
- Change the way that DOS accesses the disk drives
- Change the Shell startup options
- Creating international configurations

The next two chapters return to the subject of managing your disks.

14

MANAGING YOUR FLOPPY DISKS

Balancing DOS and Applications on Your Work Disk
Floppy Disks and Subdirectories
Backing Up Floppy Disks
Mailing Floppy Disks
Summary

Except for the invention of the microprocessor, which made personal computers possible, no other invention has contributed as much to the development and success of the microcomputer as the floppy-disk drive. The reasons are threefold. First, floppy-disk drives are inexpensive compared to fixed disks (although fixed disks are cheaper in terms of bytes of storage per dollar). In the early days of microcomputers, a fixed disk could easily cost several thousand dollars, while a floppy drive might cost just a few hundred. Second, compared to the only other cheap method of data storage—cassette tape—floppy disks are fast. Finally, floppy disks give users an easy and inexpensive way to share programs and transfer files, as well as being the perfect medium for software developers to sell their programs on. For these reasons, the floppy disk has earned a lasting place in the computing world.

How a floppy disk is used depends on whether it is the main disk for the system or only a companion to a fixed disk. In a great many fixed-disk systems, the floppy disk is not the main disk drive. In fact, in such a system, the floppy disk is used for only two purposes: to back up information on the fixed disk for off-site storage, and as a transfer medium for data and programs. In systems without fixed disks, however, the floppy disk is used as the main storage device.

This chapter will concentrate primarily on the floppy disk as it is used in systems without fixed disks. Its use as a backup for the fixed disk is explored in Chapter 13. In floppy-only systems one drive is seldom practical; at least two are required. Much of the material in this chapter assumes that at least two floppy drives are present.

BALANCING DOS AND APPLICATIONS ON YOUR WORK DISK

As you probably know, even a 1.44M disk containing DOS and all its external commands can leave very little extra room for your files. If your system has even smaller floppy-disk capacities, this problem is even worse—you have to juggle up to four disks just to have access to all of DOS. In either case, you can free more space for your own files by removing DOS files and commands that you do not need in certain situations.

Removing DOS Files And Commands

You usually do not need most of DOS's external commands and miscellaneous files when you are using your application programs. Therefore, you can free a lot of room on your DOS/application work disk by erasing the commands and files that you do not use frequently. (Remember, you should not delete files on your master DOS disks or backups.) Figure 14-1 shows a list of all of the files supplied with version 4 of DOS. Let's look at which files you can eliminate and the situations in which they can be eliminated.

4201	CPI	GRAPHICS	PRO
4208	CPI	IFSFUNC	EXE
5202	CPI	JOIN	EXE
ANSI	SYS	KEYB	COM
APPEND	EXE	KEYBOARD	SYS
ASSIGN	COM	LABEL	COM
ATTRIB	EXE	LCD	CPI
AUTOEXEC	BAT	MEM	EXE
BACKUP	EXE	MODE	COM
BASICA	COM	MORE	COM
CHKDSK	COM	NLSFUNC	EXE
COMMAND	COM	PCIBMDRV	MOS
COMP	COM	PCMSDRV	MOS
CONFIG	SYS	PCMSPDRV	MOS
COUNTRY	SYS	PRINT	COM
DEBUG	COM	PRINTER	SYS
DISKCOMP	COM	RECOVER	COM
DISKCOPY	COM	REPLACE	EXE
DISPLAY	SYS	SHARE	EXE
DOSSHELL	BAT	SHELL	ASC
DOSUTIL	MEU	SHELL	CLR
DRIVER	SYS	SHELL	HLP
EDLIN	COM	SHELL	MEU
EDTEST	BAK	SHELLB	COM
EDTEST	TXT	SHELLC	EXE
EGA	CPI	SORT	EXE
FASTOPEN	EXE	SUBST	EXE
FDISK	EXE	SYS	COM
FFORMAT	COM	TREE	COM
FILESYS	EXE	VDISK	SYS
FIND	EXE	XCOPY	EXE
GRAFTABL	COM	XMAEM	SYS
GRAPHICS	COM	XMA2EMS	SYS

FIGURE 14-1   Commands and files supplied by DOS 4

FOREIGN LANGUAGE FILES   If you speak English and use your computer in the United States, you can eliminate the following files, which are used to support foreign languages and countries:

    4201.CPI
    4208.CPI
    5201.CPI
    COUNTRY.SYS
    DISPLAY.SYS
    EGA.CPI
    KEYB.SYS
    KEYBOARD.SYS
    LCD.CPI
    NLSFUNC.EXE
    PRINTER.SYS

If you live in a country other than the United States, you can still probably eliminate all but COUNTRY.SYS. See the section in Chapter 13 on multinational versions of DOS.

DEVICE DRIVERS   If you do not need them, you can remove the following device drivers:

    ANSI.SYS
    DRIVER.SYS
    VDISK.SYS

EXPANDED MEMORY DRIVERS   If you have an 80386 but do not use expanded memory, you can remove the following files:

    XMAEM.SYS
    XMA2EMS.SYS

If you do not have an 80386 CPU, these files will not be on your disk to begin with.

THE 012345.678 FILE   You can remove the 012345.678 file. Its only purposes is as a demonstration text file.

FORMATTING AND DOS TRANSFER COMMANDS   On a work disk, you will probably not need any of the commands that are used to create new disks or to install DOS. You will usually perform such tasks with your DOS disk rather than with an application work disk. If this is the case, you can erase the following files:

FDISK.COM
FORMAT.COM
SYS.COM

PROGRAMMER-RELATED COMMANDS   Unless you are a programmer, you can remove the following files:

BASICA.COM
DEBUG.COM

FIXED-DISK COMMANDS   If you do not have a fixed disk, you can erase the following commands:

BACKUP.COM
FASTOPEN.EXE
RESTORE.COM

SELDOM-USED COMMANDS   You will probably never use the following commands:

APPEND.EXE
ASSIGN.COM
ATTRIB.EXE
GRAFTABL.COM
JOIN.EXE
SUBST.EXE

If this is the case, remove them from your application work disk. If you have a text editor other than EDLIN, you can also remove EDLIN.COM. In general, you can remove any command that you do not use.

One way to balance the needs of DOS and those of your application is to let the disk in drive A hold DOS, while you use the one in drive B to hold your application programs and files.

FLOPPY DISKS AND SUBDIRECTORIES

Because of the limited storage capacity of a floppy disk, subdirectories are seldom used with it; it is easier to keep logically separate applications on separate disks. This fact, however, is not meant to discourage you from creating and using subdirectories with your floppies. If you do use subdirectories with them, you should be aware of two ways in which their use affects performance.

First, each additional level of subdirectories increases the access time to the files in those subdirectories. On fixed disks this extra time is not much of an issue because they are so much faster than floppy drives.

However, on floppy disks this additional access time can be annoying. Use heavily nested subirectories only when you can justify them.

Second, each subdirectory uses disk space to hold its directory entries. Because space on a floppy disk is already limited, an unwarranted number of subdirectories could seriously decrease the amount of information that you could store on the disk, so watch the number of subdirectories you use.

BACKING UP FLOPPY DISKS

If you do not have a fixed disk, you must back up the floppy disks that contain your application programs and data on a regular basis. Not making copies of important data is negligence of the highest order.

Sources of Data Loss

Before discussing the backup routine, let's look at the four ways that valuable data can be destroyed.

COMPUTER FAILURE   The least common way that important information can be destroyed on a disk is through computer failure. Few machine errors will destroy a file. However, if software that accesses the information is writing to the disk, a hardware failure can destroy it. The most common causes of hardware failures are static electricity, overheating, fluctuations in line currents, and physical abuse. Age is not as significant a factor in hardware failures as it once was, because the integrated circuits now used to construct the computer have a very long mean time to failure.

It is very difficult to guard against machine errors except by trying to maintain a clean environment and a steady source of power. If fluctuations in the electrical current are a problem in your area, you might want to invest in a surge protector.

MEDIA FAILURES   The next least-frequent source of data loss is the physical destruction of the magnetic media of the floppy disk. This can result from negligence on the part of the user or from a poorly manufactured disk that simply disintegrates. Fortunately, with care, floppy disks will last a long time. However, any disk that has been in heavy daily use for more than a year is a good candidate for replacement.

SOFTWARE ERRORS   Programmers are not perfect. Hence, your application programs could contain one or more errors capable of destroying information. It is sometimes difficult for a user to distinguish between software and hardware errors. However, if data is consistently lost when you perform the same sequence of actions, software is the likely culprit.

You can often work with the developers of your application software to get these errors fixed. If not, you must find more reliable programs to use.

HUMAN ERRORS   A computer is one of the most reliable devices in use; human beings are not. The accidental erasing of important data is epidemic. Frankly, there is no way to guard against this—it is simply too easy to erase a file.

The Backup Routine

Your only protection against having the data on a disk destroyed is to establish a backup routine. As you will come to understand, it is not enough just to make copies of important disks. When to make them, how many to maintain, and how to recover from a loss are also crucial.

Many data-processing managers recommend the *rotating triad* method of backup. With this method, you have three backup disks for every work disk. The first, called the *daily backup,* is used to back up the work disk on a daily basis. You may find that it is better to back up after an even shorter period, such as every two hours, if your data is crucial. A copy of the daily disk substitutes for the work disk should failure occur.

The next disk in the triad is the *weekly backup*. Every Friday at 5:00 P.M., the contents of the daily disk are copied to the weekly disk. Thus, if both the master work disk and the daily disk are destroyed, the weekly disk can be used as a fairly close starting point.

At the end of each month, the weekly backup is retired and put in a safe place. A new copy of the daily disk is made and becomes the next month's weekly backup. The retired monthly backup completes the triad. In this way, if an error is not discovered for some time and has already corrupted the daily and weekly disks, the monthly backup can be used.

Because the nearest backup is potentially one month out of date, some managers employ the *snapshot* method in addition to the rotating triad. With this method, four disks are created for each work disk and are labeled 1 through 4. Every Wednesday, a copy of the daily disk is placed on one of the snapshot disks, beginning with 1 the first week, 2 the second week, and so on. After disk 4 has been used, the process cycles back to 1. In this way an error will not perpetuate itself through all of the disks.

Backing Up a Floppy Disk

The best way to back up a floppy disk is by using DISKCOPY. Using COPY or even XCOPY is not as good, because it permits human error—you could forget to copy a file or two.

Recovering Data

If you have to go to a backup disk, use it only to make a copy; then use the copy. If a hardware or software problem has caused the loss of a file, it could happen again, and you should never risk the destruction of a backup disk. Be sure to write protect the disk before putting it in the computer.

Remember also to restore all files, even if only one is lost, because many application programs use two or more files that work together. If these files are not synchronized, you could be heading for even more trouble.

MAILING FLOPPY DISKS

To close this chapter, a few words about mailing or shipping floppy disks are in order. The best way to mail a floppy disk is in a disk mailer. If none is available, however, place the disk between two strong pieces of cardboard, and put it in a large envelope. Be sure to write on the package, in large letters, that a floppy disk is enclosed and that the package should not be bent or exposed to magnetic fields.

SUMMARY

In this chapter you learned

- How to free space on your DOS work disk
- The effects of subdirectories on floppy disks
- How to maintain a backup routine
- How to mail a disk

The next chapter discusses the management of and backup procedure for fixed disks.

15

MANAGING YOUR FIXED DISK

How Fixed and Floppy Disks Differ
Backing Up Your Fixed Disk
Restoring Files
The Backup Routine for Fixed Disks
Using FASTOPEN
Loading Applications to the Fixed Disk
Preparing the Fixed Disk for Shipment
Summary

With storage capabilities in excess of 120 megabytes, a fixed disk is a system resource that demands attention. Most business users will not buy a computer without a fixed disk, and many home users find that, compared to floppies, the extra storage and speed of a fixed disk are worth the extra expense. In this chapter you will learn some valuable techniques to help you manage this important device.

HOW FIXED AND FLOPPY DISKS DIFFER

The most fundamental difference between fixed and floppy disks is that a fixed disk, unlike a floppy disk, cannot be removed from the drive. It is not removable for two main reasons. First, the read/write head is mounted very close to the surface of the disk and is quite delicate. Second, even if the drive head was not in this close position, the fixed disk could be easily damaged by dust, so just opening its case is a bad idea.

A fixed disk runs about 10 times faster than a floppy disk and stores from 10 to 200 times as much information. The increased storage capacity is the most important factor in how fixed disks tend to be used. Unlike floppy disks, fixed disks tend to have complex directory structures that hold a wide range of information and application programs. In a way, a floppy disk is like a single-family dwelling, while a fixed disk is like a high-rise condominium.

BACKING UP YOUR FIXED DISK

Making and maintaining copies of the information on your fixed disk is seldom as easy as it is on floppy disks because of the amount of information usually found on the fixed disk. Unless you have some sort of tape backup system attached to your computer, you cannot copy an entire fixed disk in the same way you copy an entire floppy disk. Instead, you will need to copy the information on the fixed disk to several floppy disks.

The trouble is that often even one directory on a fixed disk can contain more information than will fit on a single floppy disk. With only the copying commands you have learned so far, there is no easy and trouble-free way to back up a hard disk. Instead, you must use DOS's external BACKUP command, which you can execute from the DOS Utilities group, from the File System, or from the command prompt. BACKUP has the general form

BACKUP *source target options*

where *source* specifies the drive, path, and file names to be copied to *target*.

You can use BACKUP to back up the contents of a floppy disk, although this is rarely done; DISKCOPY is clearly superior. However, you can specify any target and any source drive that you desire (except that they cannot be the same drive) as arguments to BACKUP.

Option	Meaning
/A	Add files instead of overwriting the backup disks
/D:	Copy files with dates on or after the specified date
/L:	Create a log file
/M	Copy only files created or changed since the last backup
/S	Back up all subdirectories starting with the specified path
/T:	Copy files created or modified at or since the time specified on the given date

TABLE 15-1   The BACKUP Options

The BACKUP command has several forms and numerous options; this book examines the most common of them. The BACKUP options are summarized in Table 15-1. The examples presented in this chapter use drive A as the floppy-disk drive receiving the information, although you can substitute drive B if you wish. Drive C is assumed to be the fixed disk. You should substitute the correct drive letter if necessary.

The number of floppy disks you will need in order to back up the entire contents of your fixed disk is directly related to the amount of information on that disk. Sometimes this number can be quite large. For example, a full 10-megabyte fixed disk in an IBM XT will require 28 floppy disks. However, a full 20-megabyte disk in an AT will require only about 20 disks if you are using 1.2-megabyte floppies.

To compute the number of disks that you will need, run CHKDSK to find the total storage size of the fixed disk and the amount of free storage. Subtract the amount of free storage from the total storage, and then divide this number by the storage size of the floppy-disk drive that you will be using for backups. Rounding this number upward gives you the number of disks required. This formula in mathematical notation is

Number of disks = (total-free)/size of floppy

If you are going to back up only part of the disk, you can roughly compute the number of disks by adding the amount of space taken up by the files you are going to copy and then dividing this number by the storage capacity of your floppy-disk drive.

You must number your backup disks because you will have to insert them in order. The exact order in which the disks are written to is very important because a large file may be spread across two or more disks.

Backing Up the Entire Fixed Disk

The most important backup scenario (and by far the most common) is backing up the entire contents of the fixed disk. This is the safest way to ensure that all of the data on the disk is copied. To back up all of the contents of the fixed disk, use the following form of BACKUP:

```
BACKUP  C:\*.*  A:  /S
```

BACKUP will automatically format the floppy disks for you, but you will save time if you use preformatted ones. (BACKUP uses FORMAT to format the disks, so this command must be available for BACKUP's use.)

The \ path ensures that the backup will begin with the root directory, and the /S option specifies that all subdirectories will be copied. As the backup procedure begins, you will see this message:

```
Insert backup diskette 01 in drive A:

Warning! Files in the target drive
A:\ root directory will be erased
Press any key to continue . . .
```

As BACKUP continues, you will be prompted to insert additional disks until all of the information on C has been backed up.

If your fixed disk is very full, the backup procedure will take a fairly long time—up to an hour or more. Be prepared for this.

Backing Up Portions Of the Fixed Disk

When several people use the same computer, it may make more sense for each user to back up his or her own directories instead of the entire disk. For example, assume that this is the directory structure for a fixed disk:

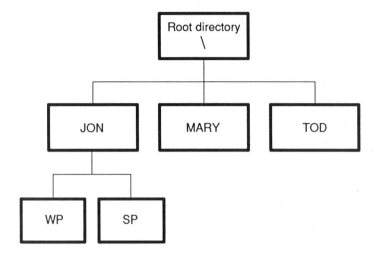

The command that Jon will use to back up his workspace, including the JON directory and its two subdirectories, is

BACKUP C:\JON*.* A: /S

In general, you specify a path to the directory at which you wish to start the backup.

If you leave off the /S option, then only the contents of the directory explicitly specified are copied. For example, the command

BACKUP C:\JON*.* A:

copies only the contents of the JON directory and not its subdirectories (WP and SP).

Adding Files to Backup Disks

The forms of the BACKUP command shown so far erase the previous contents of the floppy disks. However, suppose that you perform a complete fixed-disk backup only once a week, and you have simply added three files and left the others unchanged. How can you add these files to the backup floppy disks without having to recopy the entire fixed disk?

The answer is to use BACKUP's /A (Add) option. When you specify this option, the target disks are not overwritten—instead, the specified files are added to them. For example, to add the FORMLET.WP file to Jon's backup disks, you would enter

BACKUP C:\JON\WP\FORMLET.WP A: /A

When this command began execution, you would see the following:

Insert last backup diskette in drive A:
Press any key to continue . . .

As this message indicates, new files are added to the floppy disk used for the previous backup.

Backing Up Files Modified On
Or After a Specified Date

You can back up only those files that have been changed on or after a specified date by using the /D: option. For example, the following command copies files that have been changed on or after 5-9-88:

BACKUP C:*.* A: /D:5-9-88

The format of the date is determined by the country specified with the COUNTRY command in the CONFIG.SYS file, or as *mm-dd-yy* (standard U.S. format) if no other country is specified.

   Keep in mind that the /D: option does not prevent the target disk(s) from being overwritten. To add new files with dates after a certain date, also add the /A option to the command line. For example, the following command will add to the target disk(s) any new files modified after 5-9-88:

BACKUP C:*.* A: /D:5-9-88 /A

Backing Up Files Modified At
Or Since a Specified Time

You can tell BACKUP to copy only those files modified at a specified time or since that time on a certain date by using the /T: option along with the /D:

option. For example, the following command backs up only those files created at and after 12:00 noon on 5-9- 88:

    BACKUP C:*.* A: /D:5-9-88 /T:12:00

Again, the format for the date and time will vary in countries other than the United States. Remember, the existing set of backup disks is overwritten.

Backing Up Only Files That Have Changed

By using the /M option, you can tell BACKUP to copy only files that have changed since the last backup. As you will recall from earlier in this book, all files have an archive attribute that is either on or off. If the archive attribute is on, it indicates that the file has been modified.

The BACKUP command automatically turns off the archive attribute; therefore, only files that have been changed will actually be copied. For example, the following command backs up only the modified files on the fixed disk:

    BACKUP C:*.* A: /M /S

Adding a Log File

With the /L: option, you can create a file that lists the time and date of the backup, the path and file name of each file backed up, and the number of the floppy disk that each file is on. You can specify your own file name for the log file. If none is specified, BACKUP.LOG is used as the name, and it is placed in the root directory of both the source and target. If the specified file exists, information is appended to the end. If it does not exist, then the file is created. For example, the following command writes to the file called MYLOG:

    BACKUP C:*.* A: /S /L:MYLOG

This command uses the default BACKUP.LOG file:

    BACKUP C:*.* A: /S /L

The first line of the log file will contain the date and time of the backup. Each subsequent line lists the disk number and file name. The first few lines will look something like this:

```
9-05-88  10:30:37

001 \AUTOEXEC.BAT
001 \ANSI.SYS
001 \ASSIGN.COM
```

A log file provides a record of which backup disk any specific file is on. This can speed up the process of restoring a file, as you will shortly see.

RESTORING FILES

If a file is lost on your fixed disk, you will need to restore it from the backups that you made with BACKUP. To do so, use the RESTORE command. Assuming that you are restoring to a fixed disk, the general form of the RESTORE command is

RESTORE *backup fixed options*

where *backup* is the drive that contains the backup disk, and *fixed* is the drive, path, and file-name specifiers that tell where information will be written on the fixed disk. The RESTORE options are summarized in Table 15-2. You can execute RESTORE from the DOS Utilities group, from the File System, or from the command prompt.

During the restoration process, you will be prompted to insert one or more of the backup disks, beginning with disk number 1. When you restore the entire fixed disk, all backup disks will be read in order. If only certain files are being restored, RESTORE will search through the backup disks until it finds those files.

The RESTORE prompt tells you which disk to insert next and waits until you press a key. The first prompt will look like this:

```
Insert backup diskette 01 in drive A:
Press any key to continue . . .
```

Option	Meaning
/A:	Restore all files modified on or after the specified date
/B:	Restore all files modified on or before the specified date
/E:	Restore all files modified at or earlier than the specified time on a given date
/L:	Restore all files modified at or later than the specified time on a given date
/M	Restore all files that have been modified or deleted since the last backup
/N	Restore only those files that do not exist on the fixed disk
/P	Prompt before restoring a file
/S	Restore all subdirectories

TABLE 15-2   The RESTORE Options

Keep in mind that restoring a file means overwriting any existing file with the same name, so use the RESTORE command carefully.

Restoring the Entire Fixed Disk

To restore all of the files on the fixed disk, you must have backup disks that contain all of the files. You must have recently used a BACKUP command similar to the following:

```
BACKUP C:\*.* A: /S
```

With the disks that hold the backed up information, you should use the following form of the RESTORE command to restore all of the files:

```
RESTORE A: C:\*.* /S
```

The /S option tells RESTORE to restore all files and subdirectories. Notice that the path name you specify indicates where the files will be placed on the fixed disk, not where they come from on the backup disks.

There are only two occasions that require the restoration of a complete disk. The first—and most unfortunate—is when a hardware error destroys your fixed disk and a new one is put in the system. In this case you must reload all of your files. If you have been following a proper backup procedure (such as the one described later in this chapter), then the disruption should be minimal. However, if the fixed disk crashes and your backups are either out of date or nonexistent, you are probably in for a very painful experience.

The other time that you will want to fully recover a fixed disk is when you are bringing up another system that is intended to have the same function as the first.

Restoring Individual Files

To restore individual files, you must specify the complete path and file names. RESTORE accepts wild cards, so it is possible to restore groups of files. For example, to restore the files LETTER.ONE, LETTER.TWO, and FORMLET.ONE found in the JON\WP directory, you would use the following commands:

```
RESTORE A: C:\JON\WP\LETTER.*
RESTORE A: C:\JON\WP\FORMLET.ONE
```

Restoring Files
By Date and Time

RESTORE can restore files modified on or *before* a certain date when you add the /B: option. The /A: option allows you to do the opposite—to restore files that have been modified on or *after* the specified date. For example, the following commands restore all files changed before or on 3-3-89, and after 3-3-88—a period of one year:

```
BACKUP A: C:\*.* /S /B:3-3-89 /A:3-3-88
```

In a similar fashion, you can use /L: to restore files modified at or *later* than a certain time on a given date, and /E: to restore all files modified at or *prior* to the specified time on a given date. For example, the following command restores all files modified on 2-28-88 after 12:00 noon but earlier than 5:01 that afternoon:

```
RESTORE  A:  C:\*.*  /S  /D:2-28-88  /L:12:00  /E:17:00
```

Restoring Modified Files

The /M option lets you restore only files that have been modified or deleted from the fixed disk since the last backup was made. For example, the following command restores all files in the WP directory that have been changed:

```
RESTORE  A:  C:\JON\WP\*.*  /M
```

This RESTORE command simply checks the archive attribute of each file and restores those that have it turned on.

Similarly, you can use the /N option to restore only the files that have been deleted from the fixed disk.

Prompted Restoration

If you specify the /P option, RESTORE will prompt you when a file on the fixed disk has been changed since it was last backed up.

Special Considerations
For Using RESTORE

When you use RESTORE, you must keep in mind the following:

- RESTORE does not restore the BIMBIO.COM, IBMDOS.COM, and COMMAND.COM files. You should use the SYS command for the first two of these files and use COPY for COMMAND.COM.

- You must always start with disk number 1 to recover a file unless you have created a log file during backup that will tell you the number of the disk containing the file.

- Files stored on backup disks are not the same as standard DOS files. Do not try to use the COPY command to restore files.

- You must always restore files into the directory they came from.

THE BACKUP ROUTINE
FOR FIXED DISKS

The basic philosophy for backing up the fixed disk is the same as for floppy disks. You should still use the rotating triad method of backup (discussed in Chapter 14), maintaining daily, weekly, and monthly backup disks. The only difference is that you will use many more backup disks for each phase.

Because backing up a fixed disk that contains a lot of information is a lengthy process, after an intial backup, you should use the /M option to copy to the daily backup disks only the files that have changed, and then perform a full backup procedure at the end of the week. This will save you time and still ensure the protection of the files.

Because the nearest backup is potentially one month out of date, you should use the snapshot method of backup (described in Chapter 14) in addition to the rotating triad. In this way an error will not perpetuate itself through all of the backup disks.

Who Is Responsible?

Someone must be in charge of backing up a fixed disk if the system is used by many people. This may sound obvious, but the failure to put someone in charge of this task is the major cause of out-of-date backup disks. When no single person is responsible, everyone assumes that someone else is doing the backups. If you are a manager, make sure that someone's job description includes backing up the fixed disk.

USING FASTOPEN

The external FASTOPEN command allows DOS to quickly access files that are several levels of subdirectories deep. It is therefore particularly useful for reading the "deeper" files on your hard disk. DOS usually takes a lot longer to reach a file with a long path name than to reach one in the root. However, FASTOPEN allows DOS to remember the location of a file and therefore makes accessing that file much faster.

The general form of FASTOPEN is

FASTOPEN *drive_specifier=num*

where *drive_specifier* is the name of the drive to which the FASTOPEN command applies. (You can use FASTOPEN to provide fast access to the files on only one drive in the system.) The optional *num* argument specifies the number of files and directories that FASTOPEN can remember; it must be between 10 and 999. If *num* is not present, the default is 34.

The following command allows 34 files and/or directories on drive C to be accessed quickly:

FASTOPEN C:

FASTOPEN will display this message:

FASTOPEN installed

The following command allows the last 50 files and/or directories to be remembered:

FASTOPEN C:=50

You will usually want to use the default setting for the number of files or directories. Making this number too large can actually increase rather than decrease access time, and if you make it too small, you will not receive any benefit from it.

FASTOPEN installs itself the first time it is invoked, which means that you can execute it only once. For this reason, you should put it in an AUTOEXEC.BAT file.

LOADING APPLICATIONS TO THE FIXED DISK

No hard-and-fast rules apply to every situation you will encounter when you load applications to the fixed disk. However, some general guidelines will help you make the right decisions.

Application Subdirectories

The first and most important rule for loading applications is that each application should be loaded into its own directory. Do not put all applications into the root directory—not only will the root directory become unmanageable, but you will eventually run out of directory entries. (The root directory of a fixed disk can hold 512 entries.) It is also not wise to place all applications into one general-purpose applications directory because, again, that directory will become unmanageable.

For example, imagine that you have three applications: a spreadsheet, a word processor, and an inventory package. You should create three subdirectories, with descriptive names such as SPSHT, WP, and INVENT, and place the files associated with each application area into their respective directories.

Sometimes you will add an application that is really a subsystem of an application that already exists. For example, if you add a spelling checker to the word processor, it does not make sense to create a new subdirectory off of the root for it. Instead, you should simply add it to the WP directory because it is dependent upon the word processor. In certain situations it might even be a good idea to place it in a subdirectory of WP. In general, when one application depends on another, put the dependent one in the directory of the application on which it depends, or in a subdirectory of that application.

User Subdirectories

If several people will be using an application once it is loaded, it is best to create a subdirectory for each user, branching from the application's directory so that each user's files will be separate. Furthermore, because one user may use two or more applications, it is doubly important that individual subdirectories be created off the application directory and not the root. In this way each user can have a directory bearing his or her name in each application area.

For example, if Jon does both word processing and spreadsheet analysis, the proper directory structure will look like the one shown here:

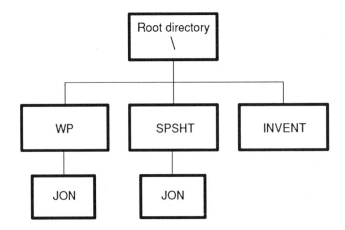

PREPARING THE FIXED DISK FOR SHIPMENT

A fixed disk must be properly prepared for travel before it is moved. The read/write head must be retracted to a position that is not over the magnetic media of the disk. Failure to do this can result in the read/write head contacting the disk, which will cause damage and loss of data. This is called a *head crash.*

The exact method of retracting (sometimes called "parking") the read/write head is determined by the type of computer that you have. However, for IBM PCs, you will find a command called SHIPDISK.COM on the Guide to Operations disk that came with your computer. To prepare your disk for shipment, simply execute that command. For IBM models 30, 50, 60, and 80, you will use the Reference Disk and select the Move the Computer option. For other types of computers, refer to your owner's manual.

SUMMARY

In this chapter you learned how to manage the fixed disk, including how to

- Back up the fixed disk
- Restore data
- Use the fixed-disk backup routine
- Use FASTOPEN
- Load applications onto a fixed disk
- Prepare your fixed disk for shipment

In the final chapter of this book, you will learn about managing the entire computer system.

16

ADVANCED COMMANDS AND SYSTEM MAINTENANCE

FDISK
SET
Recovering Files from a Damaged Disk
Advanced Program Startup Commands
Maintaining Your System
Final Thoughts

Congratulations! You have come a long way since Chapter 1. If you have read and worked through the examples in the preceding chapters, you will have no trouble using DOS.

In this final chapter, you will look at topics and commands that you will not need on a daily basis. However, you may find some of them useful in special situations. They are discussed briefly just so you know they exist. The chapter also presents is a short guide to system maintenance.

FDISK

Before a fixed disk can be formatted, it must be partitioned. A *partition* is a portion of the fixed disk that can be either part or all of the disk. A fixed disk can be partitioned for two or more different operating systems, but you will learn here to prepare the fixed disk for use only with DOS because this is the most likely situation. If your system needs to support another operating system, such as XENIX, you should refer to the specific instructions in your DOS manual.

To partition the fixed disk, use the external FDISK command. The FDISK command lets you do these four things:

- Create a partition
- Set an active partition (from which DOS loads)
- Delete a partition
- Display disk information

In general, your fixed disk is partitioned and formatted by the the supplier of your computer. If you need to use this command, refer to the documentation that came with your computer.

Warning: The FDISK command is used when a fixed disk is first brought into service or when you want to change the size of a disk's partitions. Either way, whatever is on the disk is lost.

SET

The SET command is used to create and give a value to a name that becomes part of DOS's environment. Although this name may not be of any direct value to you, it can be used by application programs. The general form of SET is

SET *name=value*

where *name* is the string that is placed into DOS's environment with the value of *value*.

The following command sets the name APPSDAT for the path \PROGRAM\APPS:

```
SET APPSDAT=\PROGRAM\APPS\
```

Once this is done, an application program that wants to know where application program data files are can check the value of APPSDAT in the DOS environment.

To remove a name from the environment, use the general form

SET *name*=

For example, the following command removes APPSDAT:

```
SET APPSDAT=
```

You can use the value of a name stored in the environment in a batch file by placing the name between percent signs. For example, the following batch file uses the value of APPSDAT to copy data files from the path specified by the value of APPSDAT into the current working directory:

```
REM copy the data files into the working directory
COPY %APPSDAT%*.*
```

When the batch command runs, it will look like this:

```
COPY \PROGRAM\APPS\*.*
```

RECOVERING FILES
FROM A DAMAGED DISK

In rare cases a disk will become damaged in such a way that part of a file will still be readable. In such cases you can partially recover the file by using the RECOVER command. This sort of recovery, however, is useful only on text files where only a small amount of text will have to be reentered. If part of a program file is lost, the program will simply not run.

The general form of RECOVER is

RECOVER *file_name*

where *file_name* is the name of the file to recover, which may include a drive specifier and a path. To recover a file named FORMLET.WP on drive C, for example, you would use the following command:

RECOVER FORMLET.WP

You can use RECOVER to recover an entire disk when the disk's directory has become damaged. When the directory is damaged, it is unreadable, so DOS cannot know which files are on the disk. In this type of operation, the program files can be recovered in a usable form, but it is best not to rely on this.

To recover an entire disk, use this form of RECOVER:

RECOVER *drive_specifier*

As RECOVER recovers the files, it cannot decipher their names because the directory is unreadable, so it puts them in files named FILE*num*.REC, where *num* is a number between 0001 and 9999.

Never assume that you can successfully recover a lost file; often, there is no way to do so. It is usually better to simply go to a backup copy. But if an accident does occur, you can try RECOVER.

ADVANCED PROGRAM
STARTUP COMMANDS

As you learned several chapters ago, when you add a program to a group in the Start Programs screen you can specify various program startup commands (PSCs). You have already learned the most important and common of these commands. This section presents more PSC commands that you might find useful.

Using a Default

The /D option lets you specify a default value that will be shown in the Parameters section of the program startup window. The general form of this command is

/D default_string

This command must go inside the brackets displayed in the window. It can be up to 40 characters long.

This command causes EDLIN to edit MYFILE.DAT by default:

    EDLIN [/D "MYFILE.DAT"]

Clearing the Entry Field

If you specify a default value for the Parameters line of the program startup window, you might also want to include the /R command. If this command is present, then striking any key other than ENTER will cause the default string to be removed. You will not need to manually erase it one character at a time. The /R command must go inside the brackets.

This command line uses the /R command:

    EDLIN [/D "MYFILE.DAT" /R]

Limiting the Length of an Entry

By default, an entry at the Parameters line can be up to 127 characters long. You can reduce this to fewer characters by using the /L command, which has this general form:

    /L "length"

This command must go inside the brackets.

The following command limits the length of an entry to 25 characters:

    [/L "25"]

Requiring Existing Files

There are two PSCs you can use to ensure that one or more files are present on a disk. The first is the /M "e" command. If this command is present in the PSC, the program will only be executed if the file name you enter at the

Parameters line exists on disk. The /M "e" command must go inside of the brackets.

You can require that a file name not entered by the user be present on disk by using the /F command, which takes the general form

/F *"filename"*

This command must go inside the brackets. The program will not execute unless the specified file name exists.

The following PSC requires that EDLIN be present and edits only existing files:

EDLIN [/M "e" /F "EDLIN.COM"]

Using Replaceable Parameters

Inside a PSC you can use any batch file command except GOTO. This means that you can use the parameters %0 through %9; the parameters that take values based on what you enter at the Parameters prompt. A parameter can go either inside or outside the brackets. For example, this PSC causes the file you edit to be printed after you are done editing it. Remember, the vertical bars are generated by pressing F4.

EDLIN [%1] || PRINT %1

You can use the value given to a parameter from the program preceding it by using the /C command, which has this general form:

/C *"parameter"*

where *parameter* is the parameter you want.

MAINTAINING YOUR SYSTEM

A computer is much like an automobile. With proper care and attention, it will run for several trouble-free years, but if you neglect the maintenance, it will be plagued with troubles. A computer system requires two types of care: physical maintenance of the computer and maintenance of the software.

Maintaining the Hardware

The golden rule of maintaining the computer's hardware is to *keep it clean*. Dust is the computer's worst enemy. It can build up on the circuits inside the computer, causing them to overheat by reducing their normal heat-dissipation capabilities. Furthermore, dust and dirt on disks reduce the life of both the disks and the read/write heads on the drives.

Although it may be hard to believe, static electricity is a major cause of computer failure. Walking across a carpet on a dry winter day can cause your body to develop a charge of several thousand volts. If you touch the wrong part of the computer, this voltage could flow into the circuits and literally blow them apart! If static electricity is a problem in your environment, you can either use antistatic sprays on the carpet or invest in a grounded metal strip that you always touch first before touching the computer.

Lightning, another form of electricity, can also damage your machine. If lightning strikes very near the computer, enough of the charge can be picked up by the circuits to destroy them. You cannot prevent a lightning storm, but you can minimize the risk by unplugging the computer. The wires that carry power act like a large antenna, which can pick up the lightning charge. If your computer is unplugged, there is much less chance of damage.

Finally, do not put liquids on top of the computer. Although this seems like a simple statement, people who are unfamiliar with computers will often set coffee cups or soft-drink cans on top of the system. Obviously, a spill can cause significant damage.

Maintaining the Software

The most important thing you can do to protect the software in the system is to maintain a rigid backup schedule. The average system usually has several years' worth of information stored in it, and the dollar value of this information is often far greater than the cost of the computer. It is a resource to be protected.

In large (or even small) offices, it is wise to restrict access to any computer that contains important information. Though deliberate destruction of information is rare, it can happen. Most of the time, however, the damage is done by someone not knowing what they are doing—the "bull in a china shop syndrome." Every employee must have a clear understanding that the information in the computer is a valued asset. Its being invisible does not reduce its importance.

Application programs are often improved by their developers, and you will want to take advantage of these new versions. To avoid trouble, you must switch to the new version correctly. First, never destroy the old version of the program. Sometimes, the new version will have an unknown problem that prevents it from being used (although this is rare). If you have destroyed the old version, you will have no way to run the application. Second, always follow the installation instructions that come with the new version. Unless you are specifically told otherwise, if you run the application from a fixed disk, make sure that all of the old programs are replaced by the new ones. Mixing different versions of the programs that make up an application can cause serious trouble.

FINAL THOUGHTS

DOS continues to evolve and change as the ways in which it is used evolve. The knowledge and understanding that you have gained about DOS will benefit you both now and in the future, because the same basic concepts can be applied to other environments. In fact, you will probably be using DOS on one computer and a different operating system on another in the not-too-distant future. You can easily generalize your understanding of DOS, and you will have no trouble using virtually any type of computer or operating system.

QUICK COMMAND REFERENCE

This appendix contains a short summary of the DOS and batch commands in alphabetical order. Its purpose is to help you quickly learn what a command does or to help you find which command you should use for a certain operation. For a full discussion of each command, refer to the preceding chapters (also see the main body of the book for information about CONFIG.SYS and device drivers).

The following notational conventions are used in this appendix. Items enclosed between square brackets ([ ]) are optional. Except where explicitly noted otherwise, the term *path* refers to the full path name, including an optional drive specifier. The term *filename* may include a drive specifier and/or a path name. Finally, three periods (...) indicate a variable-length list, and two periods (..) indicate a range (as in 1..10).

For most commands, the complete general form of the command is shown. However, commands that have very rarely used options are shown in their most common form.

APPEND

The external APPEND command is used to join one directory to another. If directory B is joined to A, it will appear to the user that directory A contains all of the A and B files.

APPEND is executed the first time in one of the following two forms:

APPEND *path1* [*;path2;..pathN*]
APPEND [/X] [/E]

The first form uses APPEND's default method of operation, in which files with extensions of .EXE, .COM, or .BAT are not appended. The second form only applies when APPEND is first installed. (APPEND is an installed command.) The /X option causes all files to be processed. With the /E option, appended paths are held in the DOS environment area. APPEND is used to allow access to data files much as PATH is used to allow access to program files.

You can see currently appended directories by entering **APPEND** with no arguments.

The following form disassociates any appended directories:

APPEND ;

The following command appends the \WP directory:

APPEND \WP

ASSIGN

The external ASSIGN command is used to redirect input/output (I/O) operations from one disk drive to another. It takes the general form

ASSIGN *drive1=drive2* [*drive3=drive4* ...]

To reverse the assignments of drives A and B, for example, you could use the following command:

ASSIGN A=B B=A

Now all I/O operations for A will go to B, and all I/O operations for B will be redirected to A.

You reset the drives to their original assignments by entering **ASSIGN** with no arguments. Remember, do not use ASSIGN with the BACKUP or PRINT command.

ATTRIB

The external ATTRIB command is used to set or examine the archive and read-only file attributes. It takes the general form

ATTRIB [+R] [-R] [+A] [-A] [*filename*] [/S]

where *filename* is the name of the file(s) that will have its attributes set or examined. Wild-card characters are allowed. +R turns on the read-only attribute, and -R turns it off. +A turns on the archive attribute, and -A turns it off. If one of these is not present, the current state of the file attributes is displayed. The /S option tells ATTRIB to process files in the current directory and any subdirectories.

The following command turns on the read-only attribute for all .EXE files in the current directory:

ATTRIB +R *.EXE

BACKUP

The external BACKUP command is used primarily to back up the contents of a fixed disk by copying it to several floppy disks. Used in this way, it takes the general form

BACKUP *source_drive[filename]* *target_drive* [/A] [/D:*date*] [/F] [/L] [/M] [/S] [/T:*time*]

The *filename* parameter may include wild-card characters.

The meaning of each BACKUP option is shown here:

Option	Meaning
/A	Add files to existing target disks
/D:*date*	Backup only files with dates the same as or later than *date*
/L	Create and maintain a log file
/M	Backup only files that have been modified since the last backup
/S	Process all subdirectories
/T:*time*	Backup only files with times equal to or later than *time* on the specified date

If executed from the root directory of drive C, the following command backs up the entire fixed disk:

    BACKUP C: A: /S

BREAK

The internal BREAK command tells DOS to check more frequently for the CTRL-BREAK key combination, which is used to cancel commands. It takes the general form

    BREAK [ON] [OFF]

where you specify either ON or OFF. Although setting BREAK to ON may seem tempting, it is usually not a good idea—it slows down the execution of all commands and programs.

The following command tells DOS to check more frequently for the CTRL-BREAK key combination:

    BREAK ON

CALL

The CALL batch command is used to execute another batch-file command from within a batch file. The general form of CALL is

CALL *batch_file*

where *batch_file* is the name of the batch- file command that you wish to execute.

The following command calls the batch file named COPYALL.BAT:

CALL COPYALL

CHCP

The internal CHCP command is used with code-page switching for extended foreign-language and country support. This command is seldom required. Refer to your DOS manual for further details should you need them.

CHDIR

The internal CHDIR (or CD) command is used to change the current directory. The general form of the command is

CHDIR *path*

where *path* is the path name of the directory you are changing to. The following command makes the \WP directory current:

CHDIR \WP

CHKDSK

The external CHKDSK command reports the status of a drive and repairs certain types of disk errors. It takes the general form

CHKDSK[*drive_specifier*][*filename*][/F][/V]

If *drive_specifier* is absent, the current disk is checked. The /F option instructs CHKDSK to fix any errors that it can. The /V option displays all files and their paths. Specifying a file name, which may include wild-card characters, causes CHKDSK to report the number of noncontiguous (nonadjacent) sectors used by the file(s).

The following command reports the status of drive A and attempts to fix any errors:

    CHKDSK A: /F

CLS

The internal CLS command clears the screen of the computer's display monitor. To use this command, simply enter **CLS** at the prompt.

COMP

The external COMP command is used to compare two files. It has the general form

    COMP *first_file second_file*

where *first_file* and *second_file* are file names that may contain wild-card characters.

The following command compares the contents of the ACCOUNTS.DAT file on drive A to the file by the same name on drive B:

    COMP A:ACCOUNTS.DAT B:ACCOUNTS.DAT

COPY

The internal COPY command copies the contents of one file into another. It takes the general form

    COPY *source destination* [/V]

where *source* is the name of the file to be copied into *destination*. Both file names can contain wild-card characters. The /V option causes COPY automatically to verify that the information was copied correctly into the destination file. This option is not available in the Shell version of COPY.

The following command copies all files that have the extension .EXE to drive C:

```
COPY *.EXE C:
```

CTTY

The internal CTTY command is used to switch console control to a different device, such as a remote terminal. It takes the general form

```
CTTY device_name
```

where *device_name* must be one of DOS's standard device names. Do not try this command unless there is another device attached to your computer that can control it.

DATE

The internal DATE command is used to set the date of the system. It takes the general form

```
DATE [date]
```

where *date* is the current date. You must use the proper date convention for the country you live in; for the United States, it is *mm-dd-yy*. If you do not specify the date on the command line, DATE reports what it thinks is the current date and waits for you to either enter the correct date or press ENTER, indicating that you accept the date reported.

The following command sets the date to June 26, 1989:

```
DATE 6-26-89
```

DEBUG

The external DEBUG command is used by programmers to help find problems in programs. For more details, refer to your DOS manual.

DEL

The internal DEL command erases files from a disk. (ERASE is another name for DEL.) DEL takes the general form

DEL *filename* [/P]

where *filename* is the name of the file to be erased. You can use wild-card characters in the file name to erase groups of files. If you specify the /P option, DEL will ask you to verify your decision before it erases the file.

The following command erases all files that begin with the letters INV from the disk in drive B:

DEL B:INV*.*

DIR

The internal DIR command is used to list a disk's directory. It has the general form

DIR [*filename*] [/P] [/W]

If a file name is present, only the files that match the file name will be displayed. Otherwise, the entire directory will be listed. Wild-card characters are allowed in the file name. The /P option pauses the display every 23 lines, and the /W option causes the directory to be displayed in four columns across the screen.

The following command lists only those files with the extension .BAT:

DIR *.BAT

DISKCOMP

The external DISKCOMP command is used to compare two floppy disks. Its most common form is

DISKCOMP *first_drive second_drive*

where *first_drive* and *second_drive* are drive specifiers. The following command compares the disk in drive A with the one in drive B:

DISKCOMP A: B:

DISKCOPY

The external DISKCOPY command is used to make a copy of a floppy disk. Its most common form is

DISKCOPY *source destination*

where *source* and *destination* are drive specifiers. DISKCOPY cannot be used to copy a fixed disk.

The following command copies the disk in drive A to the one in drive B:

DISKCOPY A: B:

DOSSHELL

The external DOSSHELL command restarts the Shell.

ECHO

The ECHO batch command is used to write messages to the screen and to turn on or off the echoing of other batch commands. It takes the general form

ECHO [ON] [OFF] [*message*]

The following command prints the message "Backing up all files" on the screen:

ECHO Backing up all files

EDLIN

The external EDLIN command is used to activate the DOS text editor, which you can use to create and maintain text files. It has the general form

EDLIN *filename*

where *filename* is the file to be edited. EDLIN recognizes the following commands:

Command	Meaning
A	Append lines (from disk file)
C	Copy lines
D	Delete lines
E	End edit and save file
I	Insert lines
L	List lines
M	Move lines
P	Display a page
Q	Quit—does not save file
R	Replace text
S	Search text
T	Transfer lines (merge one file into another)
W	Write lines (to file)
line_num	Edit the *line number* specified

For details, refer to Chapter 9.

ERASE

The internal ERASE command erases files from a disk. (DEL is another name for ERASE.) ERASE takes the general form

    ERASE *filename* [/P]

where *filename* is the name of the file to be erased. You can use wild-card characters in the file name to erase groups of files. If you specify the /P option, ERASE will ask for verification of your decision before it erases the file.

The following command erases from the disk in drive B all files that have the extension .DAT:

    ERASE B:*.DAT

FASTOPEN

The external FASTOPEN command allows DOS to remember the location of files that are in deeply nested subdirectories, thus providing faster access to these files. Its general form is

    FASTOPEN *drive_specifier*[=*num*][/x]

where *num* determines the number of files that DOS will remember. This number can be in the range from 10 to 999; the default is 34. If you specify the /x option, it allows you to use extended memory if it is present in your system. FASTOPEN is an installed command; you can only execute it once each time the computer is turned on.

The following command causes DOS to remember the location of 34 files on the fixed disk:

    FASTOPEN C:

FDISK

The external FDISK command is used to partition the fixed disk when it is first prepared for use. Refer to your DOS manual for information on its use.

FIND

The external FIND command searches for occurrences of a string in a list of files. FIND is a filter that sends its output to the standard output device, which may be redirected. The general form of FIND is

FIND [/C] [/N] [/V] *"string" file_list*

where *string* is the string searched for and *file_list* is the list of files to search. The /C option causes FIND to display a count of the occurrences. The /N option causes the relative line number of each match to be displayed. The /V option causes FIND to display the lines that do not contain the string. Notice that the options must precede the string.

The following command searches the REC1.DAT and REC2.DAT files for the string "payroll":

FIND "payroll" REC1.DAT REC2.DAT

FOR

The FOR batch command is used to repeat a series of commands with a different argument each time. It takes the general form

FOR *%%var* IN (*argument_list*) DO *command*

where *var* is a single-letter variable that will take the values of the arguments. The arguments must be separated by spaces. FOR will repeat *command* as many times as there are arguments. Each time FOR repeats, *var* will be replaced by an argument, moving from left to right.

The following command prints the TEXT1, TEXT2, and TEXT3 files:

```
FOR %%F IN (TEXT1 TEXT2 TEXT3) DO PRINT %%F
```

FORMAT

The external FORMAT command is used to prepare a floppy disk for use. Its most common form is

```
FORMAT drive_specifier [/V]
```

The disk to be formatted must be in the specified drive. The /V option causes FORMAT to prompt you for a volume label. Remember that formatting a disk destroys any and all preexisting data, so use the FORMAT command with care.

The following command formats the disk in drive A:

```
FORMAT A:
```

GOTO

The internal GOTO batch command directs DOS to execute the commands in a batch file in a nonsequential order. Its general form is

```
GOTO label
```

where *label* is a label that is defined elsewhere in the batch file. When GOTO is executed, DOS goes to the specified label and begins executing commands from that point. With GOTO, you can cause execution to jump forward or backward in the file.

The following command causes execution to jump to the label DONE:

```
GOTO  DONE
    .
    .
    .
:DONE
```

GRAFTABL

The external GRAFTABL command loads a character table that gives DOS extended foreign-language support. It requires a color/graphics adapter. If you speak English, you will not need this command.

GRAPHICS

The external GRAPHICS command lets you print graphics images by means of the print-screen function. Its general form is

GRAPHICS [*printer*] [/R] [/B/] [/LCD]

where the name of *printer* is determined according to this list:

Printer Type	Name
IBM Personal Graphics Printer	GRAPHICS
IBM Proprinter	GRAPHICS
IBM PC Convertible Printer	THERMAL
IBM Color Printer with black ribbon	COLOR1
IBM Color Printer with red, green, and blue ribbon	COLOR4
IBM Color Printer with black, cyan, magenta, and yellow ribbon	COLOR8
Printers that use 11-inch-wide paper	GRAPHICSWIDE

If no printer name is specified, the IBM Personal Graphics Printer is assumed as the default. The Epson MX-70, MX-80, and MX-100 printers are quite commonly used with microcomputers and are also specified with the GRAPHICS printer name.

By default, white on the screen is printed as black on the printer, and black on the screen is printed as white. The /R option causes black to print as black and white to print as white. The background color of the screen is usually not printed, but if you have a color printer, you can print the background by specifying the /B option. Finally, the /LCD option should be specified for computers using the IBM PC Convertible Liquid Crystal Display.

The following command enables graphics images to be printed from the default GRAPHICS printer:

GRAPHICS

IF

The IF batch command takes the general form

IF *condition command*

If the condition evaluates to True, the command that follows the condition is executed. Otherwise, DOS skips the rest of the line and moves on to the next line in the batch file (if there is one).

INSTALL

The internal INSTALL command is used to install resident programs.

JOIN

The external JOIN command joins one drive to the directory of another. Files on the first drive can then be accessed from the joined drive as if they were in a subdirectory. JOIN takes the general form

JOIN *joining_drive joined_drive\directory* [/D]

The joining drive will appear to be in the specified directory of the joined drive. The /D option is used to disconnect a join.

This command joins drive A to drive C, using the ADRIVE directory.

JOIN A: C:\ADRIVE

KEYB

The external KEYB command loads keyboard information for foreign-language support. Its most common form is

KEYB *keyboard_code,code_page*

where *keyboard_code* and *code_page* define the keyboard code and code-page code (see Chapter 13 for details). If you speak English, you will not need this command.

The following command configures the keyboard for use in Germany:

KEYB GR,437

LABEL

The external LABEL command is used to create or change a disk's volume label. It has the general form

LABEL [*drive_specifier*][*name*]

If no drive_specifier is used, the current disk is assumed. If you do not specify the volume name on the command line, you will be prompted for one. Disk volume labels can be up to 11 characters long. You cannot, however, use the following characters in them:

* ? / \ | . , ; : + = < > [ ] "

The following command changes the volume label on the current disk to MYDISK:

LABEL MYDISK

MEM

The external MEM command displays information about the memory in your computer.

MKDIR

The internal MKDIR (or MD) command is used to create a subdirectory. Its general form is

MKDIR *path*

where *path* specifies the complete path name to the directory. The path name may not exceed 63 characters in length.

The following command creates the directory \WP\FORMS:

MD \WP\FORMS

MODE

The external MODE command is used to set the way that various devices operate. MODE is a very complex command with several different forms. (Refer to its description in Chapter 13.)

MORE

The external MORE command allows you to page through a text file 23 lines at a time. It is a filter that reads from standard input and writes to standard output. Its most common form is

MORE < *filename*

where *filename* is the file to be viewed.

You can also use MORE in conjunction with other commands, such as DIR, to provide a convenient way to page through displays that are larger than one screen. For example, the following command displays the directory 23 lines at a time:

DIR | MORE

NLSFUNC

The external NLSFUNC command provides extended DOS support for non-English users. For details, refer to your DOS user manual.

PATH

The internal PATH command is used to define the search path that DOS will use to locate program files in directories other than the current one. It takes the general form

PATH *path*[*;path...;path*]

where *path* is the specified search path. You can define multiple search paths by separating each path with a semicolon. The path list cannot include spaces.

The following command defines a path to the \WP\FORMS directory:

PATH \WP\FORMS

PAUSE

The PAUSE batch command temporarily stops a batch file's execution. It takes the general form

PAUSE [*message*]

If the *message* is present, it will be displayed. PAUSE waits until a key is pressed before resuming the file's execution.

PRINT

The external PRINT command prints text files on the printer. Its most common form is

PRINT *filename filename ... filename* [/T] [/C]

where *filename* is the name of the file you want printed. The /T option cancels the PRINT command entirely. The /C option cancels only the printing of the file name it follows.

The following command prints the LETTER1.WP and LETTER2.WP files:

PRINT LETTER1.WP LETTER2.WP

PROMPT

The internal PROMPT command is used to change the DOS prompt. It takes the general form

PROMPT *prompt*

where *prompt* is the desired prompt. The prompt string can contain one or more of the following special format commands, which allow greater flexibility:

Code	Meaning
$$	Dollar sign
$b	I character
$d	System date
$e	Escape character
$g	> character
$h	Backspace
$l	< character
$n	Current drive letter
$p	Current directory path
$q	= character
$t	Current time
$v	DOS version number
$_	Carriage return/linefeed sequence

One of the most popular prompts is created by the following command:

PROMTP PG

It displays the current directory path followed by the > symbol.

RECOVER

The external RECOVER command attempts to recover damaged files. It has the general form

RECOVER [*drive_specifier*][*filename*]

If only the drive specifier is present, RECOVER attempts to recover all files on a disk. Otherwise, only the specified file is recovered. When the entire disk is recovered, RECOVER creates files named FILE*num*.REC, where *num* is a number between 1 and 9999.

Remember, not all files can be recovered. In addition, recovered program files are very unusable. It is best to use RECOVER only on text files, and then only as a last resort.

The following command attempts to recover the FORMLET.WP file:

RECOVER FORMLET.WP

REM

The REM batch command has the general form

REM *remark*

The *remark* can be any string from 0 to 123 characters in length. No matter what the remark contains, it will be completely ignored by DOS. For example, the following remark is ignored:

REM this is a test

RENAME

The internal RENAME (or REN) command is used to change the name of a specified file. It takes the general form

RENAME *old_name new_name*

where *old_name* and *new_name* are file names.

The following command changes the name of the file originally called INV.DAT to INV.OLD:

RENAME INV.DAT INV.OLD

REPLACE

The external REPLACE command replaces files on the destination disk with files by the same name on the source disk. It takes the general form

REPLACE *source destination* [/S] [/A] [/W] [/P] [/U] [/R]

If you specify the /S option, all files in all subdirectories will also be examined and replaced. You can use /A to add to a disk only the files that are not currently on the destination disk. This prevents existing files from being overwritten. If you need to insert a different disk before REPLACE begins, use the /W option, which makes REPLACE wait until you press a key before beginning. With the /P option, REPLACE will ask you to verify your decision before a file is replaced. With the /U option, REPLACE only replaces files that are older than files that will replace them.

The following command replaces the files on drive A with those by the same name on drive B, including all subdirectories:

    REPLACE B: A: /S

RESTORE

The external RESTORE command is used to restore files to the fixed disk from floppy disks that were created with BACKUP. It takes the general form

    RESTORE *backup fixed* [/A:*date*] [/B:*date*] [/E:*time*] [/L:*time*] [/P] [/S]
    [/M] [/N]

where *backup* is a drive specifier defining the drive that holds the backup disk and *fixed* is a drive and path specifier for the fixed disk. The options are summarized here:

Option	Meaning
/A:*date*	Restore all files modified on or after the specified date
/B:*date*	Restore all files modified on or before the specified date
/E:*time*	Restore all files modified at or earlier than the specified time on a given date
/L:*time*	Restore all files modified at or later than the specified time on a given date
/M	Restore all files that have been modified or deleted since the last backup
/N	Restore only files that do not exist on the fixed disk
/P	Prompt before restoring a file
/S	Restore all subdirectories

The following command restores all files with the extension .DAT into the DATA directory, using drive A to read the backup disks:

RESTORE A: C:\DATA*.DAT

RMDIR

The internal RMDIR (or RD) command is used to remove a subdirectory. It has the general form

RMDIR *directory*

where *directory* is a complete path name to the desired directory. The specified directory must be empty; it is not possible to remove a directory that still has files in it.

The following command removes the WP directory:

RMDIR \WP

Remember, you can only remove a directory if it is empty and not the current directory.

SET

The internal SET command is used primarily by programmers and system integrators to put a name and its value into DOS's environment. Refer to Chapter 16 for details.

SHARE

The external SHARE command is used in networked systems to prepare for file sharing and file locking. Refer to your networking and DOS manuals for complete information.

SHELL

The external SHELL command activates the DOS Shell. In general, this command is not used by you directly. Instead, it forms part of the DOSSHELL batch command, which you use to restart the Shell.

SHIFT

The SHIFT batch command is used to shift command-line arguments one position to the left. This allows for more than ten arguments.

SORT

The external SORT command sorts text files on a line-by-line basis. It is a filter command that reads from standard input and writes to standard output. It takes the general form

SORT [<*input*] [>*output*] [/R] [/+*num*]

where *input* and *output* are either file names, devices, or pipes. If not specified, standard input and output are used. The standard default is ascending order (A to Z). The /R option causes the file to be sorted in reverse or descending order. The /+*num* option causes the sorting to begin with the column specified by the number *num*.

The following command produces a sorted directory listing by file name:

DIR | SORT

SUBST

The external SUBST command allows you to associate a drive specifier with a different drive and directory. You can use SUBST to assign a drive specifier to a drive and directory and refer to that drive and directory by using the drive specifier. The new drive specifier is like a nickname for the other drive.

SUBST takes the general form

SUBST *nickname drive_specifier path*

where *nickname* is the new drive specifier for the indicated drive specifier and *path* is the path to the desired directory. To undo a substitution, use this form of the command:

SUBST *nickname* /D

The following command causes drive A to respond to both A: and E:

SUBST E: A:\

SYS

The external SYS command is used to copy the DOS system files to a disk. It has the general form

SYS *drive_specifier*

where *drive_specifier* indicates the drive that will receive the system files. SYS does not transfer COMMAND.COM, however. SYS must be able to read the system files off the current drive.

The following command puts the system files on the disk in drive B:

SYS B:

TIME

The internal TIME command is used to set the system time. It takes the general form

TIME [*hh:mm:ss*]

If you do not enter the time on the command line, you will be prompted for it. TIME expects the numbers 0 through 23 for the hours; it operates in military, 24-hour clock format. You can enter the time in 12-hour format, but you must enter **a** for A.M. or **p** for P.M. You need not specify the seconds.

The following command sets the time to 12:00 noon:

TIME 12:00:00

TREE

The external TREE command prints a list of all directories on the specified disk. It has the general form

TREE *drive_specifier* [/F]

where *drive_specifier* is the letter of the drive that will be examined. If /F is used, the files in each directory will also be displayed.

The following command displays the directory structure for the disk in drive A:

TREE A:

TYPE

The internal TYPE command displays the contents of a text file on the screen. It has the general form

TYPE *filename*

where *filename* is the file to be displayed.

The following command displays a file called TEST:

TYPE TEST

VER

The internal VER command displays the DOS version number. It takes no arguments.

VERIFY

The internal VERIFY command turns on or off the verification of disk write operations. When turned on, it confirms that the data written to disk is exactly as it should be and that no errors have taken place. It takes the general form

VERIFY [ON|OFF]

where you specify either ON or OFF.

The following command turns verification off:

VERIFY OFF

VOL

The internal VOL command displays the volume label of a disk. It has the general form

VOL [*drive_specifier*]

where *drive_specifier* is the name of the drive whose volume label will be displayed. If not specified, the volume label of the current drive is displayed.

The following command displays the volume label of the current drive:

VOL

XCOPY

The external XCOPY command is a more powerful and flexible version of the COPY command. It takes the general form

XCOPY *source target* [/A] [/D:*date*] [/E] [/P] [/S] [/V] [/W] [/M]

where *source* and *target* are file or path names. The operation of XCOPY is largely determined by the options applied to it. The options are summarized here:

Option	Meaning
/A	Copy only those files with the archive attribute turned on; do not change the state of the archive bit
/D:*date*	Copy only those files whose date is the same as or later than the one specified
/E	Create all subdirectories, even if empty
/M	Copy only those files with the archive attribute turned on and turn off the archive bit
/P	Prompt before copying each file
/S	Copy files in subdirectories
/V	Verify each write operation
/W	Wait until a disk is inserted

The following command copies all files on a disk in drive A to one in drive B, including all subdirectories:

XCOPY A: B:\ /S

TRADEMARKS

AT™	International Business Machines Corporation
IBM®	International Business Machines Corporation
PS/2™	International Business Machines Corporation
XT™	International Business Machines Corporation

INDEX

1-2-3®: The Pocket Reference
by Mary Campbell

All essential Lotus® 1-2-3® functions and commands are arranged alphabetically and described in a few paragraphs. Options are also listed in this invaluable resource for quick reference by the author of the best-selling *1-2-3®: The Pocket Reference.*

$5.95 p
0-07-881304-2, 120 pp., 4¼ x 7

1-2-3® Made Easy
by Mary Campbell

Osborne's famous "Made Easy" format, which has helped hundreds of thousands of WordStar® users master word processing, is now available to Lotus® 1-2-3® beginners. *1-2-3® Made Easy* starts with the basics and goes step by step through the process of building a worksheet so you can use Lotus' spreadsheet with skill and confidence. Each chapter provides a complete 1-2-3 lesson followed by practical "hands-on" exercises that help you apply 1-2-3 immediately to the job. When you've got worksheets down, you'll learn to create and print graphs, manipulate 1-2-3's data management features, use advanced file features . . . even design keyboard macros. As the author of *1-2-3®: The Complete Reference*, and a columnist for IBM® PC UPDATE, ABSOLUTE REFERENCE, and CPA JOURNAL, Mary Campbell has plenty of experience with 1-2-3. With her know-how, you'll soon be handling 1-2-3 like a pro.

$18.95 p
0-07-881293-3, 400 pp., 7⅜ x 9¼

The Osborne/McGraw-Hill Guide to Using Lotus™ 1-2-3,™ Second Edition, Covers Release 2
by Edward M. Baras

Your investment in Lotus™ 1-2-3™ can yield the most productive returns possible with the tips and practical information in *The Osborne/McGraw-Hill Guide to Using Lotus™ 1-2-3™* Now the second edition of this acclaimed bestseller helps you take full advantage of Lotus' new 1-2-3 upgrade, Release 2. This comprehensive guide offers a thorough presentation of the worksheet, database, and graphics functions. In addition, the revised text shows you how to create and use macros, string functions, and many other sophisticated 1-2-3 features. You'll learn to implement 1-2-3 techniques as you follow application models for financial forecasting, stock portfolio tracking, and forms-oriented database management. For both beginners and experienced users, this tutorial quickly progresses from fundamental procedures to advanced applications.

$19.95 p
0-07-881230-5, 432 pp., 7⅜ x 9¼

The Advanced Guide to Lotus™ 1-2-3™
by Edward M. Baras

Edward Baras, Lotus expert and author of *The Symphony™ Book, Symphony™ Master,* and *The Jazz™ Book,* now has a sequel to his best-selling *Osborne/McGraw-Hill Guide to Using Lotus™ 1-2-3.™* For experienced users, *The Advanced Guide to Lotus 1-2-3* delves into more powerful and complex techniques using the newest software upgrade, Release 2. Added enhancements to 1-2-3's macro language, as well as many new functions and commands, are described and thoroughly illustrated in business applications. Baras shows you how to take advantage of Release 2's macro capabilities by programming 1-2-3 to simulate Symphony's keystroke-recording features and by processing ASCII files automatically. You'll also learn to set up your own command menus; use depreciation functions, matric manipulation, and regression analysis; and convert text files to the 1-2-3 worksheet format.

$19.95 p
0-07-881237-2, 325 pp., 7⅜ x 9¼

1-2-3®: Power User's Guide
by Mary Campbell

Extend 1-2-3® productivity to the limit with Campbell's masterful techniques. The author of the nationwide bestseller *1-2-3®: The Complete Reference* provides you with dynamic methods that are unavailable elsewhere. This *Power User's Guide* helps you transform your intermediate 1-2-3 skills into a powerhouse of advanced 1-2-3 tricks and techniques. You'll find a complete discussion of methods for directing data management, transferring data between 1-2-3 and other software, and using advanced built-in functions. You'll devise macros to automate tasks fully, employ special techniques for multi-user applications; and use the Lotus environment as effectively as possible with enhancements provided by HAL™ and Metro™. In addition, word processing, communications, and graphics possibilities are described and various add-in, add-on, and complementary products are analyzed. With Campbell's state-of-the-art techniques, you'll be in total command of 1-2-3.

$22.95 p
0-07-881298-4, 600 pp., 7⅜ x 9¼

Quattro™: The Complete Reference
by Yvonne McCoy

Quattro™, Borland's full-featured professional spreadsheet, is now explained for novices and spreadsheet veterans alike in *Quattro™: The Complete Reference*. As part of both the *Borland·Osborne/McGraw-Hill Business Series* and Osborne's *Complete Reference* series, this title combines the best features of each: Borland's technical superiority and Osborne's top-selling reference format. *Quattro™: The Complete Reference* is the perfect encyclopedia of all Quattro commands, features, and functions. Consultant and instructor Yvonne McCoy offers beginners an overview of Quattro basics—creating, saving, and printing a simple worksheet—while experienced users are provided with detailed information on Quattro characteristics—macros, graphics, file management, and more. McCoy emphasizes Quattro's unique ability to share files with Lotus® 1-2-3®, Reflex®, R:base®, and dBASE®. Customizing Quattro to meet your special needs is another important topic that McCoy addresses in the incomparable *Quattro™: The Complete Reference*.

$24.95 p,
0-07-881337-9, 950 pp., 7⅜ x 9¼
The Borland-Osborne/McGraw-Hill Business Series

Quattro™ Made Easy
by Lisa Biow

This step-by-step introduction is just what you need if you are new to Quattro™ or new to spreadsheet software. You'll be handling Borland's new generation spreadsheet with confidence in just a few hours when you use *Quattro™ Made Easy* as your guide. Trainer and consultant Lisa Biow introduces you to Quattro concepts in easy-to-learn lessons accompanied by hands-on exercises that help you put Quattro immediately to work on your projects. Design a spreadsheet, modify data, use formulas. Biow builds on the basics as she explains graphing, database design, and macros. You'll also find appendixes that list Lotus® 1-2-3® equivalents, sample spreadsheets, and a Quattro function summary.

$19.95 p
0-07-881347-6, 400 pp., 7⅜ x 9¼
The Borland-Osborne/McGraw-Hill Business Series

Quattro™: The Pocket Reference
by Stephen Cobb

All essential Quattro® commands, functions, and features are at your fingertips with this compact reference that's arranged alphabetically.

$5.95 p
0-07-881378-6, 128 pp., 4¼ x 7
The Borland-Osborne/McGraw-Hill Business Series

Using Quattro:™ The Professional Spreadsheet
by Stephen Cobb

Here's the first official book on Quattro™, Borland's full-featured spreadsheet, that sets new standards for power, flexibility, and presentation quality graphics. *Using Quattro™* is written both for beginners who are new to spreadsheet software and for experienced spreadsheet users who are new to Quattro. Cobb, a corporate computer trainer and consultant, first eases readers into the terminology and technique of spreadsheet development, presenting the Quattro commands in a clear, detailed format. Practical examples illustrate effective use. Then Cobb delves into Quattro's powerful statistical tools and its full range of charting options. The book's last section introduces the macro power of Quattro and its custom interface features. A series of applications that combine the program's commands to demonstrate Quattro's power are also provided.

$21.95 p
0-07-881330-1, 400 pp., 7⅜ x 9¼
The Borland-Osborne/McGraw-Hill Business Series

Order Today!
Call Toll-Free 800-227-0900
Use Your American Express, Visa, or MasterCard

Quattro™: Power User's Guide
by Stephen Cobb

Stephen Cobb, author of the *Using Quattro™: The Professional Spreadsheet*, now helps you refine your skills so you can unlock the full speed and power of Borland's flexible spreadsheet program. Quattro's state-of-the-art graphics, unique macro creation and debugging features, and ability to build customized menus will be at your command. Cobb's advanced applications save you hours of computing time and make your presentations more complete and professional. *Quattro™: Power User's Guide* also covers unique ways to apply Transcript, Quattro's built-in keystroke recording system. Discover tricks that help you use Quattro's search and replace feature to edit an entire spreadsheet in seconds. All the ins-and-outs of importing and exporting data between Lotus®1-2-3®, dBASE® II and III, Paradox®, Reflex®, and other software are discussed in this guide. Cobb's years as a computer trainer and his first-hand experience with this amazing new product make him the ideal consultant around to give you the inside information you need to make the most of sophisticated Quattro features.

$22.95 p
0-07-881367-0, 600 pp., 7³/₈ x 9¹/₄
The Borland-Osborne/McGraw-Hill Business Series

WordStar® Professional Made Easy
by Walter A. Ettlin

WordStar® Made Easy the original "Made Easy" guide which has sold more than 350,000 copies worldwide, has been so successful that Osborne has published a companion volume on the new WordStar® Professional release 5. New commands and features are thoroughly described and illustrated in practical exercises so that you can put WordStar Professional to immediate use, even if you've never used a computer before. Find out about WordStar Professional's special features including footnotes, endnotes, nonprinting notes, printer support, macros, and pull-down menus. Walter Ettlin, who has written five books and taught for 23 years, guides you from the fundamentals of creating a memo or report to advanced topics such as using WordStar's calculator mode, macro commands, and Word Finder™. You'll also learn about WordStar's latest spelling checker. *WordStar® Professional Made Easy* puts you in control of your software with the acclaimed "Made Easy" format that is now used in a series of beginner guides.

$17.95 p
0-07-881354-9, 300 pp., 7³/₈ x 9¹/₄

WordPerfect® Made Easy, Series 5 Edition
by Mella Mincberg

Mincberg's special edition of *WordPerfect® Made Easy* covers all the exciting features of the new WordPerfect version 5, including its desktop publishing capabilities. When you follow Mincberg's practical applications, you'll be able to edit text, save and print a document, set tabs, and format pages. Then you'll learn how to integrate text and graphics, enhance your layouts, vary print styles and sizes, and effectively use your laser or dot matrix printer to produce professional publications. Step-by-step lessons also give you the experience that you need to run WordPerfect 5's more sophisticated features: automatic redline and strkeout, spell checker, mail merge, file management, macros, referencing, and special enhancements like windows and line numbering. Mincberg, author of the acclaimed *WordPerfect®: Secrets, Solutions, Shortcuts* as well as the original *WordPerfect® Made Easy*, draws on her years of computer training experience to transform the wide range of WordPerfect features into easy-to-understand procedures that will quickly make you a confident WordPerfect 5 user.

$18.95 p
0-07-881358-1, 492 pp., 7³/₈ x 9¹/₄

Microsoft® Word Made Easy, Third Edition
by Paul Hoffman

The top-selling *Microsoft® Word Made Easy* has been revised to include all the impressive new features of Word version 4, just released by Microsoft. Whether you're new to computing or just getting acquainted with Word, Hoffman's step-by-step format guides you from the basics to more complex techniques. Using hands-on exercises, you'll learn to create memos and reports. When you feel comfortable with those applications, you'll explore version 4 capabilities—macros, linking documents, special features for lawyers, and desktop publishing projects. Hoffman also discusses text outlining, spelling correction, indexing, mail-merge, windows, Microsoft's new PageView program, and more. You can rely on Hoffman, the author of several acclaimed computer books, to help you learn Word version 4 with ease.

$18.95 p
0-07-881329-8, 400 pp., 7³/₈ x 9¹/₄

Order Today!
Call Toll-Free 800-227-0900
Use Your American Express, Visa, or MasterCard

C: The Pocket Reference
by Herbert Schildt

Speed up your C programming with *C: The Pocket Reference*, written by master programmer Schildt, the author of twelve Osborne/McGraw-Hill books. This quick reference is packed with vital C commands, functions, and libraries. Arranged alphabetically for easy use.

$5.95 p
0-07-881321-2, 120 pp., 4¼ x 7

C Made Easy
by Herbert Schildt

With Osborne/McGraw-Hill's popular "Made Easy" format, you can learn C programming in no time. Start with the fundamentals and work through the text at your own speed. Schildt begins with general concepts, then introduces functions, libraries, and disk input/output, and finally advanced concepts affecting the C programming environment and UNIX™ operating system. Each chapter covers commands that you can learn to use immediately in the hands-on exercises that follow. If you already know BASIC, you'll find that Schildt's C equivalents will shorten your learning time. *C Made Easy* is a step-by-step tutorial for all beginning C programmers.

$18.95 p
0-07-881178-3, 350 pp., 7⅜ x 9¼

Advanced C, Second Edition
by Herbert Schildt

Experienced C programmers can become professional C programmers with Schildt's nuts-and-bolts guide to advanced programming techniques. Now thoroughly revised, *Advanced C, Second Edition* covers the new ANSI standard in addition to the Kernighan and Ritchie C used in the first edition. All the example code conforms to the ANSI standard. You'll find information you need on sorting and searching; queues, stacks, linked lists, and binary trees; dynamic allocation; interfacing to assembly language routines and the operating system; expression parsing; and more. When you finish reading *Advanced C*, you'll be ready for the slick programming tricks found in Schildt's twelfth book for Osborne, C: Power User's Guide.

$21.95 p
0-07-881348-4, 353 pp., 7⅜ x 9¼

C: Power User's Guide
by Herbert Schildt

Make your C programs sizzle! All the bells, whistles, and slick tricks used to get professional results in commercial software are unveiled to serious programmers in *C: Power User's Guide*. In his eleventh book for Osborne/McGraw-Hill, Schildt shows you how to build a Borland type interface, develop a core for a database, create memory resident programs, and more. Schildt combines theory, background, and code in an even mix as he excites experienced C programmers with new features and approaches. Learn master techniques for handling menus, windows, graphics, and video game programming. If hashing is what you're after, it's here too, along with techniques for using the serial port and sorting disk files. OS/2™ level programming with specific OS/2 functions is also covered. Before you send your programs out to market, consult Schildt for the final touches that set professional software apart from the rest.

$22.95 p
0-07-881307-7, 384 pp., 7⅜ x 9¼

Order Today!
Call Toll-Free 800-227-0900

Use Your American Express, Visa, or MasterCard

The C Library
by Kris Jamsa

Design and implement more effective programs with the wealth of programming tools that are offered in *The C Library*. Experienced C programmers will find over 125 carefully structured routines ranging from macros to actual UNIX™ utilities. There are tools for string manipulation, pointers, input/output, array manipulation, recursion, sorting algorithms, and file manipulation. In addition, Jamsa provides several C routines that have previously been available only through expensive software packages. Build your skills by taking routines introduced in early chapters and using them to develop advanced programs covered later in the text.

$19.95 p
0-07-881110-4, 220 pp., 7³/₈ x 9¹/₄

Artificial Intelligence Using C
by Herb Schildt

With Herb Schildt's newest book, you can add a powerful dimension to your C programs—artificial intelligence. Schildt, a programming expert and author of seven Osborne books, shows C programmers how to use AI techniques that have traditionally been implemented with Prolog and LISP. You'll utilize AI for vision, pattern recognition, robotics, machine learning, logic, problem solving, and natural language processing. Each chapter develops practical examples that can be used in the construction of artificial intelligence applications. If you are building expert systems in C, this book contains a complete expert system that oan easily be adapted to your needs. Schildt provides valuable insights that allow even greater command of the systems you create.

$21.95 p
0-07-881255-0, 432 pp., 7³/₈ x 9¹/₄

These titles available at fine book stores and computer stores everywhere.

Or call toll-free 800-227-0900
Use your American Express, Visa, or MasterCard

For a FREE catalog of all our current publications, call 800-227-0900 or write to Osborne/McGraw-Hill, 2600 Tenth Street, Berkeley, CA 94710

Prices subject to change without notice.

Quick Command Synopsis

DOS Commands

Command	Description
APPEND	Joins one directory to another
ASSIGN	Assigns a new drive letter to an existing drive
ATTRIB	Sets or displays a file's attributes
BACKUP	Backs up the fixed disk
CHCP	Supports foreign-language version of DOS
CHDIR (CD)	Changes the current directory
CHKDSK	Checks a disk and repairs some types of errors
CLS	Clears the screen
COMMAND	Activates a new command processor
COMP	Compares two files
COPY	Copies contents of one file to another
CTTY	Switches control of the computer to a remote terminal
DATE	Sets and displays the system date
DEL	Removes a file from a disk
DIR	Displays the directory
DOSSHELL	Activates the DOS Shell
DISKCOMP	Compares two floppy disks
DISKCOPY	Copies the contents of one disk to another
EDLIN	Edits text files (DOS's text editor)
ERASE	Removes a file from a disk
FASTOPEN	Allows faster access to disk files
FDISK	Partitions the fixed disk
FIND	Searches for a specified string in a list of files
FORMAT	Formats a floppy disk
GRAFTABL	Supports foreign languages
GRAPHICS	Enables graphics images to be printed on the printer
JOIN	Joins a drive to a directory
KEYB	Loads keyboard information for foreign languages
LABEL	Displays or changes a disk's label
MEM	Displays information about the computer's memory usage
MKDIR	Creates a subdirectory
MODE	Sets the way various devices operate
MORE	Pages through a text file
NLSFUNC	Supports foreign-language versions of DOS
PATH	Defines a search path
PRINT	Prints a text file on the printer
PROMPT	Sets the format of the command prompt
RECOVER	Attempts to recover damaged files
RENAME	Changes the name of a disk file
REPLACE	Replaces files on the destination disk with files by the same name on the source disk
RESTORE	Restores files to the fixed disk from backup copies made by BACKUP
RMDIR	Removes a directory
SET	Sets the value of an environmental parameter
SHARE	Used by networked systems
SORT	Sorts a file
SUBST	Substitutes one drive name for another
SYS	Transfers the DOS system files to another disk
TIME	Displays and sets the system time
TREE	Displays the structure of a directory and its subdirectories
TYPE	Displays the contents of a text file on the screen
VER	Displays the DOS version number
VERIFY	Determines whether file copies are verified
VOL	Displays the volume label of a disk
XCOPY	An expanded copy command

DOS Batch File Commands

Command	Description
CALL	Calls another batch file
ECHO	Displays a message on the screen
FOR	Executes a series of commands
GOTO	Jumps to the designated label
IF	Batch-file conditional statement
PAUSE	Temporarily stops the execution of a batch file
REM	Adds a remark (comment) in a batch file
SHIFT	Shifts command-line arguments one position to the left

CONFIG.SYS Commands

Command	Description
BREAK	Determines how often DOS looks for a CTRL- BREAK keypress
BUFFERS	Determines the number of disk buffers active in the system
COUNTRY	Specifies country specific information
DEVICE	Installs device drivers
FCBS	Determines number of file control blocks active in the system
FILES	Determines the maximum number of files that can be open at any one time
INSTALL	Installs resident programs
LASTDRIVE	Determines the maximum number of drives in the system
SHELL	Loads a command processor
STACKS	Specifies the system stack size
SWITCHES	Specifies a conventional keyboard instead of an enhanced one

IF YOU ENJOYED THIS BOOK . . .

help us stay in touch with your needs and interests by filling out and returning the survey card below. Your opinions are important, and will help us to continue to publish the kinds of books you need, when you need them.

What brand of computer(s) do you own or use? _____

Where do you use your computer the most? ☐ At work ☐ At school ☐ At home

What topics would you like to see covered in future books by Osborne/McGraw-Hill? _____

How many other computer books do you own? _____

Why did you choose this book?
☐ Best coverage of the subject.
☐ Recognized the author from previous work.
☐ Liked the price.
☐ Other

Where did you find this book?
☐ Bookstore
☐ Computer/software store
☐ Department store
☐ Advertisement
☐ Catalog

Where did you hear about this book?
☐ Book review.
☐ Osborne catalog.
☐ Advertisement in: _____
☐ Found by browsing in store.
☐ Found/recommended in library
☐ Other

☐ Required textbook
☐ Library
☐ Gift
☐ Other

Where should we send your FREE catalog?

NAME _____

ADDRESS _____

448-0 CITY _____ STATE _____ ZIP _____

BUSINESS REPLY MAIL
FIRST CLASS   PERMIT NO. 3111   Berkeley, CA

Postage will be paid by addressee

Osborne **McGraw-Hill**
2600 Tenth Street
Berkeley, California 94710